CW00922137

Jacking Out

About the Author

Aron Lee recently earned his Ph.D. in educational studies from McGill University, where he also worked as a researcher and course lecturer. His research investigated ways of supporting the development of students' critical digital literacy practices. Previously, Lee worked as a high school teacher and plans to return to the classroom now that his degree is finished. He is also a poet, musician, and community organizer. He grew up in Amiskwacîwâskahikan (Edmonton) and now lives in Tio'tia:ke (Montreal). *Jacking Out* is his first book.

Jacking Out

Aron Lee

Rock's Mills Press
Rock's Mills, Ontario • Oakville, Ontario
2023

In memory of Aziz Choudry (1966–2021)
and for my nieces, Aria and Elliot

In grad school, while studying the internet, I decided to spend a year offline. I didn't know exactly why, but it felt like something I had been working towards for a long time.

I made up some rules: I couldn't use the internet myself or look at online screens, and I couldn't ask other people to do things online for me.

As my year offline approached, I got in the habit of keeping a journal and wrote in it almost daily throughout the project. I have chosen some of my favourite entries to share here.

Except for public figures, I have used pseudonyms to respect people's privacy.

Before

Writers who venture beyond the most pedestrian dreary conceptions of tools and uses to investigate ways in which technical forms are implicated in the basic patterns and problems of our culture are often greeted with the charge that they are merely "antitechnology" or "blaming technology."
—Langdon Winner, 1986, *The Whale and the Reactor*

FRIDAY, SEPTEMBER 20th
We drove more than five hours, making two pretty drastic wrong turns despite having Google Maps going on everyone's phone except mine. On the way, we chatted about the cabin Darren had booked. It was very remote. I was trying to focus on the road, but Darren pulled up a map on his phone and held it in my face.

"See those little grey lines between the streets?" he said, "We're staying on one of those. There won't be internet or probably even cellphone service."

When we arrived, our phones worked perfectly. As the rest of us unpacked the car, Darren got distracted messaging a guy he'd met on Instagram.

"It's too bad there's cellphone and internet service here," I said, heavy-handedly.

"Yea," Darren replied, still on his phone.

SATURDAY, SEPTEMBER 21st
"Who's the photo for ... your followers?"

I'm sure I had a jokey, self-righteous tone and I won't

deny that I was laying on the phone-guilt hard, but I didn't think anything of it. I assumed my friends were used to my trolling. But then this evening, while I was building a fire in the pit outside the cabin, Darren came out and asked if there was something I wanted to say to him.

"No," I started, cautiously, "I'm okay…"

"Well," he said, "I just thought you might want to tell me something."

This wasn't the first time Darren had confronted me like this. We've known each other for three years and I feel like the closer we get, the more we get on each other's nerves. When we first met, we hooked up a couple times. After that stopped, we became better friends but also started bickering more.

"Just admit you're trying to hurt me," he blurted.

"What?" I was surprised – I'd thought he was going to tell me I was patronizing him, trying to teach him something, acting like I knew better, "I'm not trying to hurt you, Darren."

WEDNESDAY, OCTOBER 2nd

Today I finally did it. I've been having dreams about it all week in which the conversation gets foisted on me, unplanned. But this morning I did it on my own terms. I brought along some hummus and pita (because I've heard it's the key to his heart) and went to see our department's registrar, a stylish man in his late forties who always pours the wine at our department events. There are whispers that he's a strict and unforgiving bureaucrat, but that hasn't been my experience. Perhaps whoever said that caught him on a day when he had an especially high number of unread emails.

When I arrived, he was in the middle of filing something but said he had time for a chat. My words came out awkwardly but I made it clear (I think) that I'm studying how the internet impacts students, that I want to spend next year offline, and that I'm wondering if there's a way to register for courses without the internet.

"No."

His answer came round like a finger pointing to the door.

"You're not able to register me yourself?" I asked, "Don't you have the admin privileges?"

"If I could do it, I would," he said.

The conversation felt over, but I just sat there, trying not to stare at the hummus and pita.

"And what if I don't register for the year?"

"You'll lose your funding and get kicked out."

The registrar and I looked at each other for a moment, and then his eyes changed. He stood up and I followed him over to the desk of a woman who does the admin work for our department's Office of First Nations and Inuit Education. (She works in another cubicle in the same office.) She explained that some of the Indigenous applicants from up north live without internet, or "off-grid" as she called it. When they're registering for classes, they have the option to submit paper forms. She even gave me a copy.

As I walked the registrar back to his desk, we agreed that I shouldn't use a service that's in place to support Indigenous students, but "at least we know it's possible," he said.

SATURDAY, OCTOBER 5th
"What is it about going online that makes me want to buy things?" I asked.

"Billions of dollars in advertising," said my friend Hanni, without looking up from his computer.

SUNDAY, OCTOBER 20th
I hate when I'm doing something online and I forget what it was so I just click through tabs and windows, hoping something will jog my memory or waiting to get distracted by something new.

WEDNESDAY, NOVEMBER 27th
"As much as I can understand your decision to go offline, you cannot expect strangers around you to do the addi-

tional special work connected to the paper communication."

That's a line from an email I got today, sent by the organizers of a conference I had hoped to go to next year in Europe. They were responding to my request to sign up and attend the conference while offline. I wanted to write back something about all the strangers doing the under- or unpaid work, often in the Global South, that makes it possible to organize the conference digitally – the resource extraction, manufacturing, content-moderation, ewaste disposal... I wanted to ask whose work gets to be considered *additional* and *special*.

But instead I just wrote a polite response, thanking them for considering.

THURSDAY, DECEMBER 12th

Someone at work laughed at me today when I explained that I'm allowed to send and receive text messages during my year offline.

"You create your own rules very conveniently," the laugher said.

"But texting isn't online."

THURSDAY, DECEMBER 19th

There are less than two weeks to go now and I'm starting to get a bit anxious. The idea that I won't have all the resources in the world at my beck and call has me hoarding: I've been saving phone numbers and addresses that I think I may need, I ordered the white pages and yellow pages, I've been downloading articles, buying books. At the same time, I'm trying to remind myself that if I get stuck offline and have to navigate a situation that usually requires the internet, I'll at least have something to journal about.

MONDAY, DECEMBER 30th

One day left, and I can't get enough. I keep pulling it out when I'm sitting with friends. Normally, I consider it rude or at least weird when people are on their device around friends. But it feels like there's still so much to do.

TUESDAY, DECEMBER 31st

I didn't use the internet too much today. I've done everything I think I need to do before I go offline. It'd be funny if the internet somehow went down next year, and I was the only one prepared.

While checking my email one last time, I unsubscribed from a couple more mailing lists and tried to make sure my out-of-office response is working. It seems to be all good for my work email, but I couldn't figure out how to set it up for my personal email.

January

What happens when we refuse what all (presumably) "sensible" people perceive as good things?
　　—Audra Simpson, 2014, *Mohawk Interruptus*

WEDNESDAY, JANUARY 1st
I only had a couple drinks last night, but I was home and puking before midnight. I haven't been this sick for a while – shivering with nausea, unable to warm my feet or hands, aches all over, skin tender and wet. I feel like the guy from *Crime and Punishment*, but I haven't even killed anyone – I'm just spending a year offline.

FRIDAY, JANUARY 3rd
I've still been feeling low, but I'm planning to leave the apartment finally to pick up some ramen.

Before I go, I need to grab cash. I'm trying to emulate pre-internet times, which means I *can* use my bank card to take out money from the bank, but I *can't* use it to pay for things. It's good I looked into it before going offline because I had thought that bank cards used to work with those slidey boards that imprint your card onto carbon paper. Turns out that was just for credit cards.

SUNDAY, JANUARY 5th
People have started asking. Text messages are coming in. And I know people are just trying to be supportive, trying to

connect, trying to make conversation. But it's been four and a half days. My internetless year has been fine! It's been normal. I don't like having the same conversation over and over, even if it's a conversation I want to have. Each time I have it, the fiery part burns out a bit, and I have to work harder to get the fire going each time, or I fake it.

One of my friends texted to ask if I can still text while offline. I've been asked this three times now. People seem to have a hard time keeping track of what the internet does. Part of the confusion may be due to services like iMessage and WhatsApp that send text messages over the internet. Or it may also be confusing because text messages didn't exist before the internet. But I'm still surprised.

Of course, almost everything is blended now and all sorts of offline tasks involve online actions at some point along the supply chain, but in the most direct and straightforward sense, sending a text is like phoning someone; it doesn't use data. My flip-phone isn't even connected to the internet.

I'm realizing that one of the biggest little challenges I'm going to face in trying to avoid the internet is the casualness with which people show each other things on their phones. Last night Darren was trying to brag about a dude he slept with recently and he was showing a photo of the guy to everyone at the table. I had to look away to avoid seeing the phone.

Similarly, at brunch today, someone was showing off a photo of their dog when she was a puppy and I got scared as the photo was shoved in my face.

"Don't worry," my friend said, "it's on my phone, not online."

MONDAY, JANUARY 6th
Last night I tried to go see the new Adam Sandler movie in theatres but it was sold out. The woman selling tickets (or not selling them, in my case) told me they're planning to add

some additional show-times and she suggested I check their website to buy tickets in advance. I didn't explain why that won't be possible. I just thanked her and left.

I've always been a fan of the underdog, even before I knew I was gay. As a kid, I gravitated towards news stories about exploitation. When I learned about sweatshops in elementary from demonstrators at a basketball tournament, I stopped buying Nike shoes. In high school, when I learned about the child slaves who work on cocoa farms in the Ivory Coast, I stopped eating chocolate. And more recently, after finding out about Amazon's role in supporting ICE and the round-up of undocumented migrants in the United States, I stopped using Amazon.

In a book Neil Postman wrote in the '90s, he insisted that for every advantage a new technology offers, there are corresponding disadvantages. He added that these advantages and disadvantages are unevenly distributed in ways that benefit some at the expense of others. As I resist some of the advantages of new technologies this year, I've been thinking more about the corresponding disadvantages and who they affect.

Walking home from the theatre last night, empty handed, I was frustrated and wished I could just use the internet to buy a ticket but I also tried to think about whether I really wanted that. I started thinking about the dangerous work of sorting through ewaste, the glut of energy needed to power the cloud, the PTSD of online content moderators, the unethical mining and manufacturing that goes into our devices... Is Adam Sandler really worth all that?

TUESDAY, JANUARY 7th

When I think back over the past 20ish years – since I started using the internet regularly – there haven't been very many extended periods of disconnection. I went on a big canoe trip a few years ago and was completely out of touch for two weeks, but other than that, I've been pretty online every day. I had my own website by the time I was twelve and, around the same age, was obsessed with downloading music and burning mix CDs. In the early days of instant messaging and social media, I was all about it: ICQ, MSN, AIM, Nexopia, MySpace. In recent years, I've cut back on my social media, but I've long since taken for granted that the internet will always be part of my life. Although I know this year will be different, I don't expect spending it offline will convince me to avoid the internet forever. I don't even think that's possible.

WEDNESDAY, JANUARY 8th
Today's my first day on campus without the internet and it felt weird walking to my office. I slipped into my faculty's building and made my way up the stairs without having to stop and chat with anyone. From a distance, I saw one of my professors and my department's registrar. They both looked busy and I didn't interrupt. Not being online makes me feel sneaky, like I'm avoiding contact.

When I got to my office, I got straight to work. It felt like a rare pleasure, getting right to work on the things I had to work on, instead of checking my email and adding all sorts of unexpected tasks to my schedule.

THURSDAY, JANUARY 9th
Last night, I had my first class on Critical Disability Studies. I think it's going to be a good course. I decided to take it after presenting at a conference this summer about students' over-reliance on digital tools. The professor for this class was at the conference and came up to me after my talk to tell me she really didn't like my presentation. She pointed out how making light of people's reliance on digital tools can be ableist. Although I felt overwhelmed by her criticism, I realized I have to reconsider how I frame peoples' relationship with digital tools. So I'm taking her class.

When I approached her to ask whether I could participate in the course while offline, she was very open to it. I wonder if this has anything to do with her commitment to disability justice and providing students with the accommodations they need. When adding extra work this year in lieu of internet conveniences, I want to – as often as possible – take on that work myself. As a non-disabled student with government funding and the safety net of a supportive middle-class family, I think I can handle it.

Today I walked for twenty minutes in the cold to try, once again, to buy a ticket for the new Adam Sandler movie. Even with their added show-times, tickets were again already all sold out.

As I walked home, I thought more about the advantages and disadvantages of new technologies. I realized that doing something online seems to *replace* labour, making things more convenient, but it actually just *displaces* the labour, making things more convenient *for us* at the expense of strangers we'll never meet. By spending the year offline, I'm trying to revalue the hidden work that powers the internet by displacing it with my own inconveniences, like having to walk to the theatre in the cold and failing to buy myself a ticket.

SATURDAY, JANUARY 11th

I may have met my hussband last night. Before going to a drag show, a bunch of us were at Darren's having drinks. There were about ten of us, including three guys I hadn't met before: Darren's friend Junior, Junior's friend Jonas, and Jonas' friend Rod. It was a chatty group and everyone had an opinion on everything.

We were talking about dating apps and whether people would be open to dating someone who wasn't on social media. Almost everyone agreed that it doesn't matter. Rod, though, who's a spin instructor with a very pretty face, said he'd be hesitant. Darren and Rod started talking about Grindr and Instagram (the two "places" they meet most of their honeys) but being at Darren's surrounded by tipsy gays felt sorta like a dating app, just without the ability to curate ourselves into ideals … and with much better chances of going home with someone.

✦✦✦✦✦

As we were lying in bed this morning, Jonas started to scroll. I didn't want to explain that I couldn't look, so I just turned my head to the side and averted my gaze. If we keep hanging out, I'll tell him soon.

TUESDAY, JANUARY 14th
Being offline has started to make me feel a bit disconnected in a way I don't like. Things can change a lot in a week. I've been sleeping in more than I used to, and in the evenings I've been feeling at loose ends, like I don't have new things to discover. My procrastination has hardly any outlets. I feel stifled.

It's odd because my actual everyday life isn't much different than before.

✦✦✦✦✦

There's a sticker I keep seeing around Montreal that says, "so many likes, so little love." But if people know that social media likes aren't satisfying, why are we all on our phones so much? It feels like nobody wants to change, but I also know that social media platforms like Facebook and Instagram hire the best psychologists and marketing teams possible.

Last year I listened to an interview with a former Google employee about how social media manages our attention. He discussed the power of negative emotions and how users are more likely to stay on a platform if they're feeling down. The platforms capitalize on our sadness. They present us with photos of our friends having fun without us, profiles of people with similar careers as us but who are doing better, upsetting news stories, and anything to make us feel insecure enough to stay online. They know that if we're feeling good, we're more likely to put our phones down and log off. So they're invested in our depression, but in a twisted way where it feels like we're connecting, or working towards connecting, while constantly being reminded of how unhappy we should be.

WEDNESDAY, JANUARY 15th

I got to the airport super early. I couldn't check in for my flight from home and I was worried that the check-in process would be complicated or slow. It wasn't. The employee who greeted me said I had to use a machine. I don't know if they're online, but I assume they are.

"Could I just go talk to the person instead?"

"You first have to try the machine," he explained, "then – if it doesn't work – you can talk to the person."

I told him I'm avoiding the internet this year to prepare for my grad school research.

"Do you know if the machines use the internet?" I asked.

He didn't know and let me join the line-up for the person.

When I got to the front of the line, I didn't even need to explain myself. The employee just looked at my ID and printed off a boarding pass.

★★★★★

I'm on the flight now to Edmonton, where I grew up. Next to me, there's a woman from Cameroon who now lives in Edmonton. She is travelling with her two small children – one who's four and the other who's just one, sitting in her lap. They both seem very chill, and when the older one got a bit restless, her mom gave her a tablet to watch.

I told the woman about my project, and she shared her concerns about the ways the internet influences her kids. She talked about YouTube and how her daughter often stumbles across toy reviews, advertising to her under the guise of entertainment. And she talked about her own issues, being addicted to WhatsApp. She said that she wishes she could get off the internet, especially cause she has some exams coming up which she needs to study for. She claims the internet distracts her and takes all her time away, but that she needs it to keep in touch with family in Cameroon.

She was interested in my offline project and said she wants to try it for a month. I suggested it might be better to work towards moderation instead of a radical break, and she agreed.

"But it's not as easy."

THURSDAY, JANUARY 16th

Usually when I visit my parents, we spend a lot of time sitting around on our devices. We keep each other company but we're all also doing our own things online. Earlier today we were sitting around and nobody was on their device, except my sister-in-law. Now though, as we sit around after dinner with tea and rugelach, things have devolved and everyone is on their phones except me and my dad. He's doing something on his Apple watch, and I'm on my laptop … typing this.

My dad mentioned that, out of respect for me, he's trying not to use his device when I'm around. In Montreal, partly because I don't have wifi at my apartment, I think lots of people end up feeling that way, or something similar. Most people seem to avoid using their devices around me, even though I've never asked them not to. Sometimes people even ask my permission and I always point out that they don't need to ask me to use their phone. I act surprised, like they're being absurd, but secretly I love it.

FRIDAY, JANUARY 17th

Last night, I got together with three of my high school friends and interviewed them about their early experiences of the internet. We talked about a website called Ebaumsworld as an early internet staple, at least for our demographic of grade school boys in the suburbs. I remember it for the funny pictures and cartoons, but there was also hidden adult content. My friends explained that the porn was built into games on the site, like one where you had to answer trivia in order to see photos of a woman stripping; with each question you got right, you would see a photo of her with an extra piece of clothing removed. I don't remember these adult games. Maybe I was already aware of sexism, but it's more likely I was oblivious or just not interested in photos of naked women.

Throughout the hour long interview, the conversation often returned to sex, even though I didn't ask any questions about it. I should add that all three of the guys I was talking to are single, so that may be a factor, but there seems to be a particularly close connection between the internet and sex for a lot of people. I think for me there used to be, but there hasn't been as much of one lately. A lot of my early sexual experiences were facilitated by the internet, back before Craigslist banned personal ads. These meet-ups weren't particularly conducive to dating, but they served a purpose that I found valuable at the time. And I eventually did meet my first long-term partner online, though not on Craigslist.

SUNDAY, JANUARY 19th

Last night I borrowed my parents' car and stopped by a friend's house. Edmonton is built on a grid with fairly straightforward numbering for both the avenues and the streets. My friend, though, lives on one of the few avenues that has a name instead of a number. Because I couldn't look it up on Google Maps, I asked him the approximate avenue number and somehow he didn't know. I wonder if it's because he's always got his smartphone on him. I also wonder if this reliance is really a problem if he's always got his smartphone on him. (I mean, it was a problem for me trying to find his place.)

When I first moved to Montreal, Google Maps had my address wrong for several months and lots of my friends got lost on their way over, even after I explained the glitch. Sometimes I think it's just my generation, but my aunt and uncle were around long before the internet and they're still super reliant on their GPS. They use Google Maps every time they leave the house. Last time I visited, we went to one of their favourite Chinese restaurants that was two minutes away. When we were heading over, my uncle turned on the GPS and entered the restaurant's name into it.

I asked him, "Don't you know how to get there?"

He brushed off my question and said he was turning the GPS on "just in case."

✶✶✶✶✶

Today I was meant to fly back to Montreal but my flight was cancelled at the last minute. (I found out because the airline texted me.) I was especially frustrated because I had plans to see Jonas tonight. I tried to phone and reschedule my flight but an automated recording told me that due to a high volume of calls, the airline could not be reached. They weren't even putting people on hold or doing callbacks.

So my mom and I drove to the airport – 45 minutes away – and I got booked on a flight through Calgary ... leaving five hours later than expected. We drove back home – another 45 minutes – and my brother told me that there are flights from Toronto to Montreal every hour. If I'd known that, I would have tried to get an earlier flight to Toronto and then just gone standby back to Montreal. It's a bit frustrating to realize that the internet could have saved my mom and me a trip to the airport and I could have seen Jonas tonight. But I should just appreciate the triviality of the delay and how incredible it is to be able to make it from one side of the country to another in a day. Still, I can't shake the feeling that I've been taken advantage of. I can't help thinking that if I had internet access, I would have been able to advocate for myself more effectively.

MONDAY, JANUARY 20th

I'm at a coffee shop with Hannibal. I missed class last week while in Edmonton, so he's filling me in on what happened. The professor changed the syllabus again, which I wouldn't have known if I didn't have a friend to rely on. I feel bad having to depend on Hanni, but he doesn't seem to mind – I actually think he's happy to be able to support me. The class is about disability and we've been talking a lot about the value of embracing the ways we rely on others, or being more open to the types of collaborative existences valued in disabled communities. Hanni not only filled me in on what I missed, he's helping us get some applied practice with ideas from the course.

TUESDAY, JANUARY 21st

Last night, Jonas came over for dinner. We were trying to eat, but mostly cuddling on the couch sorta watching *Napoleon Dynamite* on DVD. It was almost 10 and we were getting particularly cozy when my doorbell rang. I paused the movie – jokingly asking Jonas if he was expecting someone – and went to the door. It turned out to be a stranger who found my address on the website I put up last year about my offline project. I don't know how they heard about it, but they just wanted to share some information about upcoming events that they're organizing. It was like getting an email in person, though I don't understand why they went to such an effort.

I was telling some colleagues about what happened and my friend Sloane said that they'd never put their address on the internet because of stalkers and scary men. I forget all the things I take for granted as a man. My supervisor, Aviva, sympathized with Sloane's hesitancy and agreed that gender is a factor, but she felt differently. She's ten or so years older than me and Sloane and said that, until a few years ago, showing up at someone's house unexpectedly wouldn't have seemed so odd.

Maybe I'm just young, but I feel like, even pre-internet, it'd still be strange to show up at a stranger's house to invite them to your community events – especially at 10 p.m. Or maybe I'm just so stuck in the impersonal individualism of internet culture that I can't open up to the kindness of strangers.

✶✶✶✶✶

After doing a bit of work this morning, I went to check out my friend Lori's art stand. Lori's one of our faculty's artists-in-residence and they host a weekly drop-in session. Around the same time I arrived, a 19-year-old student stopped by and the three of us did a drawing together. We realized we were each a decade apart (I'm 30 and Lori's around ten years older than me) and we discussed how different, and similar, our experiences of the internet have been.

The 19-year-old was talking about how much his social life revolves around group chats on his phone, even when he and his friends are hanging out in person. I told him and Lori a theory I'd heard, that the reason why the show *Friends* is so popular again now is because it feeds people's nostalgia for a time before smartphones, when people could just sit around and chat with their friends. They both disagreed, insisting that people still have plenty of in-person chats, like the one we were having. Lori agreed though that nostalgia does play a part in people's renewed interest in *Friends*, but they had a different take: "Some folks miss the days when they didn't have to think about race, or gender, or sexual orientation. They don't want to question their privilege, so they watch *Friends*."

✦✦✦✦✦

This evening I was asked to emcee my university's cellphone film festival at the last minute. I agreed but right before the event began, one of the organizers told me he had loaded the winning videos on YouTube and I just had to press play. I told him I couldn't because of my internetless project and he gave me a look like I was being ridiculous or difficult. (Or maybe I was projecting my insecurities.) I told him I was happy to emcee but that I would have to leave the room for the videos.

WEDNESDAY, JANUARY 22nd
I got a letter in the mail from Aviva about her relationship with email. She told me that she checks if there's anything new right before bed and it's the first thing she looks at when she wakes up. It's where she finds out whether her funding

applications and publications have been accepted or rejected. She described it as "a barometer of self worth."

Being off email this month has mostly been a pleasure, but it's frustrating when I'm trying to get in touch with someone I don't know very well. I want to invite a prof from another department to do a guest lecture in one of my classes. Luckily I know where his office is, but without email, I'll have to go by his office, and if he's not around, I'll have to slip a note under his door… That's actually not so bad. I've just been spoiled by email.

✶✶✶✶✶

I turned my phone to silent all day today to see how it would affect me and I loved it. I even turned off the vibrations so I don't have to deal with that cloying buzz every time I get a text message. I think I'm going to keep it this way.

THURSDAY, JANUARY 23rd
This evening I had some friends over for dinner, including Jonas. Jonas invited his friend Junior, whom I've only met once before. Junior is really easy to talk to and we realized that we both play violin. We were talking about jamming together but Junior doesn't have a cellphone number. He has an iPhone but just uses the internet. Junior is the second person I've met around my age who uses the internet instead of a cellphone plan. I got Junior's mailing address and said I'll send him a letter so we can figure out a time to jam. And I will send him a letter, but knowing my generation and how flaky we can be, I doubt Junior and I will be making music together anytime soon.

SATURDAY, JANUARY 25th
I had a nightmare last night that I went online – accidentally. I was looking something up and when I realized that I was online, I got really freaked out and tried to delete my browsing history. For some reason though, I couldn't figure out how. So then I tried to delete the computer altogether,

whatever that means. It was terrifying and I felt so much guilt.

✦✦✦✦✦

Earlier this week, Jonas was sleeping over and we were brushing our teeth. He finished first and, after rinsing, popped his toothbrush into my toothbrush cup. As he strutted out of the bathroom, he said, "I'm just gonna leave that there." His British accent was heavy with a sassy confidence that made me quiver.

SUNDAY, JANUARY 26th

Sometimes I worry that I won't hear about things because I'm offline, but I was told about today's protest twice. It was snowing rain/raining slush when we arrived. The aim was to show support against India's constitutional amendment whereby Muslim immigrants and refugees are ineligible for Indian citizenship. The march was not as well attended as other marches I've been to recently, but there were enough people to shut down traffic, feel solidarity, build momentum, and pose for videos and pictures – probably to be posted on the internet (another way I'm inevitably still online).

After the protest, I had Jonas and some friends over to play Scrabble. I was surprised how often people were pulling out their phones and shoving them in my face. I'm getting very good at looking away. Darren really wanted to show me a picture of his latest dude, a guy he had met at an after-hours venue last weekend. To be honest, I was disappointed that I wasn't able to look and feel excited for Darren.

Jonas is staying over tonight and we're sitting at my kitchen table doing work together. He's also a grad student, but studying epidemiology. Normally, if I'm sitting with someone doing work in a place where there's internet, I assume they're deep in the webs, caught up in some unpredictable space or activity. Without the internet here, I know that all Jonas might be doing is reading things he has on his computer or working on an assignment. Being in our own digital spaces but together offline makes me feel more connected to him than if we were together but online.

I just read that last paragraph to Jonas and he smiled pensively, but then got back to work without comment.

MONDAY, JANUARY 27th

I'm working with Hanni on a paper – exploring pace of life at our university and how the expectations students face around productivity can be disabling and ableist. Normally, we would probably have emailed each other ideas and references, but I asked him to meet in person.

A major challenge is that I can't do new research or look things up online. I was therefore forced to think back to other things I've worked with before or have saved on my computer. Too often, working on papers means skimming abstracts for keywords and building impressive reference lists. Without the internet, though, my process involved deep dives into readings, and finding connections between pace of life and other concepts that I've been building offline libraries about for years.

TUESDAY, JANUARY 28th

While working at the graduate student society lounge, I overheard a couple of students talking about a professor they have for environmental law who included a note on his syllabus about avoiding unnecessary emails to reduce carbon emissions. I didn't mean to be eavesdropping but because I was, I couldn't help interjecting, especially because the two people I was listening to both seemed to think that such a suggestion (that email has environmental repercussions) was ridiculous.

I apologized for overhearing them but explained what I'm studying and insisted that the internet does have environmental consequences, even if most people aren't so aware of them. They seemed skeptical and asked how sending an email could have an impact on carbon emissions. After telling them about the energy and nonrenewable resources that are needed to build internet infrastructures, they still seemed unconvinced.

They were getting up to leave so I concluded with something about how we wouldn't run the water needlessly, so maybe their professor was just suggesting to avoid sending emails when in-person communication can work instead. As they walked out the door, one of them said that she had never thought about the fact that sending an email has material impacts.

WEDNESDAY, JANUARY 29th
Every interaction I have lately seems full of "so-and-so has their email," "you can take a look on the course website," "check it out on YouTube," "if you just shoot me a message about that," etc. It almost feels like I'm being microaggressed, except I've chosen to spend the year offline, and I don't think the idea of microaggressions is for me.

★★★★★

This morning I went to a memorial for the six men murdered three years ago today at a mosque in Quebec City. One of my profs, Abdul, told me about the event when I bumped into him a couple days ago, but he didn't know the exact location. I knew which building it was in, but when I got there, I had to ask a bunch of people if they knew where the event was being held before I found someone who showed me the way. Everyone I spoke to wanted to talk about the murders though, even the people who didn't know about the memorial.

Being forced to talk to strangers unexpectedly helped me start some conversations about Islamophobia in Quebec. Overall though, not being able to look up the directions was pretty frustrating.

THURSDAY, JANUARY 30th
It's been a whirlwind day. It's almost midnight and 24 hours ago I was on a bus from Montreal to Toronto, sitting on the upper deck, trying to sleep, but a bit too cold.

I was meant to take the train to Toronto today so that I could make some sperm donations for my queer friends who are trying to get pregnant. My friend Fanny's ovulation schedule is pretty irregular though and she called me yesterday when I was at school to say that she was ovulating two or three days earlier than expected. This meant that I had to get to Toronto in 24 hours so that this month's egg wouldn't go to waste. I went home, packed my stuff, went back to campus, went to class, left early, went to the Megabus station, and boarded the 9 p.m. bus to Toronto via Kingston. The bus takes six hours and I had two seats to myself but couldn't get comfortable.

When I got off the bus in downtown Toronto at three in the morning, Fanny and Alex were waiting across the street.

"Fancy meeting you here," Fanny said.

Less than 15 minutes after getting back to their place, I came into a cup with the help of a Tom of Finland book I brought with me, then quickly passed the cup off to Fanny and Alex in the next room.

★★★★★

When I woke up, it was noon and I went into the other room where Fanny was drinking tea with a friend. I couldn't help but think about the fact that she had my semen inside her, but of course I didn't say anything. Fanny's friend was talking about why people don't invite her out anymore, speculating what assumptions people make because of social media. I wasn't sure I understood, but suggested that social media may make it feel to her friends like they *are* keeping up with each other and so spending time on social media could replace (albeit superficially) the need to invite each other out.

Then we talked about the news and how much I seem to know about despite being offline. I've noticed that, getting the same news through different friends, I end up getting different details about events – sometimes even conflicting accounts. I guess the same would be true if I was getting news online. News has become a social thing for me this year. I'm never alone scrolling through headlines, and I can't read the news in bed. Whenever I find out what's going on in the world now, it's in conversation with someone. It feels more manageable, even when it's not.

FRIDAY, JANUARY 31st

I've gone without internet for a month now and people keep asking what I've noticed. How is my life different? The two changes I've been most aware of relate to time and pace. My days have become longer and slower, and not in a lethargic or anxious way.

I don't know what I was doing online that was sucking up so much of my time, but every day now, instead of checking my email and reading the headlines, I have time for conversations with friends and classmates. Instead of looking things up and planning my week, I've found time for all sorts of things I've been putting off. Instead of buying and downloading, I find myself reading books and cooking meals. Instead of scrolling through pictures and profiles, I've been going on more walks, wandering around and noticing things, talking to strangers. I feel like I have time to think and feel and even be bored. It all sounds a bit too romantic and I'm sure there are things I'm missing out on, but I'm a full-time student, I have two research jobs, I've been dating and keeping up with my friends and family… I don't really want to be any busier than I am, even though I know that's what's expected of me.

February

And there is solace in being cut off.
—Leanne Betasamosake Simpson, 2020, *Noopiming*

SATURDAY, FEBRUARY 1st
Yesterday I was on the subway in Toronto and there were five people in the car around me, all women. The three nearest me were on their devices, but each had a different kind: one laptop, one tablet, one smartphone.

The two women sitting past them were just chatting – no devices.

I wasn't trying to eavesdrop but I heard one of them say, "She's doing her second round of IVF. The first time she got pregnant twice but had two doctor-induced miscarriages."

The other one asked, "How did that happen?"

"I'm not sure. I haven't actually talked to her for a while. I just know about it from Instagram."

The personal is public. Their conversation made me think about why I got off Facebook in 2010. I was living in Holland and had been trying to reach my friend Winston back in Canada. When I finally got ahold of him over Skype, I gave him a hard time for being so elusive.

"We haven't caught up in ages!" I said.

"I know," he replied, "but I've been seeing what you're up to over Facebook."

So I deleted my Facebook.

SUNDAY, FEBRUARY 2nd

I arrived at the station to head back to Montreal, a few minutes earlier than I normally would. I didn't have a ticket yet, just a handwritten note with the confirmation number they gave me over the phone. I stood in line for ten minutes and then showed the attendant my confirmation number in exchange for a printed ticket. It was too easy.

When I sat down on the train, I pulled out my phone. I had two outstanding text messages to reply to. Neither was serious but I was feeling anxious about responding, dreading the effort it would take. I'd been putting it off since yesterday. I took a deep breath and responded to both of them back-to-back. It wasn't so bad. I think I get stressed because I never know how long people will take to respond – or if they'll respond at all.

Some people call us the Ghost Generation. We leave without saying goodbye. Okay, nobody's calling us the Ghost Generation, but maybe they should be. We're algorithms already, data points to be sorted and coordinated. The Ghost Generation doesn't have to deal with the consequences of our actions. We've stored everything in the cloud; we're insulated against losses and it's all "free." We're remote-controlling drone strikes from La-Z-Boys, watching the action on HD smart TVs. And when it's game over, we start again. When things break, we get a new one. When things are old, we get a new one. When things are fine, we get a new one. And when we get a new one, all we have to worry about is how many dollars it costs, not how many people, how many resources, or how much longer this can last.

MONDAY, FEBRUARY 3rd

Tonight I'm having Junior over to play some fiddle. I got a call from a private number and it was him! He doesn't have a cellphone plan, so he used a Google product that can call cellphones for free over the internet. Because I was just using my phone like normal, I don't consider this breaking my rules, but it's another example of how the online/offline distinction is far from clear.

TUESDAY, FEBRUARY 4th

I'm at work today and feeling a bit out of sorts, pulled in a few different directions. Part of the issue with being offline is that when I want to check in with someone, I often rely on the drop-in, which can be a bit abrasive in a lot of people's rigidly-packed day, or just uncomfortable if you don't know the person well enough. I wanted to have a quick chat with my old supervisor who just got back from a big trip, but when I poked my head in her office, there were a bunch of other people there with her for a meeting and they all looked serious and a bit annoyed by my intrusion.

I moseyed around the building and noticed Lori's office door was open, so I popped my head in and we ended up chatting for almost an hour.

When I was leaving, Lori looked at the time and chuckled, "I've already been here for two hours and I haven't gotten anything done." I apologized for intruding but Lori stopped me. "I meant that I hadn't gotten anything done until you stopped by. Thank you."

THURSDAY, FEBRUARY 6th

After class this week, I told my Critical Disability Studies professor about an in-person Disability Arts event that my friend Leah invited me to. A few of Leah's friends are in town from a gallery in Toronto that only showcases works from disabled artists. They're giving a talk on how they try to make their exhibits more accessible.

My prof seemed surprised she didn't already know about the talk. I was surprised too, especially that I heard about it before her. Being offline, I didn't expect to feel so plugged in. She turned to her computer and immediately started typing. I didn't look but assume she was Googling, or searching on Facebook. "I don't see anything about it online," she told me, sounding skeptical.

It's like in-person events are only real if they're advertised on the internet.

FRIDAY, FEBRUARY 7th
I'm doing some reading for class and sitting across from Jonas who is doing some work on his laptop. He's been distracted by his phone a bunch, group messaging with his family about gift ideas for some of his siblings' upcoming birthdays. Jonas is a triplet and he has four siblings in total. Right now, his brother is in Zurich, and his sisters are in Leeds, Panama City, and the Swiss Alps. His parents are both in Winterslow, the village that Jonas grew up in, twenty minutes from Stonehenge. Jonas couldn't keep in touch with his family without the internet, or not in the way that he does now. It would probably make the idea of living far away from family less appealing for a lot of people. (And more appealing for others.)

SATURDAY, FEBRUARY 8th
I had a meeting today with a research team I'm on that's developing a sex-ed app focused on teen dating violence. My mom worked in schools for several decades and I was telling her about the idea. She said that throughout her career, she found that digital tools were often introduced in schools regardless of whether or not there was a need for them. The technology itself became the aim instead of using the technology for a particular aim. I hope that doesn't happen with this project.

On the way home, I noticed an older woman get on the metro and look around for a seat. There were two younger women sitting in the seats reserved for elderly or disabled people and they were both on their phones. I wasn't sure if they were just pretending not to notice the elderly woman, or if they legitimately didn't see her, but neither of them got up.

I've started noticing signs in the metro reminding people not to get too distracted by their phones. The sign depicts the distracted cellphone users as zombiefied cave-people, which is a bit ironic; I mean, I get it, but isn't there something misleading about using cave-people as a symbol for what happens when we use advanced, digital technologies?

When the metro started moving again, the elderly woman still didn't have a seat, so she moved to the bar in the centre and held on tight. I was standing nearby and wanted to say something to the two women sitting in the reserved seats, but I didn't. I love a good altercation, but I was worried about being a saviour, and I was aware that they might have a hidden disability or another reason why they needed a seat. But I was frustrated. I don't know if phones just make people zone out or if they're actually making it more difficult to be empathetic.

SUNDAY, FEBRUARY 9th
"Dear Diary, Jonas is knitting right next to me. He just finished his scarf. It looks great. Now he's onto his hat. It looks great. What a guy. Are you writing exactly what I just said? What are you writing? Knit, purl, knit, purl, knit, purl, knit." That's what Jonas just said, so I wrote it down.

Last night we went with our friend Junior to watch some of the live action shorts that were nominated for this year's Oscars. One of them was about a sexy middle-aged couple with three young kids who live across the street from a sexy younger couple. Both couples leave their blinds open and spend a lot of time looking into each other's windows, feeling envious.

I don't think it was meant as a metaphor for social media, but it could have been. Instead of being present with their partners, the couples look through their windows (almost like looking through social media) into the lives of others and project themselves onto them with fantasy and fomo. Of course the film ends with both couples realizing that they were envious of the other, which makes the envy seem pointless, like we should just be happy with what we've got. Classic.

MONDAY, FEBRUARY 10th

I made my television debut as an extra in my friend's episode of *Little America*, which just started streaming on Apple TV. Unfortunately, because it's only available online, I can't watch it. Another group of people who can't access it are viewers in a dozen countries where, although Apple TV is available, anti-queer censorship compelled Apple to remove the episode. And Apple didn't even tell my friend that this was happening!! He found out through Twitter.

★★★★★

One of the speakers at today's Wet'suwet'en protest said something that scared me. It was a quote from a protester arrested yesterday in BC. As they were being taken away, they looked at the officer making the arrest and said:

"Your spirit will never recover from this."

The speaker who shared this anecdote made it sound vindictive, like the person being arrested was putting a spell on the police. I see it a bit differently; the message, "Your spirit will never recover from this" is not a curse of what ought to happen to the police officer carrying out the arrests, but a prophecy of what is happening to all of us right now as we fail to act.

TUESDAY, FEBRUARY 11th

My professor Abdul phoned today to ask how I've been doing without the internet. He doesn't have a cellphone so I feel like he's more hardcore than I am. After I shared a bit of what I've been thinking, I asked him about his relationship to tech. Abdul is a labour activist and believes that relationships are the most important factor for movement building. He told me about a woman he works with who's had a lot of success engaging her coworkers in union work. Though she uses online tools for outreach, she finds in-person events to be the most effective organizing tactic – things like movie screenings or pub nights. She said that these kinds of events allow people to really engage with each other, telling stories and chatting about the issues of labour justice and the value of union organizing.

After getting off the phone with Abdul, I rushed to campus. While we were talking, I realized the call was going on too long and I was running late. But building relationships is worth the rush.

✶✶✶✶✶

My friend Camille helped me set up a display on campus today about my year offline. She made a sign that said "AMA: Ask Me Anything" and put together several little models to provoke conversations about the internet. We sat around and invited people passing by to chat. Some of the people we spoke with included:

- a professor who was teaching a drawing class and had bought their first Facebook sponsored ad;
- two students studying with autistic people who told me how the tactile buttons of my non-smartphone would probably be easier for people with disabilities who struggle with the smooth screen of the smartphone;
- an Iranian woman who chats with her mom twice a day because she has the internet (I wonder what she would have done 20 years ago?);
- someone who was advocating for small changes to online life (she charges her phone across the room from her now and it makes a big difference);
- a dad whose daughter doesn't like commercial television (as he calls the kind of television that has commercials, like cable) but loves Netflix. He believes she prefers Netflix because there are no commercials but I suggested some other factors: on-demand, peer culture, can watch it alone on her laptop;
- a professor who brought up the way word processing hides the process of drafting a piece of writing such that students become too attached to drafts and think they're finished when they're not;
- and another professor who said she spends the first part

of her day online every day because her grandkids like to FaceTime her during breakfast.

THURSDAY, FEBRUARY 13th
Today my friend Omar was texting me and, knowing that emojis don't show up on my phone, he wrote :insert heart: instead.

I replied with a <3.

SUNDAY, FEBRUARY 16th
When Bobby arrived from the airport, he really wanted to show me a woman he went on a date with last week, and he started scrolling through pictures. I remember seeing a cute, wide-brimmed hat before realizing that the photo was online. I looked away, but it was too late. Bobby tried to convince me that he loaded the photos earlier and so they were no longer online. He even turned his phone to airplane mode to prove it.

What's the difference, he pointed out, between looking at a photo that's already been downloaded from the internet and looking at the photo of this woman on Bobby's dating app which, especially with airplane mode turned on, is really just a photo downloaded from the internet? I didn't argue but I feel like I fucked up. I'm trying not to beat myself up about it, but I have to be more careful.

The online world is creeping in.

MONDAY, FEBRUARY 17th
This evening Bobby and I stopped by a pawn shop to see if they had an N64 console. Since I've gone offline I've been playing a lot of Mario Kart, but a couple days ago my N64 stopped working. This is the same console I've had since I was a kid so it must be at least 20 years old, probably older. It's impressive that it lasted this long but I'm having a hard time believing that it's actually broken. Bobby and I spent half an hour just blowing into the game cartridge and turning the console off and on again before we gave up.

I thought finding a new N64 would be easy, but both of the pawn shops we tried said that they very rarely get any in. If I looked online, I'd probably find loads of them. Kijiji and Craigslist are great for that. But I can't, so I'll keep going to pawn shops. Or I could try to take the console to a repair shop, but will they still know how to fix it? Luckily my Sega Genesis started working again recently, so at least I've got something.

WEDNESDAY, FEBRUARY 19th

I'm heading to Berlin next week to visit some friends. I've never been to Berlin but I've heard it's like the '90s, so I'll fit in well. I hope that being offline won't cause me too much trouble. I mean, people travelled without the internet for a vast majority of human history, but things have changed now. I'm sure I'll run into some issues – especially navigating an unfamiliar city. Luckily, I'm staying with friends, so I'll be able to rely on them.

Being offline is helping me accept that relying on other people can be a positive thing. I feel like modern sensibilities suggest that independence is the goal of our individualistic society, and all the hidden resources behind the internet can help facilitate this so-called independence. Without such online supports though, I've had to rely more on people around me, which has involved nurturing relationships so that I can be supported.

It's strange to realize that digital tools, though often discussed as obstacles to independence (people are described as relying too much on the internet), can also be obstacles to dependence, facilitating a kind of selfish and superficial individualism that doesn't make space for others.

THURSDAY, FEBRUARY 20th

This morning while I was lying in bed with Jonas, he told me that the women he hangs out with from his grad school cohort had been grilling him about my internetless project. It sounds like they were being pretty bold, suggesting that my year offline wasn't rigorous or valuable for educational research, or something like that. Why does my internetless project bother them? Jonas suggested that they may think I'm attacking the way they use the internet. Could hating on my project be a defensive move? Because people are insecure about the ways they use the internet? Because people are threatened by the prospect of losing their connection? I feel like their cynicism and critiques have more to do with their feelings about the internet and its value, and less to do with me and my project. So back off, alright? Or, even better, come right in.

FRIDAY, FEBRUARY 21st

My cellphone rang at 8:30 this morning, the robotic voice on the other line announcing that my train to New York had been cancelled. Would I be refunded automatically? Was my return trip cancelled as well? I couldn't ask any questions because the call was automated. (…it probably was the internet calling.) I hung up and looked in the yellow pages for Greyhound's number. As I was struggling to find it, Jonas (who was still lying in bed but following my small drama) had looked up the number on his phone and – without me asking him to – written it down on a post-it and passed it to me with, "I bet this is making you realize just how convenient the internet is?" He laughed. I didn't.

And that was before I ran into the first major obstacle of my year offline: the woman on the phone from Greyhound told me that I couldn't buy a ticket without an email address. Over the phone, Greyhound can still sell tickets (with a $10 surcharge) but there's no longer any way to pick them up; printing them through email is the only option. Even if I go into the station, I was told I would still be unable to buy a ticket. This seemed too ridiculous to be true; I had seen Greyhound booths at the bus station before. I hung up, and phoned the station directly (this time using a number from the yellow pages), but the call was forwarded to Greyhound. I spoke with a different person who told me the same thing:

without internet, I could not take the bus. I still couldn't believe it and thought I'd just head over to the bus station and check for myself. But then I started to worry – if everyone else on my train also got an automated cancellation call at 8:30, then everyone else would be trying to buy bus tickets or flights (with the ease and speed of the internet), and soon everything might be booked. So, instead of taking the time to go to the bus station and try my offline luck, I phoned Air Canada, waited on the line for 45 minutes, and booked a $278 one-way flight to New York City. My dad used to say that if you pay less, you pay twice. I guess this is one of those cases. The only reason I'm going to New York is because flying from there to Berlin was so much cheaper than flying out of Montreal. Not anymore.

After getting off the phone, I went to a protest in solidarity with the Wet'suwet'en blockades that are happening in BC right now, obstructing the federal government's proposed pipeline. The Wet'suwet'en protests are the reason why my train to New York was cancelled, so it felt a bit ironic to be supportive of the cause and still frustrated by the morning's events. I reminded myself, though, that there are more important things than my convenience.

I made a couple signs. One said, "Hey Canada – your colonialism is showing!" The other said, "Trudeau? ...more like LIEdeau!" I got a few smirks from people about the second one.

Decolonization may be something I support, but it will have difficult consequences for my convenient, comfortable existence. As my mom pointed out to me recently, Jewish settlers who emigrated from Europe to Canada were given lots of financial support from the colonial government. This allowed her grandparents, my great-grandparents, to prosper and acquire property and resources without considering the Indigenous displacement that they were prospering from.

As someone who has done well through this system of colonization, I am almost glad to be impacted negatively by these protests and still motivated to participate. It's easy to support something that is good for oneself in the short term; it's more difficult to support something with more long-term and collective benefits.

SUNDAY, FEBRUARY 23rd

I'm leaving for New York tomorrow on my way to Berlin on Tuesday. I'm a little nervous about travelling internationally without the internet, but I'm hoping it'll be easier to dive into the trip without online distractions.

As I was choosing a couple books to bring with, I started flipping through an old copy of Gabriel García Marquez' *One Hundred Years of Solitude.* I found a passage that I'd underlined about how upset everyone got after the first telephone was installed in town:

"It was as if God had decided to put to the test every capacity for surprise and was keeping the inhabitants of Macondo in a permanent alternation between excitement and disappointment, doubt and revelation, to such an extreme that no one knew for certain where the limits of reality lay."

Now we have this type of connectivity in each of our pockets and it's constant. The alternation between excitement and disappointment, doubt and revelation is so much more extreme and frequent that we can hardly process it, but it's changing us.

MONDAY, FEBRUARY 24th

I didn't realize how inconvenient taxis have become … at least in Brooklyn. I went for a drink with a friend in Williamsburg this evening and then spent 45 minutes trying to flag a cab. Eventually, I phoned the friend I'm staying with, and he came to pick me up.

I wonder why it's so hard to get a cab. Are there that many less of them now that Uber's so popular? Or do taxis now wait for people to call them on an app or something instead of just driving around looking for fares?

My friend had an upset stomach so went to the bathroom

as soon as we got back to his place. From the toilet, he asked me what I do during times like these.

I didn't know what he meant, "When I'm taking a shit?" I asked.

"No," he replied, "what do you do when you're waiting on someone. Like, do you go on your phone? Pull out a book?"

I laughed at his question. "Sometimes," I said, "or sometimes I just sit and think."

We started to talk about downtime – me from the couch and him from the toilet. For me, downtime is when I'm not doing anything external at all – no new inputs, just my own thoughts thinking their own thoughts. Downtime is how I process things, letting my ideas and mind settle. I experience downtime when I'm in transit, on walks, lying in bed. I don't experience downtime when I read, watch movies or TV, or when I listen to music or podcasts.

My friend said he has absolutely none of that kind of downtime in his life these days. He's always listening to something, setting or responding to reminders on his phone, checking his Apple watch, looking something up, reading.

When he finally left the bathroom, I was on my computer, writing this.

He grinned. "I knew you weren't just sitting and thinking!"

WEDNESDAY, FEBRUARY 26th

I made it to Germany. My last flight felt strange. I remember (very recently) when planes were one of the last refuges from the internet. There was that story a few years back about a woman who posted a racist tweet and then boarded a plane. When she landed, she found out that her tweet had been shared millions of times and she'd been fired from her job. Of course that's not an example of a time when being offline benefited a user, but getting on a flight used to mean being out of touch. When I looked around the plane today, I saw people FaceTiming, responding to emails, reading the news. Pretty soon, "Airplane Mode" won't be a thing anymore. Or if it is, kids won't know where the term came from.

THURSDAY, FEBRUARY 27th

I'm staying with my friends Julia and Winston and they were telling me about the way clubs here put stickers over people's cellphone cameras when they enter the venue. Winston said that it really changes the club vibe when people aren't posing for photos or taking selfies.

My friends had to work today so I spent the morning at the Pergamon Museum by myself. On the way there, I walked past a con man playing that game with the three cases and the little white ball. A bunch of tourists had gathered around to watch, but I didn't stop. When I arrived at the museum, I got into a bit of a thing with the cashier. She wouldn't let me pay the student fee because my student card doesn't have an expiry date on it. She told me I could go online and show her proof I was a student. I explained why I couldn't, and I think she even believed me, but she was not willing to make an exception. Germans, amirite?

★★★★★

My phone doesn't get data messages, so when someone sends me an MMS – like a group message or a photo – it just shows up as a blank text. Today I got a blank MMS from an unfamiliar Montreal number and I'm curious what it might've been, but I don't have a phone plan here, and I'm not about to spend the $12 it would cost to text back and ask.

FRIDAY, FEBRUARY 28th

I got a second text from the same Montreal number, this time asking me to confirm that I received their previous text. I did get it, but I'm not going to spend $12 to confirm it. I think it must be something work-related, although I told everyone I work with that I was heading out of town. Are we expected to respond even when we're on vacation now?

SATURDAY, FEBRUARY 29th

I borrowed my friend's bike and, although my map's not very good, I've been able to get around Berlin without too much trouble. My friends keep thinking I'm gonna get so lost, but so far I've only had to ask for directions once. Since the internet has become such a big part of getting around, people forget that it's not too tough to navigate without it.

✶✶✶✶✶

I just realized it's February 29th … which means it's a leap year and I get to spend an extra day offline!!

March

For a moment, the custom is shown to be not the horizon of possibility, but rather a tiny island in a sea of unexamined alternatives.

—Jenny Odell, 2019, *How to Do Nothing*

SUNDAY, MARCH 1st

Today I heard about "Post-Internet Art" for the first time. We were at a gallery, originally built as a Nazi bunker. The roof was made of four metre-thick concrete, and there were several floors connected by a double helix staircase. The woman running our tour told us that even staff regularly get lost. After the war, after being used as a Soviet prison, an exotic-fruit storage facility, and a nightclub, the bunker was bought by a couple of art collectors and renovated into a contemporary gallery with their private apartment on the roof.

Our guide kept referring to pieces as "Post-Internet Art," like a big cardboard horse cut-out, or an arrow jumping off a trampoline. *Post*-Internet? I didn't know we were there yet, but our guide claimed that Post-Internet Art has been an important part of their collection for at least a decade. It refers to art made for a world where creators have to think about how pieces will look when digitally reproduced, like on Instagram. Something about artistic intent and potential is very different when a piece is conceived of with Instagram in mind.

✶✶✶✶✶

I noticed a graffiti sticker on a bike lock today that read "Instagram is an ecological disaster." I'm not sure exactly which disaster the sticker is referring to, but I probably agree. Mindlessly scrolling on social media wastes a lot of energy and resources. Not to mention the way hype can ruin pristine nature spots, like the beach from that Leonardo DiCaprio movie, or #JoshuaTree.

A few hours later, I saw another graffiti sticker in another part of town that read "Fuck off Google!" It seems like Berliners despise big tech as much as I do.

TUESDAY, MARCH 3rd
I'm staying with my friend Osama now and he likes to watch something while he's falling asleep. Last night he started turning a video on while we were getting ready to doze off and I asked if it was downloaded or online. He lied and said it was downloaded. Luckily, I know Osama and I could tell he was lying, so I turned on my side, facing the wall, and fell asleep trying to ignore the narrator's obnoxious voice.

I don't want this offline project to inconvenience the people around me, especially if I'm somebody's guest, so I think turning away and ignoring the online video was a fair compromise.

It sorta feels like Osama is trying to sabotage me, though. This evening, I asked for his phone to text one of my other friends in Berlin. He pulled it out and handed it to me, already loaded on a conversation with Winston. I wrote my message and sent it, assuming it was just a text. Winston replied that I'd just sent him a message over WhatsApp, an *online* digital messaging service. Fuccccck.

I swear it felt like a text.

WEDNESDAY, MARCH 4th
It's my last full day in Berlin and the sun is out. My friends

are all at work, so I biked around the old Tempelhof airport and then to the Deutsches Technik Museum.

One of the exhibits at the museum featured a precursor to social media called a Kaiser Panorama. It's a stereo-pan-orama device, so it shows pictures that look 3D, and it circulates them amongst a group of viewers. With all the hype about the transformative effects of the online world, I often forget that things are still firmly repeating patterns of the past. German photographers used Kaiser Panoramas to try to get their photographs out to an audience who would sit in front of the machine, staring into the picture-holes as they scrolled around in a circle, leaning back once in a while to look at the captions written below. The one they had at the Technik Museum was massive and could seat twelve people at a time. Not quite the same reach as Instagram.

After the museum, I knew the vague direction back to Osama's, but didn't want to backtrack, so I just went for it and ended up having a lovely wandering bike ride. The city feels pretty straightforward after a week of navigating without a smartphone. I started by stumbling upon a big, hilly park (luckily I was going downhill) and biked through it, into a quiet residential neighbourhood. Then I got back onto busier streets and started to zig-zag: past an Islamic cemetery, stopping for baklava, passing smaller parks, stopping at a flower shop where I bought Osama and his roommate tulips and some yellow flowers that I think the florist called "ginsta." Then I hit the canal that leads back to their place. Now I'm here but no one's home. I think I'll snoop around and see if I can find a vase.

THURSDAY, MARCH 5th
Before getting on my flight, I had to answer questions about where I've been and whether I've been feeling sick. There are screens all over the place in the airport flashing scary headlines about special regulations for travellers coming from China. While I was waiting to board my flight, I went into one of those shops that sells magazines and newspapers –

just to peruse the headlines. I read that hand sanitizer is sold out everywhere; one newspaper I saw had a headline about online retailers selling little bottles of Purel for $79 US. I'll just make sure to wash my hands.

Maybe it's just due to travel, but I'm feeling more uneasy today than I have the whole time I was in Berlin. If I'd been online and checking social media while I was away, I wonder if I would have felt this anxiety sooner.

FRIDAY, MARCH 6th

I stopped in New York again on my way home, the so-called "centre of the universe," but it feels like I have nothing to do. I'm staying with the same friend again, but he went out of town this morning, so I'm alone at his apartment. I have plans this evening, but for now I'm just sitting here, checking out the books on his bookshelves, using his Hypervolt massager on my back, looking out the window at the grey sky and the beige building next door.

I know if I go outside, the city will come alive, but right now I feel like I'm stuck. And somehow it feels like if I had the internet – even just to look at a map of the cafes and restaurants and shops and museums in the neighbourhood – I would be unstuck.

*****

Just got back from a walk around the neighbourhood. Brooklyn is unique, but seeing the kinds of outfits and boutiques in the neighbourhood made me realize just how similar Brooklyn is to Berlin is to Montreal is to Brooklyn, etc. These hip big cities aren't international as much as they're cosmopolitan, reflecting a particular pattern of western, upwardly-mobile, hipster life and culture.

At the grocery store I had a funny and frustrating interaction with the woman in front of me in line whose credit card wasn't working. She tried a different card, and it didn't work either. She explained to the cashier that these were British cards, and the cashier was empathetic. She had lived in Europe for a few years and said her German card used to have problems in the US too. The customer didn't accept the empathy though and kept saying things like, "why don't you get new machines?!" and "I've been having these problems here all month and the management said they'd do something about it!" and "you need to take this up with your management!" all the while trying frantically to insert the card, tap the card, use the other card again, etc.

Eventually the cashier got another employee to come and the other woman was able to make it work, but she did *not* appreciate the customer's attitude, and made that clear before walking away.

The customer, all paid up now, turned to the cashier one last time: "Tell your managers to get new machines," adding, "Look how long this guy had to wait," while pointing at me.

ARON: I'm in no rush.
HER: Well some of us aren't so lucky. I have to get back to work.
ARON: Life can be hectic.
HER: If the machines worked, it wouldn't have to be.
ARON: Well, if you've been having the same problem all month, you could always bring cash?
HER: Uh … have you heard what's going on in the world?! Irregardless, I have a degree in mathematics and I program AI. There's no reason why these machines shouldn't work.
ARON: Sure. I'm just saying though that they *aren't* working, and you apparently knew that.
HER: And now you're being sexist.
ARON: Disagreeing with you doesn't make me sexist.

By that point, I was already done paying, so I thanked the cashier and walked towards the door. Somehow the woman, though in front of me in line, was still standing there, hungry for more altercation. I expect this kind of thing on the internet, but I forgot that arguments can escalate in bizarre ways in real life too. I felt silly getting caught up in her mythology, but at least it gave me something to write about.

*****

It was raining when I left to meet a friend for a drink this evening. I knew the general directions, but I asked a postal worker to make sure I was walking in the right direction.

"I'm looking for Nevins and Atlantic," I said.

She told me the most direct route, but suggested a slight detour.

"You don't wanna walk past the projects," she explained, "especially when it's raining."

I wonder whether she was being racist or helpful or both. If I were using Google Maps for walking directions, they certainly wouldn't have added that caution. Or does Google Maps steer people away from "dangerous" neighbourhoods? And if that's the case, how do they determine what's dangerous? Is it personalized? Like do Black people's walking directions steer them away from neighbourhoods with lots of cops in them?

*****

I talked with Jonas for the first time in over a week (being out of touch when on vacation is another bad and good difference of being offline) and he made me feel special in a way I don't often feel. He told me that my place has been all taken care of: plants watered, mail collected, fridge stocked. He told me that he's excited to "squeeze" me tomorrow. He said he hasn't been sleeping very well since I left.

SATURDAY, MARCH 7th

I've heard it said many times, if you see something suspicious, SAY something suspicious – like, "oh there certainly is a lot of bread on that BALONEY sandwich." (The "baloney" part is meant to be said with extra volume and emphasis.) It's like the loads of tuna, too much too loud too often. But there's certainly a chance that I'm making all this up, that I'm just stalling for time as my brain's automatons slow and slip and sweat. Swept aside one last time, I can't think of any other reason why I'd say such a thing, such a dastardly thing, such a sweet and sassy dastardly thing. For weeks now I've noticed the same patterns, the same streams of speed, but I've just this morning had it halted into play, softening as I go around and about and amidst even.

"And he has an enormous head, and a tiny body," says the boy sitting with his mom across the aisle from me on the train back to Montreal. They're reading a book, and he has a toy car, but this is going to be a long eleven hours.

WEDNESDAY, MARCH 11th

This morning, before coming to campus, I went and bought some canned food and toilet paper. I doubt we'll have a shortage of food or toilet paper, but even without social media, all the hype is starting to get me. And I don't wanna be left hungry or unable to wipe.

★★★★★

I've always had a hard time saying no and it's even harder when you have to do it in person. You don't get the luxury of master narrating the reasons in a carefully worded email, written from the comfort of home. Instead, I had to face my boss and improvise my way out of the research team. I pride myself on being good with words and with manoeuvring people but I couldn't do it. When faced with the human presences of the people I wanted to abandon, I felt guilt and decided that I could keep supporting the project without causing myself too much more frustration.

I hope though that I actually believe this, and that I didn't just fail to quit because I was scared by the face-to-faceness of it all. Email is a nice tool to hide behind and, in this case, it would have given me what I thought I wanted. But then, in person, what I thought I wanted became less clear and things unfolded as they did. It's almost like email lets us be more independently ourselves whereas non-email interactions force us to exist more collaboratively, less able to prioritize our master narrations over the perspectives of others.

✸✸✸✸✸

A friend of mine is working with a group of Grade 8 students (she's a student teacher) and they're exploring how social media influences their relationships and friendships. The actual teacher of the class is very biased against social media but my friend told me that almost all the students in the class disagree. They see social media as a healthy and effective social tool. Despite all the research I've read about the negative impacts of social media, I'm starting to wonder whether it's just that being from the generation that existed before social media makes me conservative and closed-minded about new technological change. Although, on the flip-side, these young pro-social media students have never experienced life without social media, so their perspectives are similarly limited, but in reverse.

THURSDAY, MARCH 12th

People are acting like the internet is such a lifeline right now – as if, without it, we wouldn't be able to let people stay home from school or work. And yes, the internet can help with social isolation, but in the case of massive lockdowns, it's not really a lifeline; it's more of a productivity-line. It helps people stay a productive part of the labour force, even if they have to work from home.

SATURDAY, MARCH 14th

In February, I set my ringtone to the sound of me coughing so that – if it went off in meetings or during meals – no one would really notice except for me. In the few weeks that passed since I did that, the sound of coughing has become the most conspicuous sound there is. So I changed the ringtone again yesterday to a clip of me jamming with some friends. I'm on the fiddle, Pete's playing guitar, Memo drums, and Niko keyboard.

★★★★★

Darren had a brunch this morning and invited a lot of gays and one of our girlfriends over. He made pancakes and bacon, and we all brought toppings, fruit, and drinks. Jonas and I brought strawberries, raspberries, guava juice, lemonade, apple sauce, pineapple chunks, and – that was it, I think. It was a lovely meal.

Darren announced to everyone that he recently got a flip-phone and is making the switch! I don't want to take too much credit, but I wonder how much my obnoxious badgering got under Darren's skin. He insists that it's just his own personal solution to being unable to self-regulate when it comes to Grindr and Instagram. He feels like his phone has made it hard for him to focus on things lately. He read something about dopamine being depleted or hard to regulate because of the rushes we get from listening to music and podcasts, or going on shiny apps and scrolling through pictures. With less options on his new flip-phone, he hopes he'll feel better about himself and that his ability to pay attention will improve.

We'll see how long this lasts. I give it a month.

SUNDAY, MARCH 15th

My friends keep saying that with everything moving online, my project is about to be more interesting. And it's probably true – we all love drama. But it's also frustrating and scary that I might not be able to get everything done that I need to. The fact that this development is witnessed with glee by my friends feels weird – it's like they support me, but want to see me struggle.

TUESDAY, MARCH 17th

Darren had a big win in Scrabble last night and claimed it was related to his new flip-phone, like his brain was already working better. I think his win had more to do with luck than anything, but Darren said that his memory and ability to retrieve information has improved since he made the switch.

A few minutes after he left, I realized Darren forgot his phone, so I walked over to his place this morning and dropped it off.

✶✶✶✶✶

Things seem to be going really well with Jonas, though it's definitely intense to spend so much time isolated together. Luckily my apartment has a few separate rooms. Right now Jonas is working on some mathematical modelling in the kitchen and I'm in the living room, making phone calls and journaling. I'm at that point in a relationship where I really want it to work, which makes it harder to know whether it's working. Plus, having someone to bunker down with has been very cozy – perhaps deceptively so.

WEDNESDAY, MARCH 18th
Last night I was supposed to go to my friend Tyler's for a small birthday dinner but he postponed. He said he'll reschedule later this week, but I sort of doubt it.

I had some weird dreams this morning. A childhood friend (not Jewish) was having a bat mitzvah, except it was really difficult to get there. I kept taking buses but they were indirect and I had to wait for long intervals between them. And all the while, I was having to put my socks on. The fabric was too tight and my hands and arms were too weak. I woke up with sore legs and feeling like I couldn't get the relief or release I was craving.

THURSDAY, MARCH 19th
Everyone keeps talking like they have all this extra time now. I've been asked several times what I'm going to do with all my extra time, but I feel like I have less and less time actually.

★★★★★

When I left my place to pick up my produce basket, I was surprised that there was no mail. For the last few weeks, I've gotten so used to sending and receiving letters that I'm starting to feel bad when I don't get any. I'm like one of those Instagram people who feels bad if they don't get their average number of likes on a new post.

When I got home, my friend Niko came over. As he walked in, I wasn't sure if I should hug him. Would it be safe? I asked Jonas for advice but he thought I was asking for permission, which maybe I was. He said I didn't need his permission to hug Niko, so we hugged. I do think I need Jonas' permission, though.

Niko told me about his new job. He recently started working for a big gaming company and this week, began working from home. One issue he's already run into is that he can't turn to the person sitting next to him anymore and ask questions. As a new employee, he'd been doing that a lot. Instead now, he messages the guy who used to sit next to him over Slack, but it takes longer and Niko feels bad bothering him.

"It makes it more of a formality to ask simple things."

Niko realizes he might just be paranoid, but he thinks his coworker is annoyed that he's asking so many questions. He didn't think twice though when they were at the office.

★★★★★

Hanni told me today that he keeps getting an error message that Cloudflare – an online service that helps distribute internet activity – can't access some gateway. I love the idea of internet gateways being blocked and cloudflares failing. I don't know what it all means, but it reminds me that the internet is physical and poetic.

FRIDAY, MARCH 20th

Jonas used an app to get some prescription meds he needed. Just using his phone, he was able to meet with a doctor and get a prescription, all in less than two hours. Because the app has become so popular recently, Jonas was telling me that it's been running into some new problems. So many people are using it and getting prescriptions that it's overloading fax machines. The prescriptions are automatically faxed to pharmacies from the app but the high volume of requests means the faxes keep failing.

"A clash between old and new technologies," Jonas said.

SATURDAY, MARCH 21st

Today's Saturday. On Thursday Jonas and I are driving to Toronto where I'll be donating sperm for Fanny and Alex. This is our third month trying. We're doing it at at their home, with baby-syringes, so each attempt is only 15–30% effective, but I'm still optimistic that it's just a matter of time.

SUNDAY, MARCH 22nd

I walked in on Jonas in the shower this morning. He had his waterproof smartphone in there and was watching television. (Not even porn.) I made some jokey comment about him not having downtime, even in the shower, and he said that he feels like he does get downtime while watching TV.

"I can multitask," he said, "and think while watching."

It's a different kind of thinking though, I think. I once went to a meditation course where they claimed that beyond sleep, we require a second, different kind of rest. We can get this rest through meditation. (…said the teachers of the expensive meditation course.) I don't think that we specifically need meditation, but I do think there's a psychic or mental settling that happens when we cut off external stimuli and just let our mind work with what's already there.

As the internet becomes more casually part of every aspect of our lives, we are spending more time passively listening to music, podcasts, scrolling social media profiles or news feeds, watching YouTube and Netflix. We have less and less time for the kinds of meditative, potentially boring downtime that I think is key to our mental wellness. As anxiety and stress reach new heights, we need to hold onto some of the secret, silent structures that have kept us sane for so long. As they disappear, we are hardly noticing because what we're losing never made much noise. But I really think we're losing something that we rely on, whether we're aware of it or not.

★★★★★

Just got back from a walk with Jonas. We ended up talking about the whole downtime thing and it got a bit messy.

It started when I told him about that trip I went on with Darren last year when he called me out for being patronizing and condescending for teasing him about his phone use. I was saying how funny it is to look back on that now that Darren has a flip-phone. Jonas used this an opportunity though to bring some things up. He feels like Darren may have been onto something and that I can sometimes be a bit too controlling or moralizing. He used our conversation about downtime this morning as an example. It might just be that he and I are spending so much time together that we're getting irritable, but I tried to ignore the excuse and hear what Jonas was saying.

Jonas reiterated his need to be on his phone in the mornings to be in touch with his parents. He added that he thinks it's important to stay up to date with the news.

I once again conceded that being in touch with his family is an important feature of his phone and that news – although mostly just non-updates and stuff we already know (Aron!!) – can also be important if not overindulged. I returned though with the same old idea that always having the hum of something else going on makes it hard to process life and feel mentally grounded.

He said he's okay with how he's processing life and he thinks he *is* grounded.

I retreated and made it clear that I think he isn't on his phone as much as some people I know, or we wouldn't have made it this far in our relationship. I also said that I agree he has a solid sense of self and a mental groundedness, but that it can always go deeper.

He said it still felt like I was trying to control him.

"I care about you and there's a fine line between caring and controlling," I shot back. That was a manipulative way to put it – I need to figure out how to be less controlling.

Jonas pointed out that because I'm doing research about people's everyday experiences of the internet, it can feel kind of patronizing when I talk about it, like I'm trying to tell people how to live.

"Like have I become your research subject?" he asked.

"No," I said, "or, I don't know." I paused. "Our relationship definitely comes first."

He told me that if he's a research subject, he wants to get paid.

MONDAY, MARCH 23rd

My daytimer has become a bunch of scribbled out appointments, meetings, and reminders. I'm still busy with lots of work on the go, but mostly it's all independent and any meetings I did have were shuffled around, mostly into the online or – for me – telephonic world. Today is Monday and as I opened the new page in my agenda, it was all either crossed out or wrong. Normally, having so much empty space in my calendar would be relaxing, but not now. I feel like I have an unending workload despite the lack of meetings and appointments, and the more flexible deadlines.

*****

Some of my friends have been telling me how online hook-up culture has changed lately. Because everyone's at home and glued to their devices, there's more traffic on dating platforms but there are probably less people meeting. I don't know that … I'm just assuming/hoping. People might actually be more inclined to have casual sex – even if its risky – when they're so isolated socially. I've heard that many apps, like Grindr, are warning people to avoid meeting.

Sloane told me that some polyamorous people they know are making pacts to be exclusive for the time being. Sloane's not down though.

"I'd rather be sexually frustrated," they said, "than some weird virus monogamist."

TUESDAY, MARCH 24th

I woke up late and wanted to take a bath, but managed my time poorly. The tub takes forever to fill and when it was finally ready for me, I realized it was already time to call in for a meeting with one of my research teams. I figured nobody would ~~mind~~ know if I was in the bath during the meeting, so I hopped in and made the call.

The main theme that kept coming up on the call was the idea that the internet is a great saviour. People literally said things like, "Thank goodness for the internet. Life would be so much worse right now without it." Or, "We're very lucky. We can be at home; we have internet."

✶✶✶✶✶

I love my friend Bradley but he phoned me three times today! The first time we spoke, the second time he left a message, and the third time I picked up because I thought it might be an emergency considering how many times he had already called. But no, he was just phoning to chat.

"I already called you today?" he asked, "I was just bored, looking through my phone and saw your number."

✶✶✶✶✶

I went on a walk this evening with Leah. We didn't touch but enjoyed each other's company and conversation in the snow. During our walk, we passed a phone/internet service box that was open. We looked around but there were no service people in sight. Because it was snowing and windy out, the wiring and mechanisms were getting wet. Leah was worried about everyone losing connection, so she closed the box. I wondered (jokingly) whether it might've been left open on purpose by mischievous anarchists who are trying to provoke a new global order by sabotaging our means of organizing ourselves; with everyone rushing online, they're sneaking out and leaving service boxes open in the snow!!

As we continued on, Leah told me about the Zoom calls she's been having for school and work. A month ago I hadn't heard of Zoom. Now it seems to be part of people's casual, everyday lingo. This morning a friend texted me, "let's have a call or Zoom later this week." Leah told me that she has very slow internet and that it's been even slower during this surge in use. Her experience on the Zoom calls has been pretty good, but finds she's always the one lagging. Leah's an advocate for slowing down and being careful about our pace of life, so I'm not surprised her glitchy internet feels the same way.

WEDNESDAY, MARCH 25th

Fanny and Alex are in their car at the moment on their way to Montreal. They decided to come here instead of having Jonas and I go there. It really is quite an honour when people plan a whole trip just to come get your sperm. Originally they were going to stay with me, but one of their housemates got sick, so they decided to stay elsewhere – just in case they caught something.

We're going to try three drive-by inseminations while they're in town: one tonight, one on Friday, and one Sunday. Apparently, most bodies need a couple days between ejaculations for the sperm to repopulate. You *can* come over-and-over again (or *I* can), but if you want that semen to have sperm in it, you need to wait.

For these drive-by inseminations, the plan is for me to come into a waterproof pill bottle, stick it into a mason jar with warm water (double-boiler-style), run it down to them in their car, have them drive it back to their Airbnb ten minutes away, and there, they'll have some intimate fun with my semen (or I guess it's their semen at that point). I'm a bit concerned about the amount of time it'll take to get back and whether the sperm will still be okay. If they're up for it, I'll offer to come at their Airbnb at least one of the times. I'll just make sure not to touch my face, and to wash my hands before and after.

✷✷✷✷✷

Jonas is at my place again today. He's doing work in the other room. He's been here most days for the past couple weeks. This morning though, he made a comment that upset me a bit while we were listening to the prime minister's daily address from Ottawa on the radio. As a 25-year-old, Jonas has pretty much always had internet. Plus, he needs it for school. Today's press conference was about new restrictions and Jonas said that if the government orders everyone to stay home, he'll have to go back to his place and stay there. Although it struck me as harsh at the time, I realize in retrospect how drastic it is to take away someone's internet, even if they have a bit of data. I may be used to living in an apartment without wifi, but for Jonas, it's not really surprising that it's starting to get to him.

Or maybe I'm just rationalizing it like that to protect myself.

THURSDAY, MARCH 26th

My friend Issa called this afternoon and I told her about the drive-by insemination I did yesterday. She said that she had been part of something similar, but for delivering a sourdough starter. Her friend biked over and left the starter in a container by her side door. There's a trend of baking sourdough rising on social media at the moment, but Issa assured me that her interest is unrelated. She is far from the only person who I've heard that from – that although their interests align with social media trends, there is no connection. It seems like we're all somehow embarrassed to be part of culture, the internet, the world. Or maybe people just like to downplay their connection to the internet when chatting with me.

✶✶✶✶✶

I got a note in the mail from a stranger in Montreal who had heard about my offline project. They were interested in meeting to discuss a podcast they are planning to record that will consider technologies as extensions of the body and the internet as a gigantic nervous system. We made arrangements to meet which fell through, so we planned a call instead.

On the call, we ended up having a long and candid conversation that helped me think through the potential of the internet to provide meaningful connections between people. They told me about a five year long-distance partnership they've had with a lover in Berlin. They explained that they've often felt isolated from this person because of distance. However, lately they feel like all of their relationships are long distance (even with their best friends who live nearby) and so their relationship with the Berliner has gained some validity and feels more sustainable. This keeps me bumping my head against the question of whether we can have corporeal, intimate interactions over the internet. And of course we can, and of course there's a difference, but maybe the degree of difference is getting smaller and smaller as we close the gap between online and in-person interactions.

They explained why they like describing the internet as a gigantic nervous system or a kind of mycelium, connecting us all and forming a shared processing centre. I pointed out that corporate control online makes this metaphor seem a bit limited, but they suggested that the internet still has the potential to be something organic and positive. They talked a bit about the dream people had for the internet back in the 90s and I told them about a Fred Turner book I've been reading. It explores this fantasy of a liberatory, utopic, radically free internet and shows how it was mostly a fiction sold by Stewart Brand and the Whole Earth Network (that would become *Wired* magazine).

I keep clinging to the idea that there's something better about in-person interactions than their online alternatives. Rationally though, I know that in-person things could very well just be what I'm used to, a matter of preference.

When I got off the phone, I noticed I had missed a call from Hanni. I tried to call him back but it didn't even ring. I just got a robotic voice saying, "All circuits are busy." I've been hearing this message a lot recently. Too many people making phone calls? But I thought everyone was online.

FRIDAY, MARCH 27th

One of my professors gave my number to someone in Toronto who is thinking about doing a graduate degree in our department. Actually, they've already accepted the offer to study here, but they're just waiting to see if anything better comes up in the meantime.

If they end up here, they're interested in Luddism and how people can engage digital tools more responsibly, especially in the science world. They did their undergrad and masters in theoretical physics and are very frustrated with the way people disregard the physical consequences of using digital tools. They often remind people in their lab that the materials they are using have histories and come from mountains and are mined, often by children. They shared my frustration with how people seem to think that the cloud is actually just a light and fluffy web of mist without physical, material impacts. We talked about how epic and grand data centres and server farms must be, and how most people can't imagine them – may not even know that they exist – despite relying on them daily.

Our phone connection was a bit glitchy and I was having trouble making out some of what they were saying. We tried to hang up and reconnect but the sound quality didn't improve. We didn't mind, though. It seemed fitting.

SATURDAY, MARCH 28th

- "Interesting time for you to be disconnected from social media. How are you keeping up with the news?"
- "Able to maintain your disconnect?"
- "Are you thinking of putting your project on hold? How are u keeping up with everything?"
- "I was wondering how it would have been for you when the tides really flipped and we were all on the pulse of things via the internet."
- "Must be crazy not to have internet during this time!!"

These were all text messages I got this week from different friends who I haven't spoken to in months. Everyone's getting in touch at the same time.

✶✶✶✶✶

Jonas and I joined Fanny and Alex this afternoon for a walk up the mountain to the cemetery. While entering the cemetery gates, a guy in a van drove by and coughed loudly out the window, directly at us. It was done very theatrically, so obviously a joke, but not a funny one. After the cougher drove by, Jonas and Alex both commented that they hope the guy gets sick.

While we explored the cemetery, we all had too much to say and kept getting pulled into tangents. Fanny and Alex use the metaphor of tabs, like from an internet browser, in order to talk about all the different threads of a conversation. "Let's go back to that tab for a second," "I have a new tab, but I'm gonna wait to open it," "We have too many tabs opened!" And we did.

SUNDAY, MARCH 29th
Jonas just woke up from a dream that he had gotten rid of his smartphone.

✶✶✶✶✶

Last night, Darren wanted to bring that Rod guy we met

in January over to have breakfast for dinner (Darren's idea) and play Scrabble with us. They've been chatting a bunch lately and I think Darren is trying to sleep with him. We agreed and Rod joined with his big husky. While we were playing Scrabble, Rod told us that he'd made almost half a grand in the past week by using a website called OnlyFans. Basically, it's like a premium, risqué Instagram where followers have to pay to see people's profiles, and the content is more explicit.

Rod only has a few followers but they tip generously, he explained. Darren said he would never do something like that because of his job and Rod replied that it's all private, and that, of course, people can take screenshots, but he's shared so many nudes through Grindr over the years that he's sure they're already out there. He also said he doesn't send jerk-off videos, just ones of him working out nude and stuff like that. While telling us about this, Rod was showing off a few photos from his OnlyFans account to Jonas and Darren, but – because I'm not allowed to look at internetted screens – I couldn't look. Rod's a very handsome guy and it was hard not to peek.

Jonas, Darren, and I have been playing a lot of Scrabble recently and we love learning and using new and funny words. We're not super serious Scrabble players, so instead of challenging each other on words we think aren't real enough, we just look things up before we play them. When we got to the first questionable word last night ("dint"), Rod started to look it up with Siri on his watch and phone.

Without a word or even a glance, Jonas rushed to my rescue and grabbed two dictionaries, throwing one at me. Somehow both Jonas and I managed to look up the word before Rod figured out how to make his Siri tell him whether it was a word or not. And when Rod did manage to get Siri to work, she worked on his phone and his watch at the same time, but with different answers. Jonas made some passive-aggressive comment about how much he loves these old dictionaries I have, even the one with funny conservative definitions for words like "communism" and "anarchy." I think Rod assumed Jonas was just talking about the dictionaries, but I got the subtext and was glad to have Jonas around.

✦✦✦✦✦

This morning I woke up early to do one last drive-by insemination before Fanny and Alex drive home. Alex brought over some chocolate and malted eggs as a thank you. Eggs are a funny gift considering what I'm gifting them.

I texted Fanny a couple hours later and they were already on the road. She and Alex had just passed the border into Ontario.

MONDAY, MARCH 30th

Classes start again at my university today, and I woke up with a rash or something. Whenever I get itchy bumps, I assume it's bedbugs. I haven't had bedbugs for over a decade, but still, I'm always worried. I'm hoping it's just eczema or a spider or the itchy wool sweater I wore yesterday or a stress rash or anything other than bedbugs.

I don't have any classes until Wednesday but Jonas has a full day of Zoom ahead. He's actually gone back to his place for the first time in a week and is going to do his classes from there, where he can get online without using his phone's data. One of his profs sent out instructions for the class' Zoom calls. Jonas told me that the prof wants everyone to be dressed (duh…), have their video on (Big Brother?), have their sound off, and be in a private room where they won't have distractions.

That last qualification, that people need to have a private space to Zoom from, is a bit classist. Some people will have a difficult time finding a private room to use, especially students who live with their kids or in communal situations. Jonas doesn't have a desk or table in his bedroom, so has to do his calls from the kitchen table, which means that his roommate will probably walk by. Jonas doesn't mind, but his professor might.

*****

Jonas and I had a big talk this weekend about him moving in. His lease is up in two months and his roommate is moving away, so he's looking for a new place and was planning to live alone but…

The issue is that it's really early (we'll have only known each other for five months). If we make this decision, we're both going to be more committed to convincing ourselves that the relationship is going well, which it may very well be, but it'll be harder to know once we have such an investment in it: shelter.

I tried to bring this up with Jonas but it was hard to explain. I pretty much just told him how hard I've found it to get out of relationships once you get past a certain point.

"If things aren't working between us, we have to be comfortable bringing it up," I said.

We both agreed, and we also both agreed that it's easier to commit to that kind of openness than it is to actually act on it.

*****

This afternoon I received a text message from a teacher friend who wanted to tell me about his experience teaching music over Zoom and how much he appreciates it – albeit at a high school where students all have their own devices and a quiet place to use the internet. He joked that he likes Zoom because of his love for *Hollywood Squares* and *The Brady Bunch* but then clarified that it's actually because Zoom has allowed really incredible interactions in his classes: "The introverts are comfortable enough to take risks and I have the ability to mute the extroverts if they step over the line." Although muting students seems like it's a bit much, his point about introverts reminded me that I don't get the whole picture when I imagine things only from my perspective as an extrovert.

As I get to the end of my third month offline, I've been

thinking about whether I feel like my life so far this year has been better, worse, or just different than how it might have been otherwise. It's hard to know, but I still feel like I appreciate being offline and the lifestyle and mindset it facilitates. I'm realizing though how much this is contingent on various privileges I have and how much I need to contextualize such a judgment as being highly personal to me. So, let me rephrase that: after spending a quarter of the year offline, I feel like – *as* an extroverted, non-disabled student with supportive friends and family – I prefer being offline.

TUESDAY, MARCH 31st

Our department finally sent out an email about class registration. Within moments of this email being sent, I received three text messages about it. (From Sloane, Bridget, and Anne.) Registration opens tomorrow at 12:32 p.m., and I had planned to just go in and talk to the registrar, but campus is still closed. I sent my supervisor a text asking if she can talk to the registrar for me and she said she'll try. I explained that I had already chatted with him about this but she pointed out that things might be different now.

If I'm not able to register, I'll lose my funding and get kicked out of school. It's ironically moments like these, when I feel the most precarious, that I wonder if my offline experiment may be a bit too self-indulgent.

April

TRYBORG CONCERNS: The Anthropocene, Texting, Networking

CYBORG CONCERNS: Can I afford my leg? Will a stalker, a doctor or the law kill me?

     – Cy. Jillian Weise, 2018, *Common Cyborg*

FRIDAY, APRIL 3rd

I feel like I failed. My supervisor checked in with our department's registrar and texted me his response:

"Hello Aviva – Now that we are not in the office and it's impossible to call anyone at their desks etc., this situation has become more difficult to deal with. Honestly, I haven't had much time to think about Aron's situation as email messages haven't stopped since registration opened on Wednesday.

"Given how upside down everything is just now, I'm not sure If I will be able to help Aron out. I personally can't register him. I thought I could figure out a work around, but as I mentioned, communicating with others by email will be difficult. It will be way too easy for anyone in central to say something like 'It's not possible,' 'given the current situation, why are you asking this?' etc... etc... Give me a couple more days, but he just might need to go on-line and register himself."

Aviva agrees that I should find another way to register.

I just can't get over the fact that our department's registrar isn't able to register me from his end – even if he is working from home. The permissions and privileges of these online registration bureaucracies are stingy and unforgiving.

I guess I'll give my username and password to a classmate – maybe Sabrina – and ask her to register for me. Although it breaks my rules, Aviva reminded me that it doesn't hinder what I can learn from the experiment.

"It's not cheating. It's being sensitive and adaptive."

I still feel like I failed.

✶✶✶✶✶

I was talking to an older member of my research team about the grad degree she did "a million years ago." We were discussing the digital divide between families and individuals with internet access and those without it. Because most low-income families in Montreal do have the internet these days, and because most of their kids even have smartphones, one might think that the digital divide is a thing of the past. My colleague explained though why she thinks it's as big as ever. Now it's not about whether or not someone has internet access. Instead, it's about things like how fast their connection is, how much data they can afford, what kind of device they have, and how the echo chamber or internet bubble they live in shapes their experience of the online world.

She told me a story about sitting with pregnant teens recently and trying to help them find parenting resources online. Her searches came up with genuinely helpful results, whereas the teens got trivial clickbait – even though they were using the exact same search terms. After seeing how different their results were from the ones she got, she recognized that it's "such a different internet" for everyone.

SATURDAY, APRIL 4th

Last night Darren came by to play Scrabble. While we were playing, he asked Jonas and I what our favourite thing is about each other, and our least favourite. Not to just focus on the negative (i.e. precisely to do that), but Jonas' least favourite thing about me is how much I'm on my phone, and that I zone out and stop paying attention when I'm texting. (I said he's a bad singer.)

I'm not sure if my compulsive phone use was always such an issue, but I've definitely been on it too much lately. I'm tempted to get rid of it altogether and replace it with a landline so that I can avoid the texting issue, but I know I rely on my phone when I'm out of the house, so it'd be hard. I should just learn some self-control instead of jumping to such drastic solutions.

While Darren was over, he told us that Tinder has added the free "explore" feature that Grindr has so that users can talk to people from all over the world. He's now got lots of new international dudes to share photos and videos with. He's most excited about a young guy in Kazakhstan who he's been masturbating with. Darren explained that he's been so busy with this Kazakh dude that he's not even watching porn anymore.

SUNDAY, APRIL 5th
Jonas and I took a bath today and while we were soaking, we talked about whether actions have consequences. I said they all do, every single one, like a mystery novel that never ends such that no details become central and nothing is a red herring.

Jonas said that actions may have consequences but the world is really big so the consequences of actions are often irrelevant.

ARON: But how do we know which are irrelevant and which actions really matter?
JONAS: We don't know.
ARON: So we've gotta assume everything matters.
JONAS: You mean, everything *might* matter.
ARON: Same thing.
JONAS: No it's not.

Why do baths always end up being so philosophical?

✶✶✶✶✶

Tonight Jonas and Darren are going to that Rod guy's place – the gay gym bro who somehow snuck his way into our pod – to watch the new episode of *Drag Race*. They didn't invite me and I wasn't sure why so I brought it up. "Is it cause I'm not a big Rupaul guy?"

"Not at all," they thought it was obvious, "We'll be streaming it over the internet, so you can't be there."

They were right but I was still a bit taken aback. It's not that I expect my friends to change all their social habits to convenience me all the time, but it still feels shitty to be excluded from something. Maybe I've been spoiled. Considering how much everyone I know uses Netflix and other streaming services, the fact that I made it three months without facing this kind of exclusion is actually pretty surprising. I must have some amazing friends.

TUESDAY, APRIL 7th
Some of my friends have been texting me poems this week – by Arundathi Roy, Henry David Thoreau, and some original pieces. There's something about a poem that forces me to stop and think and see things differently. On days like today, I need poems.

Fanny texted and said she took an early pregnancy test and it came back negative. I didn't expect it to hit me so hard, but I was so hopeful this month. I'm starting to think there's something wrong with my sperm. As a gay man, that was never important to me, but now that it's important to Fanny and Alex, it's become very important to me.

✶✶✶✶✶

The grocery store didn't have the Passover supplies I was looking for, not even matzah. When I got home, I phoned a couple other grocery stores in the neighbourhood (using my trusty Yellow Pages), but they didn't have any either. I phoned one of my Jewish friends who grew up in Montreal and she suggested I try the Kosher grocery stores further north in the Mile End (duh) so I went there and bought what I needed.

Searching for a place to buy matzah felt like a kind of ritual. When I was a kid at my cousins', we used to search for a piece of matzah at the end of the meal, to exchange for a prize or some money. This year the search for the matzah came before the seder, out of order.

WEDNESDAY, APRIL 8th
Today I was procrastinating and wrote a list of pros and cons for the two phones I've had recently:

Alcatel One Touch

+ Its t9 (predictive texting) is more accommodating because you don't have to be as exact.
+ Flipping a phone open is very satisfying. As is shutting it. Also, because it's a flip-phone, there's no potential for pocket-calls or butt-dials.
− Its contact list is glitchy and takes a while to load. (A long while.)

Nokia TA-1036

+ Comes with the classic cellphone game, Snake.
+ You can use your phone and send texts while you're on a call.
− When typing a text, if the recipient happens to text you, the text you are typing will be automatically sent, regardless if you've finished.

So which of the two would I recommend? Neither of them. Next time I'm going to buy an old, refurbished phone. I always wanted a Razr back in high school. Maybe I can still get one.

I started the call for class this afternoon while out on a walk and I could hardly focus on what the prof was saying. Usually in class people are on their laptops and the internet can be distracting. When class is on the internet though, the world can be distracting.

FRIDAY, APRIL 10th

I was talking to my uncle and aunt on the phone today and my uncle thinks I should suspend my offline project. He doesn't think the experiment works anymore because without inter-net, I apparently "don't have any alternative social potential." I reminded him that phone calls, like the one we were on, can be a pretty fulfilling way to connect.

People keep assuming that without the internet, I'm at much more of a loss than I feel like I am. As if without the internet, there's nothing. Not only do I feel okay (thanks to my phone and the mail and Jonas and my media collection), but I think that I can still learn from the offline interactions I'm having, even if I can't go out. I'm also talking to so many friends on the phone these days that I'm still learning a lot about what's going on, even if it's not in person.

My uncle said that at least it's good I have Jonas to use the internet on my behalf. Before I could explain that it's against my rules to ask people to do things online for me, my aunt interrupted: "But you don't understand! Aron doesn't *want* to rely on the internet. That's the whole point."

SATURDAY, APRIL 11th

Fanny texted this morning that she'd gotten her period. I re-ally want Fanny and Alex to be able to have the family that they want and I feel like I'm failing them. I know, it's not about me. It's about Fanny and Alex. I can't stop dwelling on my part though. Fanny's had fertility testing so it makes it seem like the problem must be me. And I know that these things have low chances of working, so it could be anything, but we did everything perfectly this time, so – I donno – it just feels like I'm the broken cog.

I phoned Fanny and talking to her helped me feel better. She had just been on a run and we chatted about control. We shared the feeling of wanting to have the control we can have, amidst the uncontrollability of the moment and the future. So Fanny's going to mail me an at-home fertility test, or whatever you call it for sperm, and I'll be able to check whether I'm the problem, or if we ought to just keep on trying at the whim of the world. Fanny said that even if she and Alex end up having to find a different donor, I'd still be uncle Aron. And I appreciate that, but I know it wouldn't be the same.

The other piece of control I might have over my sperm has to do with smoking weed. Although I've heard it's not very scientifically validated, some people think that sperm that's high is lazy and slow, like stoned humans. Now, I'm not the kind of stoner who gets lazy or slow when I'm high, but that doesn't mean my sperm is similarly resilient. So, for the next two weeks, until my next attempt at insemination, I'm not going to smoke. It may be completely irrelevant, but it gives me something I can control.

SUNDAY, APRIL 12th
As Jonas and I were falling asleep, we talked about our relationship. It's scary how close we've gotten in just over three months. Jonas doesn't understand why I think that it's scary.

MONDAY, APRIL 13th
This morning the radio was broadcasting an interview with the author, Douglas Coupland. He's come up with a bunch of slogans about the internet and posted them around Vancouver. Some of the ones I managed to jot down include:
- "Knowing everything turns out to be slightly boring."
- "I miss my pre-internet brain."
- "I subcontracted my brain out to the cloud."
- "A plague without wifi would be truly horrible."

After Coupland shared the last one, the interviewer responded sarcastically with, "Imagine if we had to read and talk to one another." It felt like he was defending me.

I didn't hear the end of the interview because my parents called. (You can't pause radio.) They wanted to talk about my brother because he and his wife just told us all that they're pregnant. I still haven't told my parents that I'm trying to help my friends get pregnant. I think they'll be happy for me, but I'm also aware that it'll be a heavy conversation and I don't want to pull those big slabs of emotion around until Fanny actually gets pregnant.

Luckily, now that my brother's having a baby, it'll be less of a big deal for me to tell them that I'm trying to have a biological kid who won't be their grandchild. Fanny and Alex have said that my parents can still be family (great aunt and uncle style) but if it weren't for the fact that they'll have a grandkid now from my brother and his wife, I feel like my mom, at least, might've felt a bit cheated or something.

After I got off the phone, I turned the radio back on and caught the end of the news. It was about university exams going online and the new concerns that have emerged around privacy and the protection of students' data. The terms and conditions for the software that's being used to proctor exams say that they can change the terms at any time and that they're not responsible for the mishandling of personal data. I wouldn't want to use a software that doesn't claim to protect me. Nobody should have to. And yet, students are required to opt-in if they want to complete their degrees, so agreeing to these terms and conditions is a forced choice, or not really a choice at all. The choice isn't whether they agree to the terms; the real choice (or non-choice) is whether they want to risk the terms in exchange for a chance at completing their university degree. And of course the answer most people will have to give is, "I agree," but it would be more honest if there was an option for, "I guess so," or "begrudgingly."

✶✶✶✶✶

I talked to my cousin AJ today and his 6-year-old, Cary.

They live in Montreal and I usually see them once or twice a month but haven't since I got back from Berlin.

I asked what they've been up to lately and whether they've been using the internet more than usual. AJ told me that Cary doesn't get very much screen time but some of his friends' kids spend all their time online or in front of a screen. He said he doesn't hold it against parents, especially if they're working full time, but he described the zombifying effect a full day of screen time has on these kids: "It's like watching someone get hypnotized by staring into a spinning spiral or a swinging pendulum or something." He said that on the odd day when Cary does have more screen time, he's more likely to get angry, frustrated, or act out … especially if you try to get him to put down the screen.

Because Cary can't type or read, his experience of YouTube is totally at the whim of the machine. He just chooses a random video and then watches whatever the algorithm feeds him next. AJ told me about one video currently trending among six-year-olds that features a man playing with a doll in a bathtub full of gumballs.

Although he doesn't get much screen time, AJ did install one of those internet boxes that you can talk to in Cary's bedroom. AJ read me some of the transcripts of Cary politely chatting with his Alexa while lying in bed. "That's so interesting," "Cool," "Thank you for explaining." I got Cary to put AJ on the phone and asked him if he knew that the Alexa wasn't a real person. He didn't seem to understand what I was trying to ask and gave the phone back to his dad.

TUESDAY, APRIL 14th

It's already noon and I haven't done anything yet today. I mean, I did laundry, made breakfast, took a bath, finished a Pynchon novel, wrote in my journal, and texted some friends. However, in terms of things that I've been programmed to consider productive, I've had an irresponsibly lazy day.

✱✱✱✱✱

I'm currently on day three of not smoking weed and it's a bit harder than I thought it would be. The thought of blazing keeps popping into my head and there's nobody stopping me from doing it, except me. I even still have weed in the other room, but am managing to control the urge to roll just a little joint. It's weird because I'm not even being pressured to do this by Fanny and Alex; in fact, they told me about a study that suggested weed may *help* fertility. I think it's partially just a challenge that I've set for myself after realizing that I haven't taken two weeks off smoking since I went on a trip to South Korea over three years ago. It's hard! I am, however, enjoying how much more vivid my dreams have been since I've stopped. And, now I've got something to look forward to. When I smoke again for the first time, I'm gonna get high-school baked.

✱✱✱✱✱

Jonas is over but he's lying down with a headache. He thinks it's cause he drank too much coffee and not enough water. He's probably partly right, but I pointed out that he also spent the last eight hours staring at a screen.

WEDNESDAY, APRIL 15th

Jonas was looking at his phone and had an amused look on his face. I asked what was up and he told me he'd just read a Tweet that reminded him of my little cousin Cary's relationship with his Alexa or Google Home or whatever they have.

The tweet was about a little girl who caught her dad getting angry and short with their Alexa. She apparently told him he should be nicer. He explained that it's a machine and asked her why he should be nice to it. She replied that when the computers take over, she expects they'll treat her nicely in return.

I really hope that little girl was joking but it doesn't sound like she was... We are raising a generation that doesn't really see the difference between humans and computers. I'm all for queering binaries but I feel like there *is* a rigid distinction between life and non-life, between people and machines. Or am I just being old-fashioned?

✶✶✶✶✶

I've already had to deal with one of my uncles trying to tell me that I should consider putting my offline project on hold. Now my other uncle texted me the same thing. He heard about the trouble I was having trying to register for classes and wrote:

"I was glad to hear what sounds like maybe you are re-evaluating the offline experiment. I'm sure your conclusions would be just as valuable if they supported use of the internet in a balanced way or a mixed-use tailored to the individual."

Because of the dramatic nature of going offline for a year, people keep assuming I'm *against technology* – whatever that means. But that balanced, mixed-use, tailored to the individual is exactly what I'm trying to advocate for!

✶✶✶✶✶

Darren came by this evening on his way to Rod's. They finally hooked up and Darren said it was good, though a bit awkward.

"I hope Rod and I are both on the same page," Darren told us, "and we're just sorta using each other."

I suggested he bring that up before things go too far. Jonas jokingly asked me if that's what he and I are doing, just using each other. I don't think that's what's happening. I hope not.

THURSDAY, APRIL 16th

Last night I had a long phone call before bed with Bobby. He's a very social guy, one of the few friends I have who is as social as I am, and he told me that he's been having a really hard time lately. He was dating someone but that fizzled out and now he's been left without much to do. He has a room-mate, but she lost her job and is unable to pay him rent, so she's hiding out in her room and avoiding him. He told me about the incredible amount of FaceTime calls he's been on, so many that he described feeling a sense of "FaceTime fatigue." He said it feels like there's something separating him from the people he's speaking with online. I mean, there is.

FRIDAY, APRIL 17th
I stayed in bed this morning until almost noon even though we went to bed pretty early last night, before eleven. I've been pretty good at sleeping these days, even without weed. I wouldn't say I'm depressed though, at least not in a serious way. Maybe it's okay to sleep more.

✶✶✶✶✶

Today Hanni and I worked on our final paper together, over the phone. Hanni told me that he's been making a bunch of banana bread lately and I made fun of him for following internet trends. He denied it, claiming he's been making banana bread because he's had lots of mushy bananas. Hanni especially, as someone critical of the internet, is particularly defensive about his offline motivations relating to the online world. But who cares why he made it?! He's got fresh homemade banana bread!

Jonas told me that banana bread is a particularly gay trend online at the moment. Once I shared that with Hanni, he (as a straight fella with lots of queer friends) seemed a bit more okay with being in-sync with an online trend. It's funny how it's more okay or cooler to follow trends when they're started by the queer community. If only people realized that we start *all* the trends…

✶✶✶✶✶

Niko needed to print some shipping labels, so he came by to ask me to print them for him. Because I'm offline, I bought a printer this year. It's funny how being digitally-limited by being offline actually makes me more digitally-capable in other ways.

While Niko was waiting for his labels to print, I asked how he'd been doing and he gave me a pained look. He told me about a group video call he was on last night with eight of his friends from high school and he said that the call was "unconsensual." I didn't know that video conference calling could be unconsensual but I realized that, like Bobby told me the other night, it's nearly impossible to turn down an invite for one of these online calls these days, especially in the evening when people know that most of their friends aren't working either.

Niko said that the people he was on the call with kept commenting on how uncomfortable he looked. They even took screenshots of his awkward facial expressions and shared them around, making jokes. It sounded terrible but Niko kept saying that it was actually a really nice call. But then he'd go back to talking about how it was unconsensual.

"If I didn't have to have my camera on," he said, "it would've been fine."

"Did you have to have your camera on?" I asked.

"I guess not," he tried to laugh, "but it's hard to say no. Especially after I'd already agreed to the call."

SATURDAY, APRIL 18th
Just woke up from a dream in which I accidentally checked my email. I keep having these dreams. I always realize I've done something wrong as soon as I log into my account. Strangely, in the dream I just woke up from, I only had a dozen or so emails. I hope that was a premonition and that I'll only have a dozen or so emails to sort through when I get back online. In reality, I imagine there'll be a few hundred – though probably only very few that I'll actually need to read or reply to.

Jonas and I lay in bed for a while this morning, working on our laptops. It was cute but also made me feel a bit sick – probably because of the nature of our conversations, but also because working on my computer in bed makes me feel lazy and sore.

We first talked about Amazon. Jonas told me about his uncle in Spain who has a small company that sells surfing supplies. He tried to sell things over Amazon, but his account kept getting hacked, even after he changed his password multiple times. He got in touch with Amazon but they said it wasn't their problem, so he stopped using the site.

I haven't used Amazon in over two years now – not since I made an oath with Tyler after we watched that Boots Riley movie *Sorry to Bother You*. I don't hold it against people who feel compelled to choose it as the least expensive and most convenient option. But as someone with the money, time, and ability to go out and shop, I can avoid the forced choice of Amazon. And I think that other consumers with similar degrees of choice have a responsibility to consider the impacts of using Amazon.

As Jonas' uncle's experience demonstrates, small business owners aren't always served by Amazon and many are even put out of business by the rigged competition that pushes Amazon's own versions of products. In Amazon's "*fulfillment* centres," workers report fast-paced conditions that lead to many workplace injuries. Some employees even wear diapers because they don't have enough time for bathroom breaks. Amazon also actively works against union-organizing efforts. They're just a shitty company that leads people to buy more junk they don't need.

One of the biggest issues for me though has to do with Amazon's partnership with the US government to help deport undocumented migrants. Not only does Amazon operate the servers for ICE (the US department that fights undocumented migrants), but they actively lobby ICE to invest in Amazon's own proprietary technologies – like their facial recognition tools – that could help detain and deport people more efficiently. I've done this song and dance a lot but most people I know still use Amazon on a very regular basis. As that *Sorry to Bother You* movies points out, when a problem is so big that individuals feel unable to make a difference in relation to it, they (we) stop caring – as a kind of defence mechanism. But although our individual impact may very well be negligible, collectively we are responsible for Amazon's continued success. It just takes one person, albeit several million times.

✶✶✶✶✶

Jonas had a fun Zoom call with some friends back in the UK today where they played a game that struck me as a more creative alternative to socializing than the typical Zoom calls I've been hearing about. One of his friends who was organizing the call went back through everyone's Facebook and found old photos and funny or embarrassing status updates. It must have taken a lot of scrolling because some of these were over ten years old. For each photo, the challenge was to guess when and where it had been taken. And for the status updates, the idea was to guess who had posted it.

One of the posts that was from Jonas' Facebook said "___ likes Maths." It was from when he was thirteen years old. Jonas said the game worked really well, and, even though some of the statuses were embarrassing, nothing was too over-the-top, except for one… Jonas has a friend who grew up in Germany and she had her phone stolen in 2012. When it happened, she had chased the guy down and tackled him and gotten her phone back. Afterwards, she posted a status update about the incident and had used a racial slur for the person who stole her phone. Because the person organizing the game didn't know German slang, she didn't know that the term in the status was racist. When it came up though, the German friend was very embarrassed. It's a good reminder that what people post online can last forever.

I don't have any social media accounts but I'd be interested in what someone could come up with about me if they looked hard enough and knew how to navigate the internet archive. The only thing I can think of is an interview I did for an Israeli newspaper while I was visiting the West Bank, staying with a Palestinian family in the D'heisheh refugee camp. I had been meeting with people impacted by the Israeli occupation and learning from organizations that support Palestinian prisoners. The Israeli journalist asked me a provocative question about Palestinian suicide bombers and how I feel about them "killing innocent Israeli women and children." Thinking about all the Palestinian women and children I had met who were impacted by the occupation and considering how Israelis benefit from the dispossession of Palestinian lands, I glibly responded, "Who's innocent?" With the appropriate context I stand by my response, but the article made me sound like a terrorist.

Years later when I was trying to get a job working at a Jewish high school, I got in touch with the editor of the paper and asked him to take my name out of the article. He responded that his news organization wasn't in the habit of changing history at the whim of its readers. However, after I explained my situation, he agreed. If you're good enough at surfing the web though, I'm sure you can still find a copy of the original.

SUNDAY, APRIL 19th

My aunt phoned this morning in tears. Before even saying hello she told me "Marguerite died." She let out a sob, "Oh Aron, I always thought you would get to meet her. I told her so much about you. I thought that next time you visited..."

I wish I could give her a hug. It's her 70th birthday tomorrow and I wanted to celebrate with her, but she lives in the US and the border's still closed. My aunt's definitely young for 70, but she won't have too too many birthdays left. Whenever the subject of her age comes up, she always acts with genuine surprise that she somehow got to be as old as she is. Where have all the years gone?

TUESDAY, APRIL 21st

Today I got a letter from a friend with some poems they had typed up on their typewriter. One was by Jack Gilbert. It was about being alone so long that "you would go out in the middle of the night / and put a bucket into the well / so you could feel something down there / tug at the other end of the rope." Is that what it feels like to be online?

I walk out my front door and check my mailbox a lot more often these days, and I keep finding myself pulling out my phone to see if I have any new text messages. Having internet access can make it feel like lots of other people are around – friends, strangers, governments, corporations – all lingering just behind the screen. Without it, I feel more alone.

*****

Jonas told me that he's managed to lower the amount of data he's using without actually using his phone less. He was able to check and found out that something called "systems services" accounted for a majority of his background data use. When he clicked on it, his phone told him that the most data-intensive part was "iTunes media services," so he turned it off. Jonas was quite confused by this because he doesn't know what it is and didn't even think iTunes was a thing anymore. At least he's using less data now.

WEDNESDAY, APRIL 22nd
Fanny and Alex are coming back to town today for another few shots at (squirts of?) insemination. The drive-by inseminations didn't work, so we're gonna do the deed in person (not directly *into person* though).

*****

I was feeling stressed about money things this afternoon and worrying whether I'd paid certain bills (Quebec hydro, teaching license, rent, etc.). I started wishing I could check my online bank accounts to see which had been charged already, and how much each was, and if I'd been overcharged for anything, and whether I was on track to have enough money saved in my account for paying tuition this summer.

I'm fairly sure everything's in order, but I wish I could check and reassure myself.

THURSDAY, APRIL 23rd
Last night Fanny and Alex got to town around eleven and we did a late-night insemination attempt. When Fanny got out of her car, I went in for a hug but she stopped me and suggested that I should ask Jonas to make sure he's cool with it before we hug. I reasoned that I'm getting into her car and about to try to inseminate her, so a little hug couldn't hurt. She insisted though that I'd better ask Jonas first, just to be sure we're all on the same page.

"Just because you're going to be in the car, it's not like we're exchanging bodily fluids."

I thought she was joking and waited for her to laugh but then realized she hadn't intended or even noticed the pun.

"No Fanny, exchanging bodily fluids is precisely what we're doing. That's why you just drove to Montreal."

But we decided not to hug anyway.

This morning, Fanny called to let me know that she's already ovulating, a couple days earlier than expected. She's eager for another round of Aron DNA sooner than later. The plan is for me to go back over tomorrow morning at 9 a.m., so it won't have been too too long since the egg dropped. I'm glad we ended up doing a try last night. Procreation can be so finicky.

FRIDAY, APRIL 24th
Big day today. I woke up before 8 to get to Fanny and Alex's place for another insemination attempt. Fanny's early ovulation meant that we didn't have much time so I got there by 9 and, using my trusty Tom of Finland book, pumped one out in minutes. Because porn is so easy to access with the internet, it's become an important (or at least normal) part of everyday life for a lot of people. Without the internet, porn seems less important.

Exploitative treatment of workers aside – and I realize

that's a very big aside – I'm not against porn. I've heard that porn in the early 20th century played a big part in turning people onto the female orgasm and the importance of going down on women, but now porn seems to be slipping back in the other direction, and women's pleasure isn't always a big part of what's out there. Or so I've heard.

✶✶✶✶✶

After Alex dropped me off at home, I left almost immediately to bike down to visit my cousins whom I hadn't seen since February. It was weird not hugging Cary. Usually, he's quite physical and jumps on me when I see him, or at least hits me a bunch. Today, when he came outside, the first thing he said was, "My daddy says I can't touch you."

"I know," I replied, "hopefully we'll be able to hug soon though."

Going for a walk was really nice and AJ's partner gave me a bunch of VHS tapes that her parents were throwing out.

AJ and his family live near Sloane, so after spending an hour or so with my cousins, I biked over to Sloane's place in Verdun and we went for a walk. It felt really special getting to see them. As Sloane and I were walking, we approached a park where I thought we might sit and chat. Sloane directed us away from the park though, telling me that there have been lots of cops hanging around there lately. They told me not to worry too much, though.

"We aren't the ones they're targeting."

Sloane is involved with community activism against policing. Because I live in a privileged bubble, I had no idea how much the police have been ticketing people lately for gathering in public spaces. They claim to be warning people first (like I experienced), but Sloane's spoken with a lot of people – mostly homeless youth – who've been given tickets without warning. There are a couple websites that have popped up so that people can report where they got tickets and how much the tickets cost them. Not surprisingly, low-income areas have been hit the hardest, with an Indigenous reserve in Northern Quebec being the area with the highest proportion of tickets.

One Indigenous woman that Sloane spoke with works for an organization that supports homeless Indigenous people in the city. She was working in the park – giving out masks, gloves, safe drug gear, and information – when she was arrested and put in the back of a cop car. She explained to the cops that what she's doing is an essential service and they let her go ... with a $1500 ticket. It made me feel sick to hear about this, especially considering the history that police have of mistreating Indigenous people. On my bike home from hanging out with Sloane, I saw a big group of cops on motorbikes and I wanted to say something, but I didn't.

When I was arrested in a protest against the police in 2008, I had to get a lawyer. The one I found would only agree to represent me if I'd concede that – despite being against police in the context of the protest I was a part of – I valued having police in general. I told him I did, but it's violently clear that this value is only for people like me.

Instead of any real issues, my biggest challenge today was trying to figure out how to get reimbursed from my insurance company for contact lenses without using the internet. It hardly even seems worth mentioning.

SATURDAY, APRIL 25th
Fanny and Alex came over last night before driving back to Toronto this morning. We talked about the online communities Fanny's been exploring that give people who are trying to get pregnant somewhere to share their neuroses and support each other, but in ways that might also feed some insecurities. Fanny's part of one TTC (Trying To Conceive) community where people post videos of themselves checking pregnancy tests. I don't think Fanny's made any videos herself, but she's watching other women who – even before they could possibly test positive – film themselves peeing on test-sticks and waiting to see the positive indicator. She described these women as quite ridiculous, testing just a cou-

ple DPO (Days Past Ovulation) and trying to make out the positive indicator, even though it couldn't possibly be there. (When you're pregnant, I've learned it takes at least ten DPO before it'll show up on a pregnancy test.)

Alex told us about the over-zealous supporters who watch these videos and post comments like "BFP! BFP!!" ("Big Fat Positive! Big Fat Positive!!") Although it was clear that Alex and Fanny found these videos hilarious, Fanny seemed like she was getting pretty caught up in that world. So, instead of diving in and starting to make these videos herself, she wants to avoid doing pregnancy tests this round and plans to just wait until she misses her period (hopefully).

SUNDAY, APRIL 26th

I saw a video of my sperm today! I wonder how many people can say that. Jonas and I used the fancy home-fertility test that Fanny and Alex bought. The test showed that my sperm concentration is normal and that its motility is above average. I'm at a 70%. The video really showed it too, with lots of my sperm zipping around almost faster than the camera on the microscope could trace and capture. I realize sperm are just cells but seeing them with their little heads and tails and moving on their own and at such different speeds, it was hard not to think of them as tiny creatures. I hope I don't start feeling bad when I masturbate and spill a whole slew of them unheedfully. In the bible, the main reason it's not okay to be gay is the same reason it's not okay to masturbate: the spilling of seed without reproductive potential. I guess, as a gay, my seed is always sorta wasted unless we expand what we mean by reproductive and examine what's created between two men making love. The only time I've ever been potentially reproductive in the conventional sense is when I've jerked off for Fanny and Alex. As far as religion goes, donating sperm is probably the most kosher kind of "sex" a gay guy can have. Maybe I'll go to heaven after all.

Last night Darren came over and gave us an update on the situation with him and Rod. Sounds like it's over. They've hung out twice now where they cuddled but it didn't go further. Darren said he made it clear that he wanted things to go further – not relationship-wise, just sex-wise – but it seems like Rod really just wanted to cuddle. Darren feels led-on because Rod sent him lots of suggestive text messages, including nudes. I don't think we'll be seeing Rod again.

Darren was also talking about a boy in Quebec City whom he's been chatting with. They met on Instagram. Darren's been posting lots of photos of himself working out with his shirt off. Normally, he doesn't post very much of this type of content ("thirst-traps," as he calls them) but he explained that all the gays have been more shameless lately. (Shameless or more insecure and wanting validation?) Obviously "*all* the gays" isn't exactly true – and even of the fit and vain type, I'm sure it's not everyone. Jonas hasn't been posting any thirst-traps to Instagram, at least not that I'm aware of. Although I don't think he posts much of anything on there anymore.

WEDNESDAY, APRIL 29th
Jonas was reading an email he got from our university's chancellor and overlord. She sends him and all students (including me, presumably) lots of emails. He started to read it out loud, thinking I would find it funny, but I asked him to stop.

"This is one of the reasons I'm offline, remember?"

He said sorry, and I said I was trying to make a joke. But it really is one of the problems with being online: we're bombarded by this mix of important and irrelevant messages from people who are important to us personally or institutionally, and we're expected to sort, process, and respond to them in a timely fashion. It's a lot of work, even for emails which don't require a response, even for ones that we just skim and flag in our brains as irrelevant. Being offline this year has made it a bit more difficult to be in touch with certain people, but not having to check my email has felt really good, like I'm breathing more deeply and more often.

May

It is not simply that some bodies and tools happen to generate specific actions.
    – Sara Ahmed, 2006, *Queer Phenomenology*

FRIDAY, MAY 1st

Burning Bush

Opened tulips are nasty,
like entering a fire. Once they're open,
they're awful.

Getting closer to the fire though, as the tulips open,
it's a beautiful thing,
a breath half-taken, a stop-and-stare.

But once they climax
and snare their pointy teeth, it's a breath
I don't want to finish –

A fire felt first at the fingertips,
before it gets inside you
and shows you its private parts.

✶✶✶✶✶

Darren's going to come by tonight so we can celebrate his birthday. Jonas and I (well, mostly Jonas) are going to bake him a cake. We're thinking apple because it's in one of our cookbooks and we have all the ingredients we need to make it.

Hardly any of my friends use cookbooks anymore. It's all about the internet. Though even without a recipe, Jonas and I managed to bake a delicious banana bread at 11 p.m. last night. I like that Jonas is up for impromptu self indulgences like late-night baking. We just improvised and it turned out better than I could've imagined. Jonas added cut-up pieces of caramel, which oozed to the bottom and made for a crispy, crunchy crust. We (well, mostly I) ate half the loaf before going to bed.

SATURDAY, MAY 2nd

I biked over to my friend Leila's and the two of us went for a walk. Without warning, she asked if I love Jonas. I don't know what that word is supposed to mean, but I told her we haven't said "I love you" to each other yet. I shared though that I felt a wave of affection wash over me when I went back into the bedroom to say bye to him this morning before biking over.

Last night when we were sitting watching a bunch of TV shows, I kept having this strange flashing awareness of Jonas sitting beside me. First he was a stranger, and I felt anxious and excited, and then he was my boyfriend, and I felt warm and safe. It was a bizarre back-and-forth because I hardly know Jonas and I know him really well. I think being together so much lately and spending most of our time in the same space has confused my non-conscious self. It knows I know Jonas super well spatially, but knows I don't know him very well temporally. I don't know if I love him yet, but if love is just the act of working towards intimacy, trust, pleasure, and so on, then yes, we do seem to love each other.

MONDAY, MAY 4th

Just phoned into a local radio show and had a chat with the host, along with an expert who was talking about new tech. They were discussing Zoom, so I called to share my experience being offline. I got a strong reaction and took the opportunity to ask if the expert had any advice for how people can be more responsible when adopting new technologies. His response was to straight-up avoid new technologies that aren't "necessary." He spoke about how he tried to get off Facebook but realized he needed it to stay in touch with certain people in his life. Now he only uses it when absolutely necessary.

I think I agree with the sentiment – it would help a lot if people reflected on why they use certain new technologies and tried to only use ones they really valued. I don't agree with the expert's qualification of only using tech that's "necessary" though because I think there are plenty of reasons to use tech that aren't essential needs, and I find it hard to believe he actually *needs* Facebook.

It was quite a rush calling into the radio. Without the internet, it's easy to stay in touch with friends but it's harder to interface with strangers and the big ol' outside world. Phoning into the radio made me feel connected in an impersonal but all-encompassing way – sort of like using social media. Despite being abstract and disembodied, it felt like a group hug: awkward and tentative, but warm and well-intentioned.

TUESDAY, MAY 5th

Last night Jonas and I started watching a show I downloaded before going offline called *Succession*. I noticed partway through the episode that Jonas had his phone out. I asked what he was distracting himself with and he got defensive.

"I'm just reading about the show."

I prefer watching a show without knowing much background. If it's a show I end up liking, I usually end up wanting to read about it, but not at first. I didn't say that to Jonas though. Everyone's got their own approach. My mom always reads the ends of books first and if a kid or a dog dies, she won't read it.

I'm starting to realize that Jonas might be a lot like my mom. Uh oh.

*****

I got a letter from a friend today who's a couple decades older than I am. In her letter she reminisced about some of the cool ways that letters have been used: "1) When letters were conversations between family members or artists or creative people or thinkers, 2) When letters were conversations between different kinds of people in the heyday of the 'pen pal' era and 3) When, in my teens, they were a way to share so many thoughts with my friends at school, journaling and very much 'thinking' on paper."

I know emails can serve similar purposes, but there's something about letters… I don't think it's just that they're less common now, because as my friend described, letters were special even back when they were normal. Maybe it has to do with the more physical act of writing and sending something, or maybe it has to do with waiting and the time it takes to exchange letters.

My friend feels like she no longer has time for these kinds of correspondences: "I have no idea where that time has gone," she writes, "but it may be time I spend online!" I'm not sure. Is it that the medium changed or is it the way we relate that's different? Which came first? Can we think of them separately? I want to ask everyone and know all the different ways of thinking about these questions, but as my friend said, who has the time?

WEDNESDAY, MAY 6th
Sloane texted me about a nightmare they had last night: "I was dreaming in Zoom windows and there was always this empty video that would pop up and as soon as I'd look at it, a man would run at the camera and jump through the screen at me!"

I woke up with a big bump on my leg … not a red and itchy one like I've had so many times before, but a big lump underneath the skin on my thigh. It's painful in an achy sorta way, but it's hard to notice when I'm sitting still. I have no idea what it is. Normally I'd take a look online and read what other people who've had similar symptoms think, but I can't, so I'm trying to convince myself just not to worry about it. It may even be better that I can't look it up, because if I did check online, I'd probably find out I have cancer.

If it gets worse, I'll go see a doctor.

THURSDAY, MAY 7th
Last night Darren came over to play a bit of Scrabble with Jonas and me before bed. While we played, Darren was telling us more about the new boy he's been chatting with from Quebec City. They met on Tinder and it was originally just expected to be something very casual – someone to jerk off with over webcam – but somehow they've really connected and have been chatting daily, for more than two hours each time. Darren isn't sure if the intense feelings he's having are real or not.

The last guy Darren slept with, Rod, fucked with his head. Especially when Darren found out from a friend that they had both been sleeping with Rod around the same time – this despite the fact that Rod claimed to be seeing no one other than his dog.

Rod's what I like to call an "app rat" – one of those guys whose always lurking online and has probably messaged you at least once. I had expected my gay friends' casual hook-up lives to slow down considering the added risk lately, but I was wrong.

FRIDAY, MAY 8th
I texted Fanny before going to bed and woke up this morning with a message that she'd been up since 5 with cramps and her period.

"Had my sad snuggle with Alex and we both did the (classic?) thing where we are sure it's our fault! But then just tried to sit with the knowledge that there's actually nothing wrong with trying! I hope this doesn't feel too sad or disappointing for you/but also totally get if it does :/ let me know if you wanna chat out any of your feelings too!

We are totally around and love you so much."

Lately Fanny and Alex have started telling me that if this known donor insemination doesn't work with me, they've decided they'll go with an unknown donor. It struck me as a compliment, but it's also just a comment on my relationship with Fanny and Alex. At this point, I don't think I'd be as open to going through this process with anyone other than them either. I don't know many people who are as good as Fanny and Alex at managing their feelings and expectations AND those of the people close to them.

It is very disappointing to hear that, after four attempts, Fanny and Alex are still no closer to being pregnant, but maybe that's not fair. Maybe, despite being just as unpregnant as before we started, maybe we are closer to making a baby. I can't imagine the stress of the process helps, especially with Fanny's work where she supports nurses who are trying to unionize, but this is the world that we're living in and the world that Fanny and Alex's baby will be born into if all goes well, and there's no insulating against the world. So as long as Fanny and Alex want to keep trying, I'll keep feeling hopeful.

After I got Fanny's text, I had to do something to keep my mind and body busy so I went into the kitchen and started washing dishes. Jonas and I had a cheese fondue for dinner last night so there was a pot with lots of sticky cheese hardened onto it. I also turned on the radio, but turned it right off again after a few seconds of the news.

SATURDAY, MAY 9th

The lump on my thigh is still here today, so I phoned my brother who's a doctor. He said that as long as it's not infected, I shouldn't worry. I would know if it was infected, he told me, because it'd be warm and red. All of a sudden, it's feeling warm, but I'm hoping that's just in my head. I wonder whether I would have called my brother about the lump if I'd been able to do my own research online.

★★★★★

Jonas told me he's been looking into how to connect my apartment – or maybe I should start thinking of it as *our* apartment – to the world wide web. It feels kind of terrifying, but I'm okay with making the compromise when the trade-off is so dang adorable and smart and lovely to be around. Jonas is trying to choose a smaller internet service provider, thinking that they might be a bit less unethical. He's settled on a local DSL provider who's offering 25 mb/s for $45 a month, but $25 for the first six months. It sounds like it's going to be installed soon but I didn't ask Jonas the exact date. I don't think having the internet available is going to make it more tempting to use, but I am feeling anxious.

Last night we were watching *Office Space,* and Jonas was on his phone. At first I was annoyed because he'd never seen the movie before and I thought he wasn't paying attention, but I remembered that (a) he may just be looking up things about the movie and (b) he doesn't need to pay attention all the time. Not being focused throughout a movie or having a shorter attention span is not necessarily a bad thing. I find I set standards for the people around me fairly arbitrarily based on myself. But I wouldn't want to date myself.

SUNDAY, MAY 10th

I spent most of my day so far cleaning: the dishes, the sink, the tub, the toilet, the laundry, the floor. At one point, Jonas came into the room and sat around for a while, on his phone. He was taking a break from doing an assignment and was using his phone to read the news, and not even the political kind of news – he was reading like culture/celebrity news stuff. Granted, that kind of news can be pretty valuable, and yea, he was taking a break, and I know, he made me breakfast this morning, but I still felt annoyed by his mindless surfing. I think it's more about my frustration with the way the internet demands so much attention, but it feels like I'm frustrated by Jonas.

I heard that a couple just outside of Montreal went around lighting internet or cell towers on fire recently, saying they were protecting us all from the towers' radiation. I'm not worried about having the internet in my apartment for the radiation, but I am worried how it'll change the way people feel and act when we're hanging out. I love the slower pace of internetlessness – playing Scrabble together and looking things up in dictionaries, tapping the record player when it's stuck repeating the same snippet of music, ad-libbing cookie recipes and eating them while watching a DVD. When we get the internet, will people start asking for the wifi password when they come over and then spend the whole time with their heads in their phones?

I think that may have been why I felt icky seeing Jonas scrolling his phone while I cleaned the kitchen. Articulating it and taking a breath makes me feel a bit less anxious.

TUESDAY, MAY 12th
It already feels like Jonas has moved in. When I got home, there was just this handsome, sweet, smart, quirky dude waiting for me. (Well, not waiting for me, but there – or rather, here.) We're not the most stereotypical gays, but one thing I noticed when I got home is that we have too many shoes, and the number seems to have expanded while I was out. We need to buy a shoe rack.

WEDNESDAY, MAY 13th
I got a shoe rack today and the front entrance of our apartment looks much less cluttered.

THURSDAY, MAY 14th
I woke up with way more itchy bumps and they're all over my body now. They're on the backs of my knees, near my groin, on my chest, and on the backs of my thighs. I think I may have had a similar outbreak around the same time last year, but I'm worried. Jonas doesn't have any, so we don't think they're bug bites, but it's hard to say. I phoned my der-

matologist's office and they're only taking appointments for phone consultations. The receptionist explained that I could send in photos though. I don't know how I'll send in photos, but I didn't explain that. I just thanked her for the information and hung up. Maybe I can print out some photos and mail them in? I hope these bumps just go away on their own. They're distractingly itchy. Jonas said that I may be having an allergic reaction to him.

I tried to stop thinking about the itches and turned on the radio. The news was depressing. A part of me appreciates that a bunch of mystery bumps is the only thing I have to worry about. (Well, I am still worried about that other big lump thing in my thigh too.)

SATURDAY, MAY 16th

This morning I went and got croissants and coffees for Jonas and me across the street from our apartment. They don't accept cash anymore, only cards. Credit cards *did* exist before the internet, but they weren't as universally accepted. I originally planned to avoid using them this year, but I think I have to give up on that.

After lazing about for a couple hours, Jonas and I went to meet some friends at the park. As we approached, I saw Darren and looked at the people gathered around him. I recognized our friends Yoni and Junior, but they looked a bit different. I couldn't tell if it was their hair, their weights, or just that I hadn't seen them in a while.

We sat down and I got a rush. It was weird socializing in a group after so much time in isolation. It made me feel good. But within two minutes, police approached us and made us all show them our IDs. They told us that we were sitting too close together and they took down our names and addresses. They then asked if we had already been warned. We said we had not. They told us that if they found out we *had*, they would mail us each a ticket for $1546 dollars. What an outrageous amount!!

We stayed at the park, sitting further apart from one another, but the warning put a pretty heavy blanket of anxiety on our casual Saturday afternoon hang-out. It didn't help that dark clouds had formed and the sun wasn't able to get through. I'm definitely going to be more careful now with how I behave at parks. I wonder if the cop who took down our info actually did add us to some kind of list, or if it was all just intimidation. Either way, it worked. Fuck the police.

SUNDAY, MAY 17th
I have to straddle being just comfortable enough and not feeling too itchy. Feeling too comfortable or too itchy both make it impossible to act.

★★★★★

This afternoon the radio was airing a special about the internet and how it's changing. I wasn't listening, but my friend Sabrina texted me about it, so I tuned in. Mostly it just confirmed a lot of things I'd already heard or expected. One of the experts was talking about video conferencing and said that he believes most people find this type of communication more exhausting than audio-only options. The other expert spoke about parental support for remote learning and empathized with how difficult it is to care for children, let alone facilitate online learning. She advocated for embracing opportunities to learn from life – cooking, nature walks, discussing current events – and not worrying if online learning isn't going smoothly. She focused on all the parents who are finding it difficult to support their kids' remote learning, but she didn't talk about families where parents aren't around or able to help. She also didn't mention families who just don't have the devices or the space.

I did not expect this year to be about advocating for more investments in internet technologies, but as remote learning becomes more common, I hope schools and the government can provide more internet infrastructure and supports for families that need them.

MONDAY, MAY 18th

It's a holiday today and Darren wants to go to the park again to play Scrabble but I'm nervous about getting a ticket. I shouldn't let the police ruin my summer, but it'll be hard to play Scrabble sitting a full two metres apart from each other.

TUESDAY, MAY 19th

I had another little internet nightmare last night. I was opening Gmail on my old laptop. As it was loading, I realized that I wasn't supposed to be checking my email, so I slammed the computer shut. Behind the screen, there was a person watching me, someone I recognized while in the dream, but I can still picture their face now and they don't look familiar.

Despite these recurring dreams, I don't think I'm actually worried about accidentally checking my email. (I don't know how someone even could *accidentally* check their email.) It sounds like my mind is just craving a reason to be anxious and will latch onto anything.

Speaking of which, I have more new bumps this morning. They're not as itchy as the ones I had a few days ago, but they're still driving me a bit bonkers. Jonas and I scoured the apartment, looking on every rug and cushion with flashlights (or "torches" as Jonas calls them) for bedbugs or fleas or spiders or any casings or spots that might suggest that bugs have been around. We also spent a while staring deeply into the seams of our mattress. No luck. I would hate to have a bug infestation but I was almost hoping to find something just so we know what's going on.

Fanny and Alex are back in town and Jonas and I stopped by their place last night to share some semen. We don't have a use for it but we really enjoy making it, and they have a use for it but can't make it, so it's the perfect friendship. Fanny seems a lot more chill this time around. Now that we're in a bit of a routine, it's not as strange and our expectations are a bit less rollercoastery. Jonas commented that besides me and Darren, he's hung out with Fanny and Alex more than anyone else these past couple months.

I was just texting with Fanny and found out that they had to switch Airbnbs. When they started working this morning, Alex realized that the wifi was terrible, so they got in touch with the host and he was able to move them into another property he also owns. I asked if they were liking the new place.

"Totally," Fanny said, "We're both getting full bars."

She thought I was asking about the wifi.

✦✦✦✦✦

The internet arrived today. A man came by to plug something into the wall and some other things into a box outside. Jonas ordered a modem but it still hasn't arrived, so the internet in the apartment isn't usable yet ... but it's here. I can almost feel it.

WEDNESDAY, MAY 20th

My bumps are a bit less itchy today and I don't think there are any new ones. I did a bunch of laundry, including my bedding again, just to feel like I have some control over what's going on. Fanny and Alex are going to come by in a bit for a walk and poutine. After we're all full of fries and gravy and cheese curds, we'll trek back to their new Airbnb for another insemination attempt.

Fanny and Alex heard that it's helpful for Fanny to orgasm before Alex shoots my sperm into her, not after as we had been trying before. Although orgasming after may help the sperm get to where it needs to go, orgasming before can apparently help adjust the vagina's pH so that it's more sperm-friendly. If all goes well, Fanny and I will orgasm around the same time – though in separate rooms – and then Alex will syringe my sperm into Fanny and hopefully she'll get pregnant!

✦✦✦✦✦

Jonas told me this afternoon that someone in Singapore has been sentenced to death over Zoom. I'm against the death penalty in general but it seems even more heinous without an in-person trial. Though maybe that's just my conservative ableism showing again.

THURSDAY, MAY 21st

I don't know how I amass so much to write about every 24 hours. I've been jotting notes down on my phone (well, texting myself) every time I hear or think of something I want to journal about. Now, it's 10:30 p.m. and as I finally sit down with a spare moment to journal, I look at my phone and have eleven text messages that I've sent myself in the past 24 hours. Let's see how much I get down:

I finally told my parents that Jonas is moving in and they were really excited for us. I was a little surprised they didn't say anything about it being too soon. My mom's bold, though. She said that this move must mean that I "love" Jonas. I didn't disagree when she said it, but it caught me off guard. I still haven't explicitly told Jonas that I love him, but I did tell him recently that I think I've started to fall in love with him. I think of love as a process, so I can at least say that I'm definitely in the process of it.

Because Jonas is moving in, my parents asked whether we'd be getting internet. I told them that *Jonas* is getting internet. Lots of people have been asking whether Jonas is going to withhold the internet password from me so that I can't use it. I don't know what people think, but I'm not avoiding going online by making sure I don't go anywhere that has internet access. I'm not *so* tempted that I'd compulsively use the internet if I had an easy opportunity. So no, I don't think I have to worry about Jonas hiding the password from me.

My parents also said that they were already excited to meet Jonas, but now they really *really* want to meet him. My mom told me that she's been telling her friends that I'm dating an epidemiologist and everyone's very interested. It's cute that my parents are bragging about Jonas already. Hopefully they'll be able to come for a visit in the fall with their new RV.

Tomorrow I'm going over to Fanny and Alex's Airbnb at 9 a.m. for the third (and final) insemination attempt of this cycle. It'll be the eleventh shot we've taken at this, over the course of four or five months. Fanny's on some new meds for her thyroid and feeling positive. I'm hopeful but not getting my hopes up.

I'm looking forward to the morning. I always have a really good orgasm when I come for these semen donations. I was joking to Fanny and Alex that after this I might only be able to get off when there's procreative potential. This queer family making will have ironically ruined me for gay sex!! But I kid. (Pun intended, hopefully.)

It's after eleven now and I want to hang out with Jonas before he goes to bed, so I'll leave it there. I still have a bunch of notes on my phone that I wanted to journal about, but real life is calling.

FRIDAY, MAY 22nd

Darren stopped by today and things felt tense. I didn't hug him as I normally would but he didn't seem to notice. It's hard to stand up to friends. The other day – the last time I saw Darren – he asked if I would be upset if he hooked up with a stranger from Grindr without telling me. I told him I would be.

"Oops," he laughed, "'Cause I already did!"

Darren's the only other person I've let entirely into my bubble (besides Jonas) and we've had several conversations with him about the shared autonomy that comes with bubble-sharing. It's hard to give up autonomy to a bubble but I thought Darren was down for the trade-off: he gets people to hang out with and he gives up the freedom to have casual hook-ups. I feel like ultimate freedom is always tempered by relationships; the freedom to be an individual has to be compromised with the safety of the people who you're sharing space with. Because we have Fanny and Alex in our bubble too (and Fanny is hopefully pregnant), it's even more important that I'm not sharing a bubble with someone who's exchanging fluids with strangers.

Darren didn't acknowledge that I was upset. He just shared a bunch of intimate details about the stranger he hooked up. Regardless of this new guy, Darren's borrowing a colleague's car tomorrow and driving to meet the boy he's been chatting with in Quebec City.

In other Darren news, he's given up on the flip-phone and back using a smartphone again. I was surprised when he switched to a flip-phone. I'm not surprised that he's switching back.

✶✶✶✶✶

Some new itchy bumps showed up last night, so that's fun. I finally phoned the dermatologist again. If they were still only doing appointments remotely, I was tempted to break my internetless year and have Jonas email them some photos of my bumps. Luckily, they're opening again for in-person visits on June 1st, so I can be patient.

In a bit we're going to go meet Fanny and Alex in a park for some poutine. It's become a tradition, having poutine together when they come to town. And we also all really like poutine.

✶✶✶✶✶

The modem was supposed to arrive over a week ago and it still isn't here. Jonas sent the company an angry email asking for some money back, so we'll see how that goes. Even though I'm hesitant to have internet in the apartment, I feel Jonas' frustration over how long it's taking to get set up.

SATURDAY, MAY 23rd

I biked across town today and the city was warm and lulling me with different smells. I got a whiff of driving my first car fifteen years ago, I went through a street that smelled like my first violin teacher's house, I passed something that was redolent of my childhood neighbour's basement, and as I crossed the canal, I was taken back to a warm, heavy night at a nearly empty marina on the Red Sea. While I was biking along the canal and down into Verdun, I had to dodge lots of traffic. The paths were busy, filled with cyclists and people walking with dogs or in small groups. I got a bit lost, but had a map in my bag. I pulled it out and found the spot Sloane had suggested we meet. It was a quiet, almost empty "park" (or grassy lawn) beside a baseball diamond. Although there was a small group of people playing baseball, we had the grassy area to ourselves.

Sloane was already there when I biked up. They were sitting with their roommate and our friend John. After we talked about the important stuff, I updated them all about my itchy bumps. I worked with the three of them last summer doing a gardening job and they remembered me dealing with a similar problem, although at the time I thought it was something from the garden that was biting me. John has lots of skin problems too and he told me that he's had something similar to what I was describing and it turned out to be a fungus. He said that his also returned seasonally in the late spring, until last year when his doctor gave him a pill that killed it for good. I'm starting to think that my itchy bumps may be fungal too. If it's not allergies or eczema, it'd make sense why the antihistamines and the hydrocortisone haven't been helping. And it would also explain why we can't find any little biting creatures in the apartment.

Fanny and Alex drove back to Toronto today. Last night before they left, I was feeling pretty itchy and Fanny shared a mindfulness strategy she uses to manage her chronic pain. She told me to try to be conscious of the painful itching and to notice how it changes and when it becomes more or less intense. Ironically, she said, focusing on it will make it easier to handle. I've been trying her tactic a bit already and it feels like I'm less frustrated and helpless amidst my itchy discomfort. There's something about being conscious of things we don't have control over that helps us gain some control.

SUNDAY, MAY 24th

Jonas told me that people are posting their "last normal photo" to social media. The trend was started by the BBC and has spread to people's personal networks.

The last photo Jonas had taken before everything closed was of me sitting in the grad student lounge near our offices on campus. Looking at the photo of myself, sitting on campus so casually, sitting where I might have been sitting now if nothing had changed, I look too casual. Now, sitting at home and typing on my couch, life feels casual too, but in a different way. The world of Jonas' "last normal photo" felt expansive and connected in a way that I no longer feel. The repetition and routine of the last two months has made my world feel small and cut-off. I'm sure being offline hasn't helped either.

★★★★★

Just got home from a final sweep of Jonas' apartment. We had a dinner picnic in his living room, seated on the hardwood floor. I have so many memories of picnics in empty apartments and the memories are always from times of transitions – moving in or moving out. Jonas was saying that British apartments are usually furnished so this was his first empty apartment picnic. The first of many?

MONDAY, MAY 25th

Jonas and I had a cute, lazy morning in bed (which is always a bit thrilling and naughty feeling on a Monday). I accidentally told him that I think I love him. I was silly about it and made it sound tentative and playful. But he probably knew I was serious. He didn't say anything back to me, which has to be intentional. Normally, Jonas is the kind of guy who gets a compliment and returns it. I guess telling someone that you love them isn't about complimenting them (or that's not the intention anyway) but still, I expected something back. We did have sex after. That's not what I mean, though. I respect him for not parroting the "I love you" back if he isn't feeling it yet. Regardless, I'm still feeling a bit more precarious now, and today felt a bit unsteady despite being a nice, straight-forward day.

I can't believe we live together. It's weird to contrast the newness of our connection (5 months) with all the old friends who I talk to on a regular basis. Today I had four phone calls with people I've known for years. I talked to Will (whom I've known for 8 years) and Issa (10 years) about Vancouver's teacher union election that's happening this evening. They're both running and the election has been moved online which makes everything more complicated. But, because it's virtual, way more people are planning to attend. Usually they only have around 100 people vote at the meeting but this year over 600 are registered.

I had a long chat with Omar (14 years) who's back at work now at the daycare his family owns. He recently got an email from a parent raising concerns about radiation in the daycare due to cellphone towers. It seems like these conspiracies about 5G have really taken off. The parent's email cited alleged research from a university in Dublin.

I also had a long chat with Yuki (17 years) and she told me about a new TV show she's making for a friend's stream-ing service. I told her that this was one of the first times I've actually been disappointed that I'm not able to go online. She said she'll try to download her episodes and send them to me on a USB stick. I hope she does! I've had a few friends tell me they'll send me digital files to watch, but so far only one – my ex in Vancouver – has followed through with it. I love the idea of sharing offline libraries. Easier said than done though when everyone else has access to the internet's endless streams.

Darren (3 years) came over this evening with a funny request. He wanted me to set a four-digit parental lock code so that he could only check his Instagram and Grindr for a limited time each day: one hour for Instagram and 30-min-utes for Grindr. I asked him if I had to go online to set up the parental lock code and he assured me it was just on his phone locally. He even turned his internet off while we set it up.

When he was leaving he thanked me and said that hopefully, in a few months, he'll have more self-control and won't need the help. I said that I didn't mind helping and that it's good to rely on people.

TUESDAY, MAY 26th

The internet has finally arrived. Let the bells ring and the banners fly! Jonas got his modem in the mail this afternoon and plugged it in. Voila! Our apartment is jacked into the world wide web. I joked to Jonas that I'm worried about losing him to cyberspace, but he knows I'm not really joking. He asked me what he should make the wifi network's name. I love it when I see clever, raunchy, or political wifi names, so I suggested BILL21isRACIST or ACAB but Jonas wasn't comfortable with those choices. He said I could choose the password though. "Ask me later," I replied. He understood my joke and set that as the password.

THURSDAY, MAY 28th

I had a meeting today with the three professors on my supervisory committee. Before we started, I chatted privately with my main supervisor, Aviva, but her son kept interrupting. He's in Grade 1 and his teacher hardly knows how to use Zoom, but the students are expected to log in every day and participate in classes. This morning, he was supposed to be in French class but kept coming into Aviva's home office to complain. He's a gifted 7-year-old but part of his smarts involves knowing how to get out of stuff he doesn't want to do. Aviva tried to ignore him and sent him back to his room to work. She told me that he had turned his camera and microphone off and was pouting. Online learning isn't easy. And this is a kid who has all the resources to facilitate online learning (space, good wifi, supportive parents, enough computers, etc.).

When the other two profs joined us, they took turns giving me feedback. Each of the three professors recommended, at some point on the call, that I look something up on Google, only to remember that I couldn't. To "google" has started to seem like the default way of gaining information. I think that if you can discern relevant sources from popular ones, Google can be useful, but there's more to a website than its usefulness.

FRIDAY, MAY 29th

Jonas was beside me in bed looking at Twitter on his phone when I woke up this morning. I asked, without intending any passive aggression, whether he thinks he'll use the internet more now that he has wifi in the apartment. He said he thinks he was already using it a lot.

Jonas told me that Twitter is particularly interesting today because a tweet posted by the president of the US has been censored. I didn't peek, but Jonas explained that the tweet is still there, just hidden. I bet that brings more attention to it even as it makes it less accessible. It definitely gets people talking.

The president's tweet was directed at protesters in Minneapolis who have been demonstrating after video footage emerged showing the murder of a Black man by police in the city. The tweet featured some rhyme threatening to shoot protesters if they start looting – a quote taken from an infamously racist police chief. Jonas explained that Twitter hid the tweet but included a message that read:

"This tweet violated the Twitter rules about glorifying violence. However, Twitter has determined it may be in the public's interest for the tweet to remain accessible."

I wonder whether Twitter did this because they were worried about the backlash from the president if they censored the tweet entirely, or whether they left it accessible with a note because they wanted people to see how violently racist the president is. I'm hoping it's the latter because I want to believe the internet can still foster decentralized power and democratic debate. Twitter is huge but it's one of the few popular online spaces that hasn't been bought out by one of the big tech giants. If Twitter can hold out against the president too, well then the internet may still have a chance.

Later, we were hanging out with Darren and I asked if he'd heard about the president's censored tweet. He said he had but rolled his eyes.

"Everyone already knows you can't believe what you read on Twitter," he said.

I hope that most people are skeptical of what they read online, but I still think people absorb lies or hate on some level, especially when coming from authority figures, or when they're repeated over and over again.

✷✷✷✷✷

We found fleas!! Jonas spotted them while working at his desk in the middle room of our apartment. They were on his ankle. Fleas are not ideal, but at least now I know what's been biting me. I immediately went out to the pharmacy and bought liquid bleach to mop with. Tomorrow morning we're going to buy a better vacuum.

SATURDAY, MAY 30th

We woke up and got right to work. We first went to the hardware store we like and bought a fancy new vacuum. We carried the purchase home and proceeded to destroy the apartment. I led the charge, starting in each room with the vacuum, and then Jonas followed behind with a bleachy mop. At the end of it all, we both had slight headaches (despite opening all our windows), but the place feels cleaner than it has in years. I hope the fleas and their eggs are gone. And I hope that my itchy bumps weren't caused by anything other than fleas.

✷✷✷✷✷

Tyler texted today to let me know that he filled a jump drive for me. He put a few movies on it, including the Adam Sandler one I've been wanting to see. I'm feeling a lot of love for Tyler. He knew I wanted to see it and knew that one of his friends already had it downloaded, so he gave the jump drive to a friend, who passed it along to the friend with the movie, who passed it back to his friend, who gave it back to him, and now he's ready to give it to me.

✦✦✦✦✦

I got text messages from a couple friends today about a protest happening in Montreal tomorrow against the racist police violence in Minneapolis and against racist cops here in Quebec. The radio makes it sound like the protests in the states are getting bigger and more aggressive. Also, there are apparently white supremacist groups who are joining the protests covertly and trying to incite violence and burn down historic buildings in Black neighbourhoods. So fucked.

SUNDAY, MAY 31st

It's not even noon and I've already hung out with two friends this morning. I met up with Leila for a walk and on my bike ride home, I passed by Tyler's and texted to see if he was home. He was, so we walked around the block and he gave me that jump drive.

While Tyler and I were walking, a woman came up to us and started chatting. I thought she knew Tyler but she didn't. She asked whether we were coming this afternoon. After we realized she was talking about the police protest, we told her we'd be there. She was glad.

"We need some white faces walking with us," she said.

I loved getting invited to the protest like that. Of course social media can reach way more people, but when someone – even a stranger – invites me to something personally and in person, I feel way more inclined to go.

I'm a bit stressed about the protest. I can't watch the online videos that are going around of police violence (which may be okay as I'm already on side) but Jonas told me about a video that an American congressperson posted of riot cops in New York ramming a group of protesters with a police vehicle. I don't think things could get that out of hand here in Montreal, but Sloane isn't so sure. They texted that they're going to the protest but they're worried the Montreal police will "start beating the shit out of people and arresting them." Hanni's too nervous to join us and said he'll find other ways to contribute. I think Darren and our friend Yoni will be there. I don't know if Jonas will come. It doesn't sound like he's too keen – he said he doesn't want to get deported.

✦✦✦✦✦

Just got home from the protest. My head is hurting. So many people. It was a bit of a shock. It felt urgent and pent up, but everything went smoothly, albeit confusingly. Unlike most protests I've been to, the march didn't coordinate its route with the police. Walking around downtown and up St. Laurent felt like we really were disrupting things. With the police helicopters circling overhead, cars stuck at intersections, and people as far as the eyes could see, I felt connected in a way I haven't for a while.

I'll write more tomorrow when my head isn't pounding.

June

Would-be activists may turn to their computers rather than their communities, drafting a text rather than calling for a meeting.
– David Meyer and Deana Rohlinger, 2012, *Big Books and Social Movements*

MONDAY, JUNE 1st

Jonas and I finally watched that Adam Sandler movie last night. It had been hyped up a lot, so I expected it to be more intense, but I appreciated the hecticness. I love it when characters talk over each other, like in Altman movies. It makes for a more challenging viewing experience, but I sort of like the discomfort.

After so many months of trying to see the movie, I wish I had something more interesting to say about it.

*****

I just found out that yesterday's protest got chaotic after I left. The police were shooting rubber bullets and tear gas, people started looting, and around ten people were charged. I think everyone's okay. (I know systemically everyone is not okay, but I don't think anyone was seriously hurt.) I don't celebrate looting or violence, especially when the shops that get fucked over are small, local businesses. However, I can still empathize with the brokenness and desperation that may have led some of the rioters to riot. I've seen *Do The Right Thing*.

I heard on the news that before the protest, Montreal's mayor and the police both tweeted in support of the cause. After things took a "violent" turn, the mayor and others have made statements commending the actions of the *peaceful protesters* and condemning the *criminal minority who took things too far.* Civil disobedience has come so far that it's become obedient. It can be celebrated by politicians and police, neatly separated from actions that intend to break the law.

Sloane and I were texting about it and they wrote, "it seems fucked up that people get more upset about violence against cops with riot gear and windows and shit than they do about constant and oppressive systemic violence."

Bradley – who grew up in Minneapolis – phoned earlier and said something similar, that looting and property damage isn't violence. Even if protesters came yesterday without any fancy theory to justify the pain, rage, or zeal that brought them there, even if they fully intended to "fuck shit up," I still feel like we can gain more from trying to empathize with their frustrations and desires than by condemning them.

TUESDAY, JUNE 2nd
I woke up a bunch throughout the night itching and went to the bathroom to put calamine lotion and tea tree oil on the new bumps covering my feet and ankles. I hope they're somehow from before Jonas and I cleaned, but I have a feeling the fleas survived. I'm frustrated, but compared to everything else going on, my problems are trivial.

A friend/ex-student phoned earlier and I was telling him about Sunday's protest. He told me that people online are shaming any white people who haven't posted anti-racist content. I agree that it's important to be actively anti-racist, as opposed to just passively not racist, but shaming others for not being anti-racist on Instagram seems a bit superficial. I was telling Jonas about what my ex-student has been noticing, and he said it's a bit of a catch-22; he's seen white people making anti-racist posts and being shamed for creating their own posts instead of sharing content from Black people. Either way, I don't know whether online shaming is the most effective approach to changing the world.

And then there's the issue of fragility. In this cacophony of shame, some people (my ex-student included) have deleted their Instagrams and Twitters and are now being shamed for being too insecure in their privilege to face the realities of racism. I know that fighting for real equity and racial justice may make those of us who've always had privilege feel oppressed and get defensive or insecure, but that's different than feeling insecure because people are bullying you online for failing to signal wokeness in superficial ways.

*****

I went for a walk with Leah and she told me that Quebec's premier responded to Sunday's protest in Montreal by saying that Quebec's institutions are not racist.

"There is no systemic racism in Quebec."

Leah was upset but I tried to remind her that someone who has been responsible for the racism of Quebec's institutions is obviously going to deny it. This is the man who pushed through a "secularism" bill that forbids public employees from wearing hijabs, turbans, or kippahs, but that still allows them to wear small crosses.

*****

I can't believe how intense things are getting in the states with these protests. Over 5000 people have been arrested, lots of major cities are under curfews, and the president is calling for the army to attack its own citizens.

WEDNESDAY, JUNE 3rd
I finally spoke with Fanny and Alex yesterday before bed. Fanny thinks she might be pregnant. She's ten or eleven DPO now and on Monday, she woke up in the middle of the night thinking she had her period because it felt like she had peed herself. Upon closer inspection, it wasn't blood or pee, or anything she'd ever had gush forth from her body before.

This new, mysterious liquid was odourless and colourless, and – I don't want to jinx it, but at the very least … something's happening.

I asked Fanny and Alex if they've seen any online shaming about anti-racism and told them what my ex-student and Jonas have been noticing. Alex said that they've actually seen it taken one step further and turned into a real catch-22 where white people are being shamed for speaking for Black people if they post their own content, but if they repost things Black people wrote, they're being told they should think for themselves to prove they're real allies.

Despite all this, Alex and Fanny insisted that online spaces are very crucial right now. They talked about the firsthand accounts from protesters being shared over Twitter. And they explained that online tools have been the main way they've been able to engage so many people in the anti-racism network they organize with. They added that telephone calls have been more effective than emails at getting people involved initially, so they've started using phone trees alongside their online approach.

We talked a little bit about the difference between the armchair activism that's common online (what Fanny called "slacktavism") and the kinds of slow, difficult community organizing efforts that take advantage of the internet. I had a perfect example of the superficial kind: my friend Will texted me this morning with, "I'm going through TikTok and liking every single Black creator despite what they do." I didn't reply with anything harsh, because I'm not the arbiter of what meaningful online activism looks like, but I feel like Will's anti-racism strategy is not going to help anything. Just "liking" someone because they're Black seems a bit reductive. But hey, it may teach AI some inclusive tendencies that could make machine learning less likely to reproduce racism?

On my walk with Leah yesterday, she said that she's fed up with appeasing white people's guilt. She said that too many of her white friends reach out to explain comments or actions they've been criticized for as white people, wanting her to say she understands so their fragility doesn't unravel. She said she's not going to do it anymore.

"I'd rather my friends sit with their mistakes and consider how to change."

I've often been worried about leaning on my non-white friends during times of fragility but I hadn't thought about how I could also be complicit on the other side, helping white friends verbalize their guilt and wash their hands of it. Like when Will told me his anti-racism strategy for TikTok, I probably should have said that it sounded really superficial and ineffective.

✶✶✶✶✶

I walked over to the mailbox earlier to send my sister-in-law a birthday card and when I got back there were two letters in my mailbox – one from Jonas' mom and one from a friend who lives in the Yukon. It's always weird when you send and receive mail in the same day. It almost makes it seem like email. Of course, the letters I received today have nothing to do with the one I sent, but as long as I'm keeping busy, it's all the same to me.

Jonas' mom's letter was charming and made me more excited to meet her. My friend's letter was a bit distressing. She had a concussion a month ago and was told to limit her screen time to only an hour a day. She couldn't do work on her computer, watch Netflix, do Zoom calls, anything. She said that people kept saying, "I'm so sorry," and "this must be so hard for you," but she was secretly loving it. I hadn't before considered concussions as a reason why there need to be alternatives to online ways of doing things.

Tonight, Darren is coming for dinner along with the newest fella he's been sleeping with. I met him already at the protest and he was very quiet. Bringing him over for dinner seems like a big step, but Darren said they've explicitly discussed that this is a casual thing and it's not building towards a relationship. I feel like that's how all of Darren's relationships start. (Gays have complicated relationships with relationships.)

THURSDAY, JUNE 4th

Memo and I got burgers for lunch today and ate them in a park. When I got home, Jonas was on the phone with his family and they were using FaceTime, so I couldn't pop my head in to say hello. I felt sorta rude about it, especially after Jonas' mom sent me such a lovely letter, but I asked him to pass along my gratitude, and I think they understand why I can't join.

While they chatted, I stepped out front on the sidewalk and tried to clean the gunk out of my bike chain with an old toothbrush. As I was working on that, I phoned my aunt and then my mom. Then I went inside and did the rest of the dishes (Jonas had done a bunch while I was out), put the sheets in the laundry, vacuumed the mattress, the couch, some cracks in the floor (I'm still getting bites), and – once I finished that – found a dead squirrel decomposing in the shed on our balcony so I put it in a garbage bag. It was a baby squirrel and when I picked it up, it was light as dust. It made me feel ill to touch, even through a dustpan.

I don't know how I'm also supposed to keep up with school on top of all this. I feel like I'm expecting too much of myself. And it's not even that much.

★★★★★

I saw one of my Quebecois friends today for the first time in a while. After catching up, we started talking about anti-racism and all the things he's seen online this week. He told me that a woman he went to university with posted something calling out the white men from their class who hadn't posted anything about anti-Blackness. He felt like she was targeting him in particular … so he made nine Instagram posts about it. He clarified that making nine posts is because that's the amount – on Instagram – you need to take up an entire page.

"Aesthetically-speaking, nine is ideal."

My friend's posts were about the issues of publicly shaming people. He wrote about the so-called "solidarity chains" he's been invited to, where someone challenges ten of their friends on Instagram to post about racism and responded that these "solidarity chains don't break the chains of oppression." It's a cute line but bolder than I would have chosen in the context. I brought up the idea that his impulse to post defensively may have come from feeling unsure how to hold the responsibility he's feeling to communities less fortunate than him. I felt patronizing, but he listened to me.

FRIDAY, JUNE 5th

We went to my friend Mark's birthday gathering tonight. Four of the six people there were from Edmonton, where the local football team is called the Edmonton "Eskimos." Mark told us that the Eskimos tweeted their support for the Black Lives Matter protests. I don't think a team that's refused to change their racist name can be an ally against racism. It reveals how superficial some of the anti-racist messaging going on is. Ulterior PR motives are one of the worst kinds of superficial. It hides how capitalism is complicit in colonialism and racist violence, and helps the status quo continue unscathed by critique.

One of the conversations that came up at Mark's was the one I keep having, about the value of the online activism happening alongside the recent wave of anti-racism protests. I swear I didn't bring it up. Someone commented that it seems like there's more police violence all of a sudden. There was an awkward silence and I gently pointed out that we were all white. The only thing there's more of is awareness.

Someone else said that, even if there is some "annoying" stuff happening online, Black people are totally justified acting however they need to after all the racism and police violence they face. It's our job now to listen. All the focus on how people are acting online draws focus from the real issue: racism.

Currently, Black and Indigenous people are four or five

times more likely to be stopped by Montreal's police than other people in Montreal. And that's not some social media estimate. That's the official stat from the city. Montreal's police chief had been invited to the upcoming anti-racism march but he was uninvited after some of the co-organizers intervened. I think it's better not to involve the police chief in a protest against the police. Once he takes action to address racial profiling, then he can join the march. Although if he really does take action, we won't need to protest.

SATURDAY, JUNE 6th
Fanny had her period again. I feel like this happens every month! I was sad when she told me, and a bit frustrated. I'm still hopeful though – at least that's what I'm telling myself. I think Fanny and Alex want to go the clinic route now, so Jonas and I are planning a trip to Toronto in the next few weeks and I'll have to come a bunch of times while we're there.

✶✶✶✶✶

This morning when we woke up, we sprayed poison all over the apartment and then went out for a big bike ride. I really hope the fleas are gone now. The past couple days, they've been devouring me, but I'm using Fanny's strategy of being mindful about the level and quality of the itching from moment to moment. It doesn't stop the itching, but it helps.

While we were on our bikes, Jonas and I had a long conversation and I felt like we were able to be especially open and gracious. Jonas called me out for calling him out too often for how much he's using his phone. I apologized and told him that I realize I can be overbearing, especially when it comes to tech stuff.

"I know I can be too much," I said, "and I'm working on it."

SUNDAY, JUNE 7th
Just got home from another protest. It felt even bigger today than last week's but it's hard to estimate. Jonas and I

marched with Tyler and one of his friends who's studying carbon emissions. I asked him if he does any research about the internet's environmental impacts. He said that they're hard to calculate and that depending on where data centres are located and what type of energy they use, the amount of emissions they produce varies widely. Even just looking into where different companies house their data is more difficult than he expected. He's currently trying to figure out whether Facebook has any data centres on the east coast where coal is still widely used.

After the march, we stopped at Darren's to pick up some plants he propagated for us – a spider plant and a monstera. He asked whether things had gotten hectic like at last week's protest. When we told him they hadn't, he seemed disappointed. At first this made me uncomfortable, like all Darren cared about was drama, but he explained that he doesn't think protests work unless things get out of hand. I know that most people feel the other way around, but I agree. Not that things have to get out of hand, but just that the more friction protests cause, the more people might notice and make changes. Most people I know care more about comfort and security than justice, but those are likely people who've never had their own comfort or security threatened by injustices – racial or otherwise.

There was a sign at today's protest that a Black protester was holding: "If you're tired of hearing about racism, just imagine how tired we are of experiencing it!" It reminded me of what I was journaling about, how people get caught up complaining how anti-racism on social media is expressed instead of addressing the actual racism being opposed. Focusing on *how* people protest can get in the way of the more important question of *why*.

Darren didn't seem too interested in talking about the protest but he gave us an update on his dudes. He's pretty much stopped talking to the Quebec City guy, although they still keep saying they should FaceTime. He also isn't texting his dinner date from a couple nights ago anymore because he's worried he was leading him on. He said that instead of putting his energy into boys, he's been devoting a lot of time and attention to his plants.

He brought up Grindr and how it's impacting his mental health – all the rejection, even amidst lots of validation. He thinks he might have to give up Grindr altogether because he doesn't know if he can use it in moderation. It takes up so much time and it's not really geared towards finding a partner, which is what Darren says he wants.

I think a lot of things online are similar – porn, social media, or the hybrid that is Grindr – they're all about the illusion of endlessness: there's always something (or someone) better. It's more about fantasy than reality.

MONDAY, JUNE 8th

I had a really sad phone call with Fanny today. It sounds like I won't be able to be their donor anymore. She and Alex spoke with their fertility clinic and were told it'll cost around $15 000 to go with a known donor, and that amount doesn't even guarantee success. Last time they were at the clinic, the doctor gave them an overly optimistic spin on things and wasn't clear about the price. He must figure that people will pay anything to make a family, which isn't fair when the same services he offers would be practically free if Fanny and Alex were a hetero couple with their own sperm who just needed help getting pregnant, or if we had lied and said that Fanny and I were a couple.

Fanny kept saying that if they try another route, they'd still want me to be a part of their family, but I know it won't be the same. I felt down but told Fanny (a couple times) that the goal of this process is for her and Alex to have a kid and I will support whatever option makes the most sense for that.

I know it was never really about me, but it's hard to imagine that this adventure may be over … for me. I do still hope I can stay as close with Fanny and Alex as I've been feeling throughout the last few months. Even if we didn't make a baby together, we made something.

*****

I heard yesterday's protest did get hectic after all. When I was leaving, it seemed like everything was over, but a handful of people – including Tyler's girlfriend – stuck around. They didn't get aggressive or change their behaviours or tactics. They were just peacefully obstructing traffic and the police used tear gas as easy crowd control. Tyler suggested he thinks it's more important to be there at the end of protests to support and witness what happens after the crowds and cameras go home, after the state-sanctioned part of the protest is over, once the friction and resistance begin. Next time, I'll try to show up late.

Jonas told me that Minneapolis is going to dismantle their police and put together smaller community-based safety units instead. I wonder what that will look like and how it can be designed to resist replicating the previous police force. Will all the same people be able to keep their jobs just within a new institution? Part of the systemic problem of racism is the system's infrastructure and composition, but another part is the way people think about police – including cops themselves. That won't change if the new force is made up of the same people.

*****

Today is the tenth Global Day of Remembrance for Victims of Foxconn, one of the companies in China that makes a large portion of Apple's iPhones and iPads. Foxconn employs over a million people who live and work in factories with "suicide nets" hanging from the roof. Almost one in five employees has experienced beatings at work, and even those who haven't are forced to endure a military-inspired work routine. In some workshops, people are not allowed to speak to one another or lean against the backs of their chairs.

Labour costs account for less than 2% of the money we spend on Apple devices, so I'm not surprised that Foxconn's working conditions are so poor. But it's hard to reconcile that reality with our lives where we need our phones and laptops for more and more of everything.

Since at least 2010 when this memorial day began (after a particularly large cluster of suicides), plenty of people have known that something needs to change. I think most people I know are aware of the radical imbalance between our consumer comforts and the struggles of the people who make them possible. But then how has Apple managed to hold onto their reputation as a responsible and caring corporation? And what about us – the ones accepting these labour conditions and continuing to buy the latest devices? I think we may really be as evil as we seem. It's just hard to notice as we scroll through cat and dog memes or social justice-themed TikTok videos.

TUESDAY, JUNE 9th

It was really nice to hang out with our friend Junior yesterday. He finally got a phone number, so it's been easier for me to reach him. He told us about a new guy he's seeing and the stressful new job he has at the hospital. I asked whether the work stress had been connected to all the stuff happening online around anti-racism and police violence. Junior said that it's definitely added to how he's been feeling. He said that, as a Black person, it's been really hard to engage with everything that's being shared on social media. However, he said he definitely thinks what's happening online is good overall.

I'm amazed at how much my perspective can change in such a short time. (These days especially.) Less than a week ago I was being so critical of online spaces and suggesting that they were too dominated by "annoying," "self-righteous" content and that there were all these catch-22s whereby nobody could say anything right. Now, though I still acknowledge these problems, I realize that focusing on them in the wrong way can detract from the issues of anti-racism and police violence. Focusing on people criticizing the way others are contributing to the conversation sounds more and more like fatalistic fragility that won't make anything better.

There's a big difference between avoiding the negative dynamics of social media and ignoring them. It's still important to reflect on why people are so drawn to the drama of calling out others online (horrified and loving it), but instead of focusing on this drama, we can try to promote a more careful and caring judgment. We can listen more. We can consider context.

✶✶✶✶✶

I had a long call with my friend Yuki this morning and appreciated her perspective on the anti-racist conversation. She thinks it's "lucky" and "unfortunate" that I can't go online to witness the constant stream of violence between police and protesters. She said it's been really exhausting and important.

I asked Yuki if she feels optimistic about news out of the States – like the dismantling of Minneapolis' police force. She said that she's only seen white people posting about that and doesn't think it's real news.

✶✶✶✶✶

I talked to my cousin AJ today. He told me a story about a woman in Seattle who had been at one of the anti-racism protests recently. According to AJ's story, after returning from the protest, the woman was maced and arrested in her driveway while her kids were sitting in the backseat of the car. Police announced they knew she'd been at the protest and where she lived because of data gathered from her phone. I don't understand why this woman in particular was targeted amongst the thousands of protesters in Seattle, but it's messed up that police, government, and phone companies work closely enough to facilitate this kind of operation. Next time I go to a protest, I should leave my phone at home. (I probably won't, though.)

WEDNESDAY, JUNE 10th

I heard on the radio that anti-racism advocates in Canada are calling on the RCMP to collect "dis-aggregated" data on arrests and crime to measure the extent to which non-white people are being targeted by police. Currently, they don't collect very much data on the race of the people they fuck with. It's a bit ironic when you think that the RCMP was founded with a very race-based aim: "solving" the "Indian" "problem."

★★★★★

I wish I could go online right now. Doing research is hard when you can't look anything up. I've been working on a new paper the past couple days and I keep hitting dead ends when I find something I want to read or reread. I have a lot of content already saved, a lot of books on my shelf, and a lot of friends who I can borrow things from, but when it comes to specific sources that I hear about and want to check out, I'm mostly at a loss. There is an upside though. Because I haven't been gathering any new sources this year, I've had the space to thoroughly and critically read older articles and books. I know I need to engage with the latest research too, but for now there's a part of me that's very happily limited.

Omar called today to talk about … anti-racism. It's almost like there's nothing else going on. We got going on the question of online activism and Omar said he doesn't think there's anything wrong with people who are ignorant and phony making posts against racism. I pushed back and suggested that superficial actions might make people feel like they've done something helpful in a way that convinces them they don't need to do more. Omar reminded me that the people who are posting superficially aren't going to do more in the first place, so at least they're posting.

I haven't watched Fox since I was a kid, but Omar sometimes turns it on to watch the news and find out what people on "the other side" are seeing in their echo chamber. The other day he had it on and saw a graph comparing the amount of people who die annually in the US from police violence with the amount of people who die annually from falling furniture. The person on the news was asking why there aren't protests against falling furniture. I can't believe Fox's viewership is willing to accept this logic. How can someone think that protesting against racist policing is the same as protesting against gravity?

Omar also said that Fox was celebrating how much the stock market is going up at the moment. Citing the Rodney King riots in the '90s, it pointed out that this always seems to happen after major waves of protests by Black people. Is that even true? Why would that be true? I thought uncertainty was bad for the economy. Or is it only uncertainty that impacts white people?

Immediately after getting off the phone with Omar, Sloane called. I was having conversation fatigue, but I couldn't not answer Sloane's call, and I'm glad I did. They had a ridiculous story to tell me about … anti-racism on the internet. And I think it shifted my opinion again.

Sloane was called out through a public Facebook post made by a Black woman who they hardly know, saying Sloane isn't doing enough to fight racism. The woman making the post claimed it was a "calling in" not a "calling out" and suggested some ideas of how Sloane can take action, including donating $150 to her personally. I shouldn't scoff at the ways people respond to racism, but I feel defensive of Sloane. They do so much to challenge racism materially and ideologically with their research and as a volunteer. Not to mention that Sloane, though white-passing, is part Indigenous.

Sloane felt guilty and smeared. It seems like it actually *is* important to discuss online dynamics as part of talking about racism. Sloane said they don't have the energy to care about the public perception of their work, but I know they're aware that lots of young, queer academics and activists follow them online. I feel like both of these attacks – on their self-confidence and their online character – make it harder for Sloane to do the important work they do. By publicly calling out someone who does anti-racism work without knowing their story, the caller-outer could be working against their own team.

Sloane ended up privately messaging the woman and received a patronizing response saying that Sloane must not be far enough along on their "decolonizing journey." I'm still not too worried about virtue signalling except when it makes people feel like they're off the hook. But I now see why it might be important to call people out for calling people out.

✦✦✦✦✦

I talked to Niko on the phone this evening and he told me he signed up for one of those online monthly food baskets that have become popular lately. I thought he was telling me to prove how grown-up he'd become since finishing grad school and getting a fancy tech job. But then he explained that the basket comes with candy, fizzy-drinks, and salty snacks – all from Japan.

I think I'm done journaling for today. It always feels good when I finish – like when you really have to pee and finally do. I got all my memories out and can relax now. I like writing in my journal but I'm getting too obsessed with making sure I don't miss documenting anything important. It's almost like having social media.

THURSDAY, JUNE 11th

Alex phoned this morning and explained that they and Fanny DO want to keep trying to use my sperm after all!! Such a relief to hear this. However, there are still a bunch of hurdles. They don't want to pay $15 000 only to find out that my sperm doesn't work, so they've asked me to get tested here in Montreal before we plan anything else. I phoned a fertility clinic that was willing to book me an appointment next week on Tuesday. It'll be $200 and they only test sperm, so I'm going to have to find another clinic that does blood tests. It's exciting and disconcerting how easy it was to book a sperm test. When clinics are for-profit, there are less bureaucratic obstacles.

The fertility clinic would normally ask me to "produce my sample" at their facility, but that's not allowed right now. They instead are recommending I produce it at home, and then take a 20-minute cab ride to the clinic with the sample tucked under my arm, so it stays warm. The sample has to be less than an hour old, and figuring out the timing is stressing me out. My appointment's at 9:00 a.m., so I'll masturbate at 8:20ish, get the cab at 8:30ish, arrive at 8:50ish, and drop off the sample at 9. They said I have to make sure I don't ejaculate for two days beforehand BUT I can't have gone more than three days without ejaculating, so basically that means I have to ejaculate on Saturday. Should I put it in my calendar? I think I will.

I spoke with Alex on their own because Fanny is busy preparing for a 500-person Zoom call she's hosting this evening for the anti-racism network that Alex and Fanny organize with. It's hopeful to hear that so many people are trying to be part of anti-racism organizing efforts, but I wonder if people will lose steam after this current surge of online interest passes.

✶✶✶✶✶

I walked into the room where Jonas was sitting and started talking to him, but quickly realized he was on the phone with his mom. He wears those cyborg earrings, the wireless bud-style headphones that Apple's trying to push on everyone. Usually, he just uses them to listen to music or podcasts, so I forgot he could also use them to talk on the phone.

After Jonas finished his call, we went to buy him a bicycle from Kijiji. He gave it a test ride and it seemed pretty good – it certainly looks hip, all black and speckled with a design made to look like white dust. It cost $400 but it felt like a decent deal.

As we biked home, Jonas was talking about how much he likes being able to buy things used from sites like Kijiji.

I agreed but then told a story about one of my students in Vancouver whose uncle was murdered over a Craigslist deal while trying to sell his ex-wife's engagement ring.

"Are you saying I shouldn't buy things secondhand from the internet?" Jonas asked.

"Not at all! I'm sure that kind of thing hardly ever happens."

I shouldn't have said anything, but it's not as fun to talk about life when everything goes normally.

FRIDAY, JUNE 12th

I used to keep a big list of all the passwords I had for different online accounts and websites. I had saved various versions of this list in different places and always forgot which was the most current. To confuse things further, the lists were inevitably out of date and included all sorts of old account usernames and passwords that I was afraid to remove from the list, just in case. I realized today that I haven't had to look at the list yet this year.

I hate having so many different usernames and passwords to remember. Since starting my year offline, the only password I've needed is the one that lets me unlock my computer and log in. Besides schoolwork, the only things I have saved on this computer are journal entries, so I don't even care about having a lock and a password. But I haven't bothered figuring out how to turn it off.

Passwords only exist because we're afraid of malicious people seeing our private stuff, exploiting it or us, and scamming us out of money. Without the internet, it turns out there are way less opportunities to get fucked over by strangers.

SATURDAY, JUNE 13th

My mom phoned today and asked me how she could get involved in fighting systemic racism in Edmonton, where she lives. I told her about a couple things to read, but suggested she should ask one of her close friends, who's Black. She might have names of organizations to volunteer with. My mom responded that she doesn't want to burden her friend with more work, so she hasn't asked her. I was proud that my mom was hesitant to ask a Black person to do anti-racist work for her, but told her I think she can still ask her friend for ideas in a way that doesn't compel her to do anything if she doesn't feel up to it.

My parents still get the newspaper delivered daily, and my mom told me about an article she read this week about Edmonton's police chief and systemic racism. In the article, the chief is quoted saying that the police would have to fire some of their more junior officers if their funding decreases and they've done a lot of diversity hiring in the past few years – of non-white people, queer people, etc. – so those officers would be the first to go. Is that a threat?! What a reminder of how racism, although systemic, is perpetuated by individual police officers, especially those in positions of power. It's not that the Edmonton police chief explicitly thinks less of Black people (though he might), but his unwillingness to proactively address systemic issues is how they continue.

SUNDAY, JUNE 14th
This morning I noticed a flea biting my ankle and squished it to death. I had thought they might be gone, so I felt frustrated (and now itchy). I talked to my landlord and he told me that he's not obligated to help but suggested I catch a flea for him to take to an exterminator. It's confusing that he's offered to do that after telling me he's not going to pay for the exterminator, but I'll try to catch one.

TUESDAY, JUNE 16th
I'm nervously awaiting the results from the fertility clinic. After the sperm test, I went and did the blood and urine tests that Fanny and Alex needed me to do. They cost over $900 … which Fanny and Alex will pay me back for, but which will have been for nothing if it turns out that my

sperm doesn't work. Hopefully it's all good and I don't have to worry.

It's hard to write in my journal as I wait by the phone. I'm more anxious than normal. I didn't sleep well last night. And there's an obnoxious beeping noise coming from outside that keeps starting and stopping and making my head hurt.

When I was getting my blood tests earlier, I had a strange conversation with the nurse. I had to do eight tests, so I was there for a while. I told him about the sperm donor thing but he seemed confused as to why I was getting these tests. He assumed for some reason that the couple I was helping were gay cis men and didn't understand why they needed *more* sperm.

After I explained that the couple both have ovaries, he asked if I had heard about Harry Potter. (Uhh … what?) It turned out he meant had I heard about J. K. Rowling's transphobia. He went on to ask – in a way that felt a bit transphobic but mixed with what seemed like an openness to having his views complicated – how trans women fit into feminist movements.

"Isn't feminism about the shared struggles that women have?" he said.

I reminded him that trans women *are* women and also share these struggles, that they're actually more likely to experience sexual violence and discrimination than cis women.

He said "good point," and seemed to mean it.

I phoned Fanny on the walk home from the clinic. We talked about my conversation with the nurse and how he lumped together all trans (and I guess queer) people once I mentioned a couple having two ovaries.

"Like the leap from ovaries to Rowling's transphobia is … bizarre," she said, "and also far from our genders."

I wanted to tell her more about the appointment but we ended up talking about racism instead. Fanny shared her theory that to really get rid of exploitative race relations, we probably have to abandon capitalism. If the current move to fight racism in the US and Canada leads to prison reform and an end to the current manifestation of slave labour here, companies will just turn to the sweatshops of the Global South for cheap labour instead. Considering the current momentum, I can actually fathom legislation that challenges racist laws and policies in Canada and the US. However, as long as capitalism's still driving things, North American companies will figure out how to respect that legislation but keep the ol' profit machine going ... i.e. our exploitative reliance on the Global South will have to get worse.

*****

It's after 6 p.m. now and the fertility clinic didn't call. I tried their number, but they're closed. The receptionist this morning told me twice that I'd hear from the doctor by the end of the day. Did I do something wrong?

WEDNESDAY, JUNE 17th
Immediately after waking up, I phoned the fertility clinic. I waited on hold for half an hour, and then they hung up on me. I phoned back, got put on hold again, waited another half hour, and then they hung up on me again. So so frustrating!! (I think their hold system times out after half an hour.) I called again a few hours later and finally got through after just a few minutes on hold. The receptionist took my number and told me a nurse would call me back. And finally, several hours later, they called back:
"Your sperm is normal."
What a rollercoaster for such a simple message. A lot of the bureaucratic frustrations I've dealt with lately have been because I'm not using the internet. In this case though, being online wouldn't have made a difference. The only way to get my results was over the phone.
So much to feel good about today! When I checked my mailbox this afternoon, there were five letters in there. Five! None from a computer or return-to-senders, straight-up five personally written letters from friends. Two included

art, one included a photograph, and two included clippings or print-outs of articles that my friends knew I'd want to read. It's such a badass feeling to receive and open letters. I don't think I ever felt this way after getting emails. I'm sure if I received five personally written emails, I'd feel pretty good. But that immediate pressure to respond would be there, which ruins it a bit. I love the pace of letters.

One of the letters I received today, from Mark, included an article about the "Majority Illusion" in social networks. It was a bit more mathy than I'm used to, but it looked at the way people generalize from what they see of their social contacts to imagine what society is like more generally. It showed how rare or fringe opinions can seem popular if the people who hold them are socially well-connected. If just a few really well connected people think the earth is flat, it might seem like tons of people know flat-earthers, when it could just be that lots of people know those few really well connected fools.

I think I'm a pretty well-connected person. I wonder how much I'm skewing people's understanding of society towards believing that Luddites are more prevalent than they really are. Even if I know a lot of people though, being offline might limit the amount I can impact their imagined understandings of the world. Now that I think it through, if these imagined communities are based on perceptions gleaned from online networks, then Luddites are probably grossly *under*represented and people might think we don't exist at all. (If a tree falls in a forest and nobody posts it on the internet, does it really fall?)

★★★★★

I talked to my little cousin Cary on the phone today. I asked him what he thinks the internet is and he started talking about lightning bolts. Cary asked why I'm not using the internet and I tried to come up with a really simple answer. I asked whether he knew that the internet didn't exist before he was born, like when his Daddy and I were his age. He was surprised. I told him that because the internet is still pretty new and because it became popular so fast, I'm spending the year offline to check which parts of it I like and which parts I want to be more careful about using. I don't think he totally understood but he was interested in talking more about what it would be like to visit the time before he was born.

"It's like you're a time traveller," he said, "It'd be way cooler though if you could travel all the way back to meet cavemen."

I agreed, but told Cary that I'm not not prepared to spend a year without electricity. Or language.

✶✶✶✶✶

Jonas and I learned one of the reasons why we get so many squirrels on our balcony – digging up our planters, eating our herbs, and nibbling on the strings of lights we've put up around the railing. Our neighbour has been feeding them!! He's an older, Quebecois guy who sells weed and lives with his ex-brother-in-law. Super friendly ... but maybe too friendly? Jonas was on a Zoom call with some of his friends from the UK when he noticed squirrels going right into the neighbour's kitchen window. He called me over to see and we realized that they weren't just sneaking in. Our neighbour was actually inviting them in and giving them peanuts. Fuckk...

Jonas' friends wanted me to join for their Zoom call but Jonas explained that it would break my rules. Part of me is sad that I wasn't able to meet Jonas' friends but another part of me is glad that I didn't have to meet them for the first time over Zoom. In-person will be much nicer. (This offline project has really been the ultimate excuse.)

✶✶✶✶✶

I spoke with Aviva this morning about the work she's trying to do around pressuring our university to take meaningful action against institutional racism. She prepared a letter with a couple of our colleagues and it sounded really focused and clear. I suggested to cut out some of the theoretical parts and focus on concrete actions. Anyone who doesn't already agree with her is more likely to engage with suggestions for what the university can do than analysis of how neoliberal spaces are normed for white, non-disabled, straight, cis men.

Aviva is aware that, as a white person, she needs to work with non-white people on this and she's partnered with an Indigenous student to write the letter. She also reached out to a couple of the Black and Brown professors in the department. Abdul – a prof that I'm close with – replied with a short message about non-white scholars being accoutrements or cushions for white scholars. Aviva didn't understand what he was trying to tell her. I don't think I do either – not yet. Even if Abdul and Aviva have irreconcilably different perspectives on this, there's a lot I can learn from both of them.

THURSDAY, JUNE 18th

This morning Jonas and I were sitting outside on the front porch when our mail-person came by.

She had a package in her hand but, because we were on the stairs, she just passed it to us saying, "I have a package for Aron."

I took the package, but noticed it was addressed to Jonas and didn't have my name anywhere on it.

"How did she know my name?" I asked Jonas, "Do you think she memorizes all her client's names?"

Jonas replied that she probably remembers my name because I get so much mail. I hadn't considered before that the amount of letters I've received this year is probably a bit unique. I doubt there are too many people who receive so much personal mail in the age of email. I feel famous … at least to our mail-person.

FRIDAY, JUNE 19th

Last night my parents called. I expected it just to be a normal check-in, but – as my mom told me as soon as I said hi – my dad lost his job. He sounded less upset about it than my mom, but he did seem a bit incredulous. He'd been working for the same tech company for 19 years and they let him go at a moment's notice, reading from a canned HR script. After finding out that he'd been let go, he posted a note about it on LinkedIn and was overwhelmed by all the warm messages he got from contacts on there. I'm glad he at least had that to mark his departure. After 19 years though, it just doesn't seem right. It's moments like these when I wish I lived closer to home.

I listened to the economic report on the radio this morning and heard that unemployment rates in Quebec are just under 20%. It's hard to believe that nearly one in five Quebeccers is out of work at the moment. I don't know what the stats are in Alberta, but my dad's situation probably isn't unique. It seems so different though when it's someone I know and love.

SATURDAY, JUNE 20th
Tyler's been having relationship problems so I went over to hang out with him tonight. When I got there he was crying, so I asked if I could give him a hug. He agreed. I hadn't hugged him for three months and – not to sound creepy – but it felt way better than I expected it would. I mean, I was hugging him because he was upset, but having been pretty limited in my selection of hug recipients lately, hugging someone new, someone who I really care about and who was hurting – it was intense. Maybe I'll come out of this year really appreciating hugs. Or maybe I'll be scared of them. Or maybe I'll just get used to them again and forget how special they can be.

SUNDAY, JUNE 21st
I called Niko to see if he was up for a hang but he's busy playing a video game that was released on Friday called *The Last of Us II*. It's one of the most highly anticipated games

of the year and has received amazing reviews from critics who played it before the official release. However, it has a very low score from fans. The original *The Last of Us* was an incredibly popular zombie game that followed a 14-year-old woman and her father as they struggled to survive the apocalypse. In the new game, the young woman is now 19 and the story opens with her father dying. Shortly afterwards, she comes out as a lesbian, making out with another woman and sharing a joint.

Niko explained that the reason the game has such terrible reviews from fans is because a group of homophobic people have "review-bombed" it, without even trying the game. The bombers think "politics" has no place in games. Niko said he hasn't found the game to be preachy or overtly political. It just has a main character who is gay and a woman. He's worried that the bad reviews will dissuade people from playing the game. Controversy sells though, so the campaign to lower this game's rating might actually boost sales.

On the topic of internet users banding together in sneaky ways, Niko and I also talked about a grassroots TikTok campaign that a bunch of teens organized to troll the president of the US last week. They had loads of people reserve tickets for his re-election rally without any intention of showing up. Then, when the actual event happened, there was hardly anyone there.

Although the trolls messing with the president are very different than the trolls review-bombing *The Last of Us II*, they both show that the internet can still shake traditional power structures and decentralize things. I thought that this potential was waning as Google, Microsoft, Apple, Amazon, and Facebook take over every corner of the web that they can, but it turns out that internet users still have the ability to make changes collectively from the bottom-up – for better or for worse.

I told Jonas about *The Last of Us II,* and he'd already heard about it but for different reasons. It's apparently the most accessible video game ever created, with accommodations to suit as many disabilities as the designers could imagine. For example, if you're low vision, there's a text to speech option or you can set the game to highlight the enemy characters in a certain colour. Or if you have motor or physical disabilities, you can set the game so that you don't need to tap buttons repeatedly.

Growing up, I was never a fan of zombie games. But maybe I just hadn't found one that aligned with my values.

MONDAY, JUNE 22nd

I found a flea on my leg this weekend while watching TV with Jonas. We put it in a plastic container and this morning my landlord came by to take it to an exterminator. The exterminator confirmed it was a flea but said there's no way we could have fleas without pets in the apartment. We assured our landlord that we don't have any pets.

"I don't know what to say," he replied, "I'm just telling you what the exterminator said."

✶✶✶✶✶

I talked to my dad today and he told me about a job interview he had this morning. Because his expertise relies on companies having their own server instead of saving things to the cloud, my dad thinks of himself as "basically a dinosaur." However, the company that's considering him is unionized and they don't want to lose the IT jobs that would disappear if files were all saved remotely instead of on local servers.

TUESDAY, JUNE 23rd

Sloane texted me this morning to check if I'd already heard what happened to the letter Aviva put together about racism and systemic discrimination at our university. When I spoke with Aviva about it last week, she wanted to get some other people from our department to sign onto it. She had gotten in touch with the Black Students Network and they were supportive of the letter. But Sloane explained that someone who Aviva shared the letter with posted it to social media and it spiralled into a full-on public petition. And that's when the Black Students Network asked gently for the petition to be taken down.

My first reaction was frustration. I talked to Sloane about it though and they pointed out that letters to our university's administration are pretty useless: "The principal isn't gonna do fuck all and there's way better work to be doing right now." She said that she still wants to support Aviva, but that it might be more supportive to tell Aviva to focus her efforts elsewhere. Can we change the system or do we have to look beyond it? I keep thinking about this lately, in relation to the university, to police, the government, the internet, capitalism...

SLOANE: I was just reading a piece about Canadian mining and activism that was engaging with the argument that no one can say shit about extractive capitalism because we all have smartphones

ARON: Throw it out the window!! DO IT!

SLOANE: Hahahah

ARON: jk ... that'd be too easy.

SLOANE: I'd just be one of those weird pretentious eco anarchists.

ARON: I think there's something about using digital devices to help fight extractive capitalism that's hypocritical, but there's also something pragmatic about it. You told me that anarchists would say we can't use means that misalign with our goals, but I think that idea doesn't work in cases where a problem has become central to almost every possible means of addressing it.

SLOANE: I mean I also think there's something in anarchist thought about doing what you can while acknowledging that capitalism actually doesn't allow us to live the way we want yet.

I don't think we can fully address issues related to the internet without using the internet. We need to learn about and work within online infrastructures in order to transform them. Avoiding the internet may seem like it makes change, and it may seem like a choice, but my actions alone aren't the change, and spending a year without internet isn't really a choice for most people.

It's funny that I'm the one arguing pragmatism as I'm halfway through spending a year offline. My stunt this year makes people think I've got a radical message but I try to always clarify that I don't think everyone should (or could) try to reject the internet so absolutely. Spending a year offline isn't a lifestyle choice; it's a gesture, a performance – it's about bringing attention to something so that we can make changes together, slowly but surely. Any solution that can be scaled and sustained needs to be collective and it needs to engage with the problems it's trying to solve – not just reject them. I'm just as cynical about the possibility of a revolution happening as I am about the possibility of the status quo working.

WEDNESDAY, JUNE 24th

Memo sent Jonas an email asking if we could meet up this weekend to discuss the camping trip we're planning with Hanni and Kat. The four of them (minus me) have been emailing back-and-forth a bit and just want to hash out the details in person. It always seems like it'll be easier that way. And from my experience, it usually is. I'm surprised though that it has been so difficult for them to make a decision about when we're going where and how we'll get there.

If I were online and involved in the email chain, I would just do a little research, make some decisions, and email it around to everyone for approval before booking things. Because I can't look up campgrounds and car rentals, I have to leave it to everyone else. As the person who often takes the lead on these kinds of things, it's a bit frustrating to see everyone just calmly floundering, unwilling to be the one to make the decision. It's probably a good learning experience in patience and sharing control (especially as a white cis dude) but I'm finding it difficult and frustrating. Deep breath.

✦✦✦✦✦

I drank a coffee this morning and it got me going, so I decided to write a cheeky little manifesto on how I've been feeling about the internet:

We will not accept the internet as it is.

We will change and we will change it.

We will not give up privacy because "we have nothing to hide."

We will learn how others are implicated in the ways our data is used.

We will not believe everything we read online, or dismiss it either.

We will think about why who's posting what and where.

We will not trust algorithms as neutral or objective.

We will demand transparency and better data.

We will not perform to an echo chamber.

We will confuse our way out of filter bubbles.

We will not overlook prejudice online.

We will complicate conversations.

We will not accept boys' clubs in Silicon Valley.

We will call white supremacy by its name.

We will not "consent" to the terms and conditions of big tech monopolies.

We will collaborate and seek out more marginal players.

We will not use search engines or cloud storage just because we can.

We will find out where the information and files we access are stored – and how.

We will not ignore the mining, manufacturing, and disposal of our phones and computers.

We will remember that displacing labour does not replace it.

We will not shop on Amazon.

We will never shop on Amazon!

We will not buy a new device as often as we do.

We will acknowledge and try to overcome our hypocrisies.

We will not respond to work emails after work.

We will leave our phone outside the bedroom.

We will not do extra work just because mobile technology makes it possible.

We will keep aiming for balance even as we keep missing it.

We will not scroll infinitely or lose ourselves in Wikipedia wormholes.

We will forgive ourselves when we do.

We will not assume newer, faster, and more convenient is better.

We will be patient. (But not too patient.)

THURSDAY, JUNE 25th

I still hadn't heard anything from the clinic about my blood tests so I called earlier and was told that my results were available. However, the woman on the phone said she couldn't fax or email me the results. I had to pick them up in person. I've had a lot of STI tests in my life and I've never had to go into the clinic to get my results, unless— Fuuuuuck.

I went in immediately, but the receptionist seemed really confused. He couldn't find a file with my name and said he didn't have any results for me. I phoned the same number as earlier and the same woman picked up. She said she'd resend the results. And then I waited.

After waiting for twenty minutes, the guy behind the counter asked if he could help me.

"Yeah," I said, "the fax. Has it arrived?"

He looked confused. "Did they resend it?" he asked.

"Yes."

"Well then we should have received it. Just a minute," and he got up to check.

Behind his desk was a sign explaining that verbal abuse isn't tolerated and that service will be refused to anyone who breaks that rule. I never thought I'd be the guy who that sign was directed to … and I wasn't – I remained calm, but I felt frustrated and indignant.

When he came back with the results, I quickly scanned the page. Everything was negative. All that for nothing, as usual.

Before I left, I got him to fax the results over to Fanny and Alex's clinic in Toronto. Fax is pretty much exactly like email but for some reason it still exists even in spaces where everyone also has internet access. Why is that? They seem to be mostly used for medical administrative purposes nowadays. My guess is that faxes offer more security and privacy than email, but it could just be that people don't want to bother updating old infrastructures. If only I could go online to read the Wikipedia entry on fax machines. (I could fax someone and ask them to fax me back an explanation?)

When I got home, Jonas and I took turns spraying some of the flea poison that our landlord brought us all over the apartment. We had to move around our furniture in order to get at all the cracks and corners. Then, we went out for fish burgers with Memo. Right as we got back, Fanny and Alex phoned and we spoke with them for a good hour.

They've booked us a place to stay in Toronto, a rental car, and they'll be able to get me an appointment at their clinic on Tuesday morning. They want to act fast so that the sperm will be ready for Fanny's next ovulation. All of a sudden everything's moving very quickly!!

FRIDAY, JUNE 26th
This morning, I made a stack of books, assignments, papers, and other stuff I have to get through in the next few weeks for grad school work. It reminded me of being a kid and coming home from school with loads of homework. Before I got down to it, I'd always make a big pile of everything I needed to get done and show it to my mom. I don't know if I did that to brag, self-deprecatingly, about the burden of

homework, or if it was just a physical measure of how much work I had to do.

Homework isn't as physical or bulky anymore. Most assignments are digital. Students can't brag about how much work they have to do by showing off a stack of books. It's good they don't have to strain their backs anymore, lugging heavy textbooks back-and-forth between school and home. But I miss it.

✶✶✶✶✶

I biked down to Verdun today to see Hanni and Kat's new place. Hanni just quit his job as a mentor for a computer programming bootcamp. When he started the job, he used to meet with a group of students several times a week, build relationships with them, and then help them succeed in technical and emotional ways. After the course was moved online, he started to feel like an anonymous support person. Students from across Canada would log on for help and get assigned a random mentor. Hanni said that people wouldn't even introduce themselves, and many people left their cameras off.

"It's a call centre that calls itself a school."

Hanni was hating on the way this new format lacks an in-person component so I asked whether that could be ableist. It prioritizes a type of social interaction that some disabled people can't participate in. Hanni thought about it but said he feels the issue isn't whether it's in-person or not, but rather whether there's some continuity or consistency in terms of which students he's mentoring. Without that, it's hard to build a relationship and without developing a relationship, he finds it much harder to teach, or for students to learn. He also resents how precarious and replaceable he feels.

I love the relationship I have with Hanni where I can ask critical questions without worrying that he'll feel attacked.

SUNDAY, JUNE 28th

The police in Montreal have released a statement defending themselves against claims of systemic racism; *although individual police officers may be racist, the police system is not deliberately racist.* But isn't the point of systemic racism to uncover how racism isn't deliberate?!

✶✶✶✶✶

Jonas and I leave for Toronto tomorrow. I borrowed a map of Canada from Hannibal and Kat and it has zoomed-in sections for each province. I'm a bit worried about getting out of Montreal and onto the highway tomorrow, but I feel like the rest of the trip should be pretty straightforward, even without Google Maps. We want to stop for a picnic on the way in Prince Edward County on the beach at Sandbanks National Park. I found the little dot on the map that represents Sandbanks. Normally, with internet support, I'd have really specific and detailed directions – turn-by-turn – to help me get there. However, I really don't feel too anxious about finding it with paper maps.

I got in touch with some friends in Toronto to let them know I'll be in town next week. I'm excited for Jonas to meet them and for them to meet Jonas. I also told my brother and his wife that we're coming (and why), but I asked them not to mention it to my parents yet.

MONDAY, JUNE 29th

I'm supposed to pick up the rental car at noon and it's 11 now. I've been on hold with my insurance company for over two hours waiting to ask if I'm covered for car rentals. I was on hold first for an hour and twenty minutes and then the hold music stopped and the line went dead. I called back and now I've been on hold for another hour. I feel stressed and I don't know if it's cause of this repetitive hold music or the prospect of going to Toronto after hibernating these past three months.

*****

Still on hold. It's been almost three hours now and I have to go. I'm considering changing insurance providers, but I can't if they won't let me talk to anyone. Imagine if keeping people on hold is part of some twisted customer retention strategy…

TUESDAY, JUNE 30th

Six months down, six to go. I love having a reason to celebrate, and being halfway through this project seems special enough.

*****

I had my first appointment at the fertility clinic in Toronto this morning. It lasted over three hours and I was busy almost the whole time. When I arrived, a nurse took my temperature and then brought me to an office to fill out a lot of paperwork. So much paperwork. There were seven or eight documents, some over ten pages long.

One of the forms just asked me a whole load of questions to determine my risk level – questions like "have you used cocaine intravenously in the past 3 months," "have you taken any form of treatment for an STI in the past 3 months," and "have you gotten a tattoo or piercing without adequate sanitary standards in the past 3 months?" I answered yes to just one question: "Have you had sex with a man in the past 3 months?" It offended me to see a question like that included amongst so many more directly and objectively risky criteria, but I wasn't surprised. Fanny had told me that one of the nurses at the clinic tried to talk her out of going with me as her donor because I'm gay and therefore at a higher risk of getting STIs. I appreciate that Fanny sees me as more than a statistic.

After finishing the paperwork, I did a urine test, a sperm test, a bunch of blood tests (nine vials-worth), and I had a physical. When they finally let me leave, I felt drained but ready to keep going.

✶✶✶✶✶

This trip has been hectic in the best kind of way. I don't really care about many cities themselves but I love people and there are lots of people I love in Toronto. It was really nice to catch up with two of my old friends tonight, although we ended up talking about the internet more than about what's going on in our lives. One of them was excited to tell me that he doesn't use the cloud anymore so that he has more control over his files. He just saves things on an external hard drive. Like me! He also told me that he finds Zoom calls exhausting and terrible, especially for work.

The other friend felt differently. He works for a big tech company and has to do 6+ hours of Zoom calls every day. He said he doesn't mind. He admits that he's been sipping the Kool-Aid and is pretty optimistic about lots of the new infrastructures that his company promotes. He knows that they gather the shopping history of all their users, but he doesn't think that this data is sold or used for anything. (Then why do they store it?) He also bragged that his company has lots of high profile politicians' credit card information but claimed that it's all very secure.

In all his tech-optimism, my friend also insists that our devices are NOT listening to us. He shared a theory that could explain why people see ads for things they haven't searched for – things they've just spoken about in the presence of their all-knowing smartphone. The theory has to do with relationships. If someone who your phone knows is close with you (or close to you) searches something, your device might show you ads for it too – even if you've never personally searched for it.

Jonas had an experience with something similar recently. We were talking to our friends about going camping and Hanni sent Jonas an email asking if we could help him and Kat find sleeping bags, a tent, and a camping stove. Hanni specified that they were more interested in renting equipment than buying it. Mysteriously, after reading the email,

Jonas started seeing ads for camping stuff on all sorts of web pages. Then things got even more precise; he received an email from a store he'd never heard of before advertising camping equipment rentals. It featured three ads: one for sleeping bags, one for tents, and one for camping stoves. What makes this even stranger is that Jonas has very strict and effective anti-junk mail sorting settings turned on so that he only gets personal emails. However, this camping equipment ad somehow snuck its way in. How much do advertisers have to pay to break into people's inboxes?

July

"I AM WHAT I AM." My body belongs to me. I am me, you are you, and *something's wrong.*
 – The Invisible Committee, 2009, *The Coming Insurrection*

WEDNESDAY, JULY 1st
Today is Canada Day and although I try not to celebrate (despite benefiting plenty from this colonial project), we had a pretty full day. Jonas and I went for a lunch BBQ in my brother's backyard. He and my fairly pregnant sister-in-law made us a lovely lunch and we spent a few hours lounging in the shade. I'm glad Jonas got to hang out with my family a bit. It makes things between us feel more real.

After lunch, Jonas and I met one of my childhood friends and one of her friends and the four of us went for a long walk along Lake Ontario. As we were walking and talking, Jonas mentioned my journal.

"Aron writes down every notable conversation or encounter he has," he said.

I wonder whether realizing that I'm trying to document my year offline changes the way people act when I'm with them. It's like the way surveillance or social media changes how people act when they think they might end up online. We're not able to be as creative or take as many risks. It's harder to try an idea on for size when we know we may be held accountable for that idea forever.

We chatted about the issue of Canada Day. My friend's friend is an immigrant from Poland and said that, having been born under "communism," she's very appreciative of Canada. Although I'm endlessly appreciative of the privileges I have as a result of my citizenship, I try to remember that that these privileges operate at the expense of Indigenous communities. Canadians have lots of amazing opportunities, but it's irresponsible to forget that these are connected to the catastrophic disruption of Indigenous life. Celebrating Canada Day seems like it's almost flaunting this disconnect. My friend and her friend both said they totally agreed, but was it because they knew it might end up in my journal?

After the walk, Jonas and I met with Fanny and Alex for a picnic in a park. There were tons of families there and some of them were setting off fireworks. At first it was cool, but then it became noisy and obnoxious. When we were leaving, we saw a group of teenagers having a fireworks fight – running around, shooting roman candle flares at each other. It seemed unsafe, especially as there were lots of younger kids in the park too. One of the flares shot right towards Fanny and barely missed her head. She walked right over to the guy who shot it and told him to stop.

"That was incredibly dangerous," she said.

"Aw, go home lady," he said, "what are you 40? 50?"

"Is that supposed to be an insult?" Fanny shot back.

The altercation escalated, culminating in Fanny threatening to fuck the guy up.

"It's a good thing you're a girl," the boy said, "otherwise you'd be sorry."

"Oh yeah," said Fanny, "then why do you seem so scared?"

As we left the park and the rowdy teens, we talked about what the best way to respond might be in this type of situation. Shooting fireworks at people *is* dangerous, but we didn't think police should be called in to intervene. Instead, we discussed the value of having teams that people could call on made up of parents or people from the neighbourhood who know one another and have a sense of the community. It seems pretty basic and easy to orchestrate if enough people get behind the idea. It could even be volun-

tary, with different people assigned different shifts throughout the month.

Who can argue against safety teams that are cheaper and
more personalized than the police? Well … lots of people,
I'm sure. But there's something promising about how mainstream the idea of defunding the police has become.

THURSDAY, JULY 2nd

Jonas and I drove to Niagara Falls today. Neither of us had
been there before and we were pretty impressed. We took
a few selfies and Jonas said he'd heard that people die every year at Niagara Falls taking selfies. It sounds more like
a scary legend people tell their kids to make sure they stay
away from the edge. But I do love the idea of a horror movie
where selfies are somehow the villain and they manage to
knock off the main characters, one by one.

We stayed at the Falls for a couple hours and ate some
snacks on a blanket overlooking the water. We could see
the American side and all the Americans across the way. It's
strange to be so close but unable to get there. It's the first
time since I was born that the border between Canada and
the US has been closed. It may be the first time ever.

On the drive home, I was careful not to accidentally go
towards the bridge to the States. I hope I don't jinx it, but I
love how easy it's been to get around so far with just paper
maps and road signs. It's almost like the roads were designed
to be easily navigable even without a smartphone.

FRIDAY, JULY 3rd

For the past twenty years, anytime I felt lonely or insecure or
anxious, I'd just go online and read something, play a game,
or send someone a message. This year, I didn't have that option but I also haven't really felt too down. I had thought
that being lonely/insecure/anxious came first and that the
internet was a remedy. Now I'm wondering if the internet
contributed to the negative feelings I thought it was reliev-
ing. In giving me easy and immediate access to stimuli and

connections, I ended up feeling like I needed them all the time. Now that I've weened myself off the internet, I seem to have become much more comfortable and content in my own skin. (I'm sure having Jonas in my life this year hasn't hurt either.)

✦✦✦✦✦

My mom phoned and it was weird to talk to her from Toronto when she thinks I'm in Montreal. It feels dishonest but I'm in too deep now. I'll explain everything if (when!) Fanny gets pregnant. Although maybe I'll give it a month or two of gestation before I make the call.

SUNDAY, JULY 5th

I'm glad I was able to see so many friends while I was here, and introduce Jonas to them. I feel a bit guilty that I don't feel more guilty about how unproductive I was, in terms of schoolwork. The trip hasn't been totally unproductive though, not for Fanny and Alex. I sure hope not, at least.

It's hard to get work done when it's so hot out. There's no AC in our Airbnb, so it's been hot inside too. I've been man-spreading whenever I get the chance, trying to cool down and ensure that my sperm doesn't curdle or whatnot. I told Fanny and Alex and they appreciated it. Alex said it was probably the only feminist form of man-spreading possible.

MONDAY, JULY 6th

I had my last appointment at the fertility clinic this morning and decided to check what porn they had on the big television in the collection room. I was disappointed to see that it just had PornHub. Even though I'd be accessing it through the television, PornHub is online. Luckily, I've been doing just fine with my Tom of Finland book and a little imagination.

✦✦✦✦✦

$300. Fuck. My fault, but everyone was speeding. I was apparently going 139 in a 100 zone. Next time I'll just go 120. Patience! I haven't gotten a speeding ticket since I was in high school, so I probably deserve it. But it doesn't feel like it. Makes me resent the police and government, as if I'm not someone who's well served by those institutions. Are they really encouraging me to drive more safely though or just trying to make a quick buck? I wasn't swerving in and out of lanes. I wasn't tailgating anyone. I was just going fast. I know, I know, the fox condemns the trap not himself. Better a frustrating fine than a tragic collision. Words, words, words.

TUESDAY, JULY 7th

I biked down to hang out with Cary today. I wanted to pick up the drawings he had made me. When I arrived, he was already holding them and excited to show me. One was of lightning, which he said can make the internet go really fast or really slow. The second was of his favourite internet activities: video games, Netflix, YouTube, etc. The final image, and my favourite of the three, featured me, looking bored. Cary told me that it's because life would be boring without the internet.

I reminded him that a lot of his favourite things are offline; Cary loves playing sports and swimming, he loves reading, and he's recently become obsessed with playing cards and board games. I asked him why he thinks he'd be bored? He looked confused and didn't answer.

"Let me ask you a different question," I said, "What do you think the internet does?"

This time he answered right away. "So boring! All it can do is give you internet. What can it do?!"

"Do you know what the internet is?" I asked.

Cary paused to think and then said, "It gives you internet to watch things on internet." I tried to get him to tell me a bit more and he said, "It's something that helps things."

Most adults can't really explain the internet either. We don't know how it does what it does. We hardly know what it does. We take it for granted like a lot of the things we rely on: the environment, financial systems, waste disposal, the Global South, and now the internet.

We've got to look more closely at the things that support us. Otherwise we're like Wile E. Coyote when he runs off the edge of the cliff, thinking there's still solid ground below. We may hang around for a little while, but pretty soon we're going to fall.

WEDNESDAY, JULY 8th

I'm still waiting to hear from Fanny about how many vials of sperm I produced while in Toronto. The first try, I made four, which they said was above average. The second and third time, I don't think I produced as much fluid, but apparently it's all about concentration, so I could still have made three or four vials. They're hopeful it'll be enough for a second kid too.

Now that I've given my sperm to the clinic to freeze, my role is pretty much done until I get to be Uncle Aron for the little scion. Even if I didn't make a full twelve vials, I'll be okay with nine. Anything less will make me feel a wee bit inadequate. It's stupid that I care – seems like some BS primal masculinity delusion – but somehow it feels important. I've already bugged Fanny about it a couple times and she's been bugging the clinic, so now all I can do is wait.

*****

I went out this afternoon and bought my mom some beehive-shaped earrings, an overpriced chocolate bar, and a birthday card. Tomorrow I'll go to the post office and mail it. Although it would have been more convenient (and allowed me to be more productive) if I had just picked something out online and had it shipped to my mom, I think she appreciates effort more than actual gifts, so sending her something online sorta defeats the purpose. I appreciate that I have the time to be inefficient.

segment
segment
segment
segment
segment
segment
segment
segment
segment

THURSDAY, JULY 9th

After exactly four hours of waiting on hold, the line went dead. They hung up on me!! I phoned back, but this time I didn't listen to the automated options. I just hit zero repeatedly. It took another hour, but the call went to an operator. I told him I'd been on hold for five hours and he put me right through to someone. I should have just cancelled my contract, but after so many hours on hold, I didn't want all that effort to go to waste. I cut my losses and pretended everything was fine. I added Jonas to my renter's insurance and renewed the policy for another year. Capitalism works just well enough to keep me coming back for more.

FRIDAY, JULY 10th

I finally heard from Alex and Fanny today. Thirteen vials!! That means I made more on my second or third attempt than on the first one. Maybe the more I come, the more I produce?

✶✶✶✶✶

I was out of the house for twelve hours, from 10 a.m. until 10 p.m. When I got home, Jonas pointed out that this was the longest we'd been apart in months. After my meeting this morning, I biked to Verdun and met up with Sloane, Hanni, and Kat. Niko joined for lunch and we all grabbed Viet subs to eat by the river. It was boiling out, but it felt nice to have everyone together and there was a cool breeze coming off the St. Lawrence.

Everyone seemed like they were in a happy mood, even Niko, who tried to explain why his job and love life are terrible and unfair. I feel like he's been getting more and more negative lately. Either that, or I've been getting less and less patient.

MONDAY, JULY 13th

Jonas and I went for a walk last night around the neighbourhood. It wasn't completely dark out so it must have been before ten. We were up by Laurier metro station when a young, nervous-seeming guy approached us. He was around twenty, Brown, and he looked hip in a bro-ey Quebeçois way. I assumed he was about to ask us for spare change or a cigarette but instead he explained – in French – that his phone died. He asked if he could borrow one of ours to text someone.

I said sure and pulled out my little Nokia brick phone.

He looked at it, disappointed, and asked, still in French, whether I had SnapChat on there.

I said no, and he started backing away. I asked Jonas if he had SnapChat on his phone. He said no too.

The young guy thanked us, but looked dejected as he went to find someone else to ask.

As Jonas and I continued walking, I started talking about how strange it is that young people communicate on Snap-Chat these days instead of over regular text messages.

Jonas had a completely different reading of the situation. He thought the guy was trying to steal a smartphone and had just made up the SnapChat excuse when I pulled out my non-smartphone. In London, where Jonas lived before Montreal, phone theft is more common, but Montreal's a big city too with plenty of desperate people. I just can't imagine this boy stealing my phone. He had a sweet face and looked more scared than angry. Do I trust strangers too much or is Jonas too paranoid? And how might the way the guy looked have played into it?

*****

This afternoon, Jonas' friend Chris told us a strange story that happened while he was hanging out with his best friend, a Black woman, and a white friend of theirs. His friend, the Black woman, had picked up beers for the three of them and they asked her how much they each owed.

"$30 altogether, so $10 each."

They pulled out their phones and sent her etransfers. She accepted them but Chris noticed a funny look on her face... The other guy had sent her $90!

"You sent me too much money," she said.

"No, no, I meant to," he responded.

"Why? What's the extra $80 for?"

"Reparations."

"But we're friends. I mean, you don't have to pay me for–"

Chris said that his friend was so uncomfortable she didn't know what to say. If personal donations are meaningful as reparations, I don't think $80 would cut it. I think throwing money at his friend though just lets this guy feel like he did something and can stop feeling guilty or thinking about the Black communities who struggle as a result of his privilege.

Chris' friend said it's been exhausting trying to navigate all the white people who've been reaching out over social media and text messages looking for absolution. She's not god or the arbiter of racism, but some white people are really bad at processing their privilege and end up reasserting it by asking Black people to figure everything out for them. It's a painful kind of irony.

WEDNESDAY, JULY 15th

Twitter was hacked and whoever did it managed to use Twitter's system to scam at least a hundred thousand dollars out of some opportunistic Twitter users. People are calling it a "smash and grab" scam because it only worked for a few seconds before Twitter caught on and shut it down. But it was creative. The hacker posted from a bunch of rich celebrities' accounts – Jeff Bezos, Elon Musk, Kanye West, etc. The phony tweets said something about "giving back" and had a link for people to transfer $1000 in crypto-currency to the celebrity with the promise that, once received, the celebrity would send back $2000. Of course, the money was just sent to the hacker and nothing was sent back to anyone. Twitter claims the scam was stopped within minutes, but a hundred thousand dollars is quite the steal, especially for such a quick operation.

I just finished listening to an interview with an experimental psychologist from the University of Waterloo in Ontario. He studies how external storage devices impact our memory. Most of his findings were commonsensical and unsurprising, but it was cool to hear them from an expert who has done so much to back up his claims. He has proven that when we learn something that's easy to look up – either online or in a reference book we have on hand – we're less likely to store it and remember it than something that's harder or impossible to look up. So if I learned the capital of Zimbabwe, I'd be less likely to remember it than if I learned my boyfriend's brother's middle name, for example. Currently, I don't know either of these … or at least I don't remember them.

✶✶✶✶✶

We played Scrabble tonight with Darren. Jonas won. After Darren left, Jonas and I were sitting on the couch watching TV and I said, "You've been on your phone a lot tonight."

He gave me a sour face but put his phone down.

"Thank you," I said, "I like it when you're here with me."

He pushed back a bit: "But I *was* here with you."

"It didn't feel like it."

It's become so normal to be casually on the phone all the time that I feel like the unreasonable one for asking Jonas to put his down for a bit. And although he did put it down, I think he also feels like I'm the unreasonable one. At least we agree?

THURSDAY, JULY 16th

Jonas and I have fallen into a pretty strange but effective schedule lately. Jonas wakes up at 8 a.m. and goes to bed around midnight. I sleep in until 11 a.m., but I stay up after Jonas goes to bed and do work for a few more hours, going to bed around 3. I find I'm good at getting schoolwork done late at night. I also just love having that alone time; the world feels still in a magical, almost sad way.

I know there's something socially unacceptable about

going to bed late, and there's something even more stigma-tized about sleeping in, but I think I like this set-up. Living together and both working from home, Jonas and I are not alone very often. Having three hours of uninterrupted time to ourselves every day feels important. On the weekends though, we compromise and go to bed at about 2, waking up around 10, so we also have a couple nights a week where we get to fall asleep and wake up together. That feels important too. We'll see if we keep this schedule going in the fall, but it seems to be working for now.

I love adjusting social expectations a bit here and there and playing with conventions to personalize them. It reminds me of being a little kid and building pillow forts out of cushions from the couch. The difference here is that if I like what I create, I don't have to put the cushions back when I'm done playing.

FRIDAY, JULY 17th
I had an internet nightmare last night – the first one I've had in a while. I was looking something up online, but didn't notice what I was doing until after I closed the browser win-dow. When the realization hit me, I was jolted awake. There was a big storm crashing around outside the bedroom win-dow, so I'm not sure if the dream woke me or the rain.

When I first started having scary dreams about accidentally going online, they centred around my email. More recently, most of the internet nightmares I have are just like this one – I'm looking something up online, but it's never clear what I'm looking up, and I never realize that I'm not supposed to be using the internet until it's already too late. What made this dream a bit different was that I wasn't alone. A friend was there with me and he saw me go online. The feelings I got when I realized I had messed up *and* that I'd been caught were awful: regret, frustration, self-loathing, dismay, incredulity.

When I woke up, I was glad to find myself offline. How-ever, I started to think about what my brain might be working through as it forces me to endure these uncomfortable dreams. Maybe it has something to do with the fact that I'm still connected to the online world even as I try not to use the internet. The distinction between online and offline is fairly arbitrary and porous, and it's like my dream brain is trying to remind me that I'm still complicit in all the issues I'm trying to critique – internetless or not.

I also feel like my dream brain is revealing the way going online has become second nature, something I only notice doing after the fact. As we accept the internet as normal, it's even more important that we don't also accept it as neutral. Its repercussions need our attention and thinking about these consequences can't just be an afterthought. I'm glad my dream brain keeps reminding me of this, even when my waking brain lets things slide.

SUNDAY, JULY 19th
Eventually, I think there's only going to be one social media platform, and it won't have a name.

MONDAY, JULY 20th
I've been going back through my old journal entries and it's been cool to read about my life just a few months ago, but it's also painful. I didn't expect such discomfort. It's not like I was going through anything traumatic at the time, so I don't know why I feel such anxiety when I look back.

★★★★★

I'm sitting on my back balcony and a marching band just came by through the alley! There were about a dozen people playing different instruments: a trumpet, a trombone, a tuba, a banjo, guitars, drums, and singers. Everyone had so much energy on their own, but they managed to play and move in sync with everyone else. There were a few people following the musicians, and one had a sign with some internet links that probably explained more about the group and their performance. I'll never know.

It felt really good to have music coming up from the alley. I can be a bit cynical and stand-offish sometimes, but after only a moment of hesitation, I leaned right over the railing and smiled at the musicians as they passed. The trumpet player looked up in my direction and I felt like she was playing directly to me. She very well may have been. Lots of the neighbours were out on their balconies though too and I smiled and waved at one of my neighbours who I've never noticed before. I feel much better about the world now than I did ten minutes ago.

*****

When I started my year offline, I made a distinction between friends using the internet on my behalf because I had asked them to (= against my rules) versus friends using the internet on my behalf without me asking (= unavoidable, so not against my rules). To be safe, I added the clarification that I couldn't suggestively or indirectly ask someone to use the internet for me – like an orthodox Jew with their shabbos goy. Even with these rules though, I'm still finding myself in murky waters.

Like I'm reading a book Leah lent me and it mentions a website called Revver, which I hadn't heard of. I texted Leah to see if she knew what it was, and she didn't, but – without checking back with me first – she looked it up online and texted me a description, that it was like YouTube but shared proceeds with creators more transparently and it has since gone out of business. I didn't ask her to use the internet for me and I really thought she might be able to answer my question without going online, but because she didn't know, my question ended up directly compelling her to use the internet for me. Does that break my rules?

I'm sure Leah truly didn't mind being helpful. She was probably even happy to help me out, but I'm still uncomfortable with these types of exchanges – even if they don't break my rules. I'm still not entirely open to reliance and depending on people, still too caught up in the fallacy of glorious and free individualism and independence. I just need to relax and embrace the *Internet of Friends*. (The Internet of Friends is a lot like the internet, and works through the internet, but the interface just involves chatting with friends. And it can be yours too, for the low, low price of ... making some friends.)

*****

My mom and dad attended an online circumcision today for the 8-day-old grandson of one of their close friends. He was having his bris – the religious ceremony for male Jewish babies to get their foreskin snipped surrounded by family and friends. Because large gatherings are still forbidden, the ceremony was broadcast online through YouTube Live.

"It was very well filmed," my dad said.

My mom explained that the mohel, who performed the circumcision, wore a full haz-mat suit. She said that the baby's crying sounded especially shrill over the computer speakers and my dad had to leave the room.

"Why didn't you just turn down the volume?" I asked.

TUESDAY, JULY 21st
I remember games – SkiFree, CandyStand, Acrophobia, You Don't Know Jack...

Stealing music and videos – Napster, Limewire, Mega-Video, The Pirate Bay...

I remember late nights – ICQ, Nexopia, MSN, AIM, Chat Roulette, Facebook...

And feeling guilty – Hotmale, Craigslist, Plenty of Fish, Dudes Nude, OK Cupid...

I remember silence.

*****

Leah shared a collection of articles about digital storytelling with me. I read one today about a man named Michael Current who wrote and emailed a story to his friend in the early days of the internet, back in 1994. It may have been the last email he sent, because – as his friend who wrote the article explained – he died the next day. I don't think he knew he was going to die though because in the email, he asked his friend for comments:

"Please be gentle, this is not something I am used to/ comfortable with."

The story he wrote and emailed to his friend is beautiful. It describes him sending an email and feeling concerned about "the detachment of thought and affect from the fleshbones-andblood." The narrator wonders how much of ourselves we can communicate in an email – physically, intimately, even sexually. It's a vivid story and ends with a wet dream that reminds the reader how powerful virtual fantasies can be ("... naked in my bedroom before my terminal, reading the text of his desire. His mind is touching mine..."). However, it simultaneously affirms for the narrator that "we must not abandon the body." One of the characters in the story wonders whether the narrator can see "the irony in discussing embodiment by email." And then there's me, reading an email about an email about what the internet can carry.

The friend who received the email explained that he sends Michael's email out now on the anniversary of his death every year. He said Michael died the day after sending him the story so I flipped back to the previous page to check when the email was originally sent. July 20th, 1994. Which means the anniversary of Michael's death is—

I just got shivers.

*****

I decided to read more from the collection Leah gave me and found out about a creative surveillance project that puts my daily journaling to shame. Because of all the unwanted attention he was getting in airports after 9/11, Hasan Elahi started tracking every aspect of his life – where he went, what he ate, how he spent money – and he posted photos online for anyone to see. This protected him from "redneck paranoia," as he called it, while also critiquing the systems of surveillance that kept misidentifying him as a terrorist.

The interview with Elahi that I read was published in 2006 and, at the time, he had been tracking himself publicly for two and a half years. As he jokes about in the interview, "maybe one of these days [he] won't need to monitor [him] self anymore because Big Brother will be doing it for [him]."

He was partially right. We've now nearly got the government panopticon of Big Brother, but there's also the mutual surveillance of social media, and the private surveillance capitalism of big tech companies, banks, advertisers, insurance firms, etc. I wonder what Elahi's project might look like in today's online world where what he was doing – posting photos and daily updates – has become normal.

WEDNESDAY, JULY 22nd

My hometown football team changed their name, just months after publicly saying they wouldn't. The Edmonton Eskimos will now just be the Edmonton football team, or the EEs, until they come up with something new. One of their big donors was threatening to pull funding if they didn't make the change, so before we celebrate too much, let's be clear that they weren't all-of-a-sudden listening to Inuit communities. Any chance they'll ask Indigenous folks to help them come up with the team's new name? I wonder if the idea even occurred to them.

THURSDAY, JULY 23rd

Tomorrow we leave for our camping trip and I still don't think anyone's figured out where to go hiking, whether there's a campfire ban, what the weather's supposed to be like, or anything really. I doubt anyone's even looked up where the campsite is. Part of me is annoyed with my friends, but another part of me is annoyed with myself for getting annoyed with my friends. I can't be expecting other people to do things online for me.

I wonder if my friends haven't looked anything up yet because it's usually my role in the friend group? Or is everyone leaving things to the last minute because of the expectation that they'll be connected to the internet throughout the trip anyway, so they don't need to look anything up ahead of time? I hope there's no cell service at the campsite.

★★★★★

Bradley phoned today and told me about the "Gestapo," as he called them, in Portland. He was referring to the secret police who've been rolling up to anti-racism protesters in unmarked vehicles and abducting them, without charge or warrant. They're apparently heading to Chicago next. The US is so fascist at the moment. I suppose it's nothing new, though; they've always acted like this abroad, and in relation to Indigenous people. I guess now they're just widening the net.

SUNDAY, JULY 26th

The stars looked like spilled sugar. We spent a lot of the evening with our heads tilted back, marvelling at how much there was to see. The campfire had a similar draw. We depend so much on screens when we're in the city, their flashing lights alluring us like the fire and the stars. When the campfire died down and the only light was a blanket of glowing embers, the stars seemed to shine even brighter. We leaned back on our borrowed folding chairs and felt content. We didn't even need to talk.

There were four of us – Jonas, me, and our friends Memo and Chris. And then on Saturday, Leah, Hannibal, and Kat drove up just for the afternoon. City people are different when we leave the city. We all seemed happier and more relaxed – walking through the trees, wading in the lake, perching on rocks, roasting marshmallows. The only downsides are the prep and clean-up … and the mosquitoes. (At least with these itchy bites, I know how I got them – that somehow makes their itch less uncomfortable.)

The trip was fairly free of online technologies. When I picked up the rental car, the guy at the counter told me that the contract would be sent to my phone and I could sign it with my finger and send it back. I asked if there was a non-digital option and, of course, there was: I signed the contract with a pen on a piece of paper. Then, while I was driving, Jonas and Memo took turns navigating using paper maps. I didn't even ask them to, but I had the maps suggestively propped up in the front seat and they seemed eager to give it a shot.

When we got to the campsite, our phones hardly worked. We all had a bar or two of service, but nobody's data was working at all. It was like everyone was on my level for a change. I think being offline helped us notice things – a growling in the woods, birds' songs, leeches in the water, rabbits, raccoons, a lone deer. We even found some little glowing green bugs that flashed and floated in the air. It looked like their bodies were pulsing LEDs, their pre-digital glow made me think of the internet – those little green lights on modems that let you know everything's okay. Except here these bugs' green lights didn't signal anything, at least not to us – except maybe that nature is digital enough.

One of our friends, Chris, was on his phone a lot throughout the weekend, even though he could only call and text. He and his boyfriend have the type of relationship where they're constantly checking in and sending each other messages. I didn't mind because there were other people to hang out with, but whenever Chris went into his phone, he'd disappear from the conversation. At one point, I had to drive into town to buy some supplies and Chris asked to join me. He admitted that he wanted to get back to somewhere with better cell reception. When we got to town, he seemed quite relieved.

The weather was perfect for most of our trip – not too hot but hot enough. Last night though, it rained relentlessly. It's hard to sleep with the constant crackling and crashing. The stifling humidity inside the tent was too much and I started to panic. I opened the door a crack and gulped down a few mouthfuls of fresh air. Jonas was awake too and we held each other in a cliché kind of way as the rain beat down on the tent. I imagined it was energy from the stars, falling back to us.

As we drove home to the city, I was a bit damp, but refreshed.

MONDAY, JULY 27th

There was a letter in the mail today, addressed to me, but it had no return address. When I opened it, I found a cute handwritten note but no name. The letter was about the sender's experience losing their job in Montreal and heading to BC to pick cherries for the summer. They told me a story about getting a university admission offer by email while they were working. Because they were busy in the field, they weren't online very often and almost missed the deadline to accept the offer. They said it felt "weird – like the next four years of [their] life were gambled at that very moment."

At the end of the letter, it was signed, "miss u x." I have a couple guesses as to who sent the letter, but I don't know if they left off their name accidentally, or if they thought it'd be funny. Unlike an email, if you send an anonymous letter, there's no way of responding. It'd be like setting up a fake social media account, sending someone an anonymous message, and then deleting your account so they couldn't respond. Though that wouldn't be quite as cute as an anonymous letter – it would actually be pretty creepy.

*****

My dad called, which is always a bit of a shock. I got worried that somebody died, but the call was good news. He got a job! The contract is only until December but he sounded excited. I'm relieved he's found a new job so quickly. There were 250 applicants and they chose him. It's fun to feel proud of my pa.

*****

I had a weird dream last night: there were a bunch of people

I didn't know in a computer lab (all women) and they were each commenting with surprise about how much they were enjoying the internet.

I was looking over their shoulders though and the websites they were scrolling through were way clunkier than actual websites these days, and everything was glitching. But all the women seemed perfectly satisfied. The weirdest part of the dream (although it didn't seem strange at the time) was that everyone was wearing red outfits covered with white stripes and polka dots.

I have no clue what my brain was trying to work through but I do sometimes imagine what the internet might look like if it hadn't been homogenized by a bunch of men working for tech monopolies. We can dream…

TUESDAY, JULY 28th

Sloane invited me to join them this weekend at a protest that our university's Black Students Network is organizing. The protest is to challenge the legacy of our university's namesake, a businessman and trader who had Black and Indigenous slaves. It's being held beside a statue of him, right in the heart of campus. Yesterday Darren was over and when I told him about the protest, he tried to argue that slave-ownership was just the way things were at the time; it wasn't a choice, and we shouldn't criticize people for owning slaves if we don't know whether they did other problematic things in their lives. (!!!???!) I disagreed. Even if owning slaves was seen as neutral and normal by many people, I'd hazard to guess that Black and Indigenous folks didn't feel the same way.

When we celebrate the things slave-owners accomplished (like funding my university), we forget that they didn't actually make their fortunes – slaves did. How can we fight racism without compensating these people's families? Without re-framing the legacies of slave-owners and the enslaved? How can we challenge white supremacy without changing the economic or social supremacy that the families of many slave-owners continue to benefit from?

Darren argued that we should just get rid of all statues because all social change is collective and focusing on individual heroes distorts this. I again disagreed. I mean, I agree that change is always a group effort, but it can still be helpful to highlight the efforts of individuals who collaborated towards change. We can aim for collective action and simultaneously celebrate the parts played by individuals within these collectives. We just shouldn't celebrate slave-owners.

I think Darren's arguments may have been influenced by his family. I know he's on side with fighting systemic racism; he even hung a big banner from his front balcony that says, "WHITE SILENCE IS VIOLENCE – Black Lives Matter." But I know he also wants to maintain a relationship with his Republican parents in the US. It's hard to be critical while also trying to connect with parents who are fed up with the "anarchists" destroying statues of colonial figures. I know from my experience critiquing Israel that it's not easy to navigate important political commitments when they diverge from what one's family thinks. But, though I may empathize with why Darren is taking a less black-and-white stance on the slave-owner statue removal question, I still think it's a pretty black-and-white issue – even literally.

I texted a few friends and classmates to invite them along to Saturday's protest. A couple sound keen to join but others replied that they aren't up for it. My first instinct was fuck them, but I need to stop being so critical so quickly. A lot of people don't realize how much we continue to benefit from the legacy of slavery, or even from ongoing slavery today – like cocoa farming in Ivory Coast, cotton picking in Uzbekistan, or coltan mining in the Congo. Though slavery in Canada is no longer legal, we're all too ready to accept the involvement of slaves or slave-like conditions in the industries we benefit from as Canadians. Some people have argued with me about this: "In less industrialized countries, that's just the way things are." Or, "It's all part of the processes by which these developing countries will transform into an economy more like Canada's or the USA's." But I don't think we should support working conditions that we wouldn't accept for ourselves or the people we care about. I'm all for reconsidering moral questions for different contexts, but morality isn't endlessly malleable. Slavery is wrong.

★★★★★

I got my credit card statement in the mail today and I went over all the purchases to make sure there was nothing unexpected. Reading through the list felt like going through a journal of its own. There were a few transactions that I didn't remember so I went back through this journal to make sure everything added up. (It did.)

★★★★★

I had a funny experience while waiting for some chicken sandwiches to go at a Yemenite restaurant tonight. I pulled out my phone to text someone and the shop owner recognized the model.

"Is that a Nokia?" he asked.

"Yup."

"Like the old one?"

"It's a new phone," I explained, "but it's like the old one."

"Wowwww," he said, "I had that phone. I thought Nokia went out of business."

He was very impressed. I showed him that it still has Snake on it.

"So epic," he said.

He told me about his memories with the phone, back when he and his wife did a cross country trip to Vancouver in an RV. He started talking about all the places he stopped along the way, about meeting Matthew McConaughey with his shirt off at a trailer park, about getting his camera stolen. Maybe it was just nostalgia, but seeing my phone really got him going. He said he missed the days when cellphones were different, when things were less hectic, when we didn't carry the internet in our pockets.

"So epic," he kept repeating, staring at my phone, "So epic."

WEDNESDAY, JULY 29th
I received a letter from a woman I don't know who had heard about my year offline and wanted me to send her more information. I was curious how she found out about my project, but the letter didn't explain. It just had her address and a recipe for vegan zucchini brownies. At the bottom of the recipe, she included a note about how much she loves cooking. She wrote that she has tons of cookbooks, but prefers to get her recipes from the internet. I'll write her back and ask why she finds online recipes more appealing … and how she heard about me.

✶✶✶✶✶

Jonas told me that several big tech CEOs are testifying to the US congress today, but they're calling in remotely. The government is worried that big tech has too much control. (Duh.) Jonas listened for a while but said they had to recess due to technical issues. Even the biggest tech moguls can't guarantee a good internet connection.

THURSDAY, JULY 30th
The internet isn't actually infinite, but it feels like it. No single person could look through it all, so it might as well be endless. It certainly has endless potential to distract. I read that the average person my age checks their phone 150 times a day even though they get far fewer calls, messages, or notifications. The internet isn't actively interrupting us. We interrupt ourselves in anticipation of what the online world might be buzzing about. We check our phones 150 times a day proactively!

Without the internet, when I want to procrastinate, I read, clean, or do something active. I can't just sit and scroll. And when I want to work, I'm much more focused than I used to be. I'm realizing that it wasn't online messages and content that used to distract me persay. It was just that I couldn't concentrate as deeply knowing that there could be messages and content out there that I might want to check out – that I felt compelled to check because I could. Avoiding the internet is much more than being offline. It's being cut off from that rumbling cloud of potential that's blowing in our faces; it's a clear sky and a deep breath.

FRIDAY, JULY 31st
According to a book I'm re-reading by Langdon Winner, most people care if a new tech gadget can do its job efficiently and cheaply, but not how it might impact our lives, other people, and the environment. But all that has to change now that the world's ending.

✶✶✶✶✶

SABRINA: Has anyone told you yet about the new online portal we're supposed to use as research assistants?
ARON: Nope – uh oh, haha.
SABRINA: The way they track employment is moving to a different system, so you won't have access to all your pay-stubs anymore. You have to download them all before August 31st.
ARON: Thank you for letting me know! Oy...

Granted, I'm getting this information secondhand, but I'm not exactly clear on what's changing. Do I need the pay stubs that apparently won't be available when I get back online next year? I don't think I can justify breaking my internetlessness to ask Sabrina to download something for me that I don't even know if I'll need. I wish these changes weren't so normal and abrupt. We go along with every new tech innovation without asking questions. We assume they're in our best interests. Anyone who is critical of these kinds of changes must be an enemy of "progress."

August

This isn't the kind of fight we win, it's the kind of fight we fight.

– Cory Doctorow, 2019, *Radicalized*

SATURDAY, AUGUST 1st

When I arrived, there was a Michael Jackson song blasting from a giant portable speaker and there were more journalists and TV cameras than protesters. Something felt uncomfortable. Well, a few things did. Once the protest got underway a few more people showed up, but in total I think there were under 50 demonstrators.

I'm not sure why it felt disappointing. I've been to protests in the past with way fewer people that still felt good. It could just be that the last few anti-racism protests I've been to have been so huge that this one felt off in contrast. I'm worried that the recent surge in outrage against anti-Black racism may have passed its peak, that it's no longer in vogue to be out at protests. The other protesters at the event seemed a bit deflated too. Everyone was quiet.

Despite the low energy, I was glad to be there. When hundreds of people show up, I never feel like I'm contributing much anyway. Bigger protests may seem more important, but it's more important to go to smaller protests.

In honour of Emancipation Day, one of the aims of gathering was to demand that our university take down the statue of the enslaver who our school is named after. (Makes me sick with pride.) The emcee began with a list of all the things he's tired of as a Black person, like having to walk past the statue on his way to class, and being harassed online for speaking out about it. He talked about the university founder owning Black and Indigenous "slaves" and then kept correcting himself and saying Black and Indigenous "enslaved people." I appreciated the slip-up – if he had just said "enslaved people" to begin with, I wouldn't have considered the difference. (I also learned to use the term "enslaver" instead of "slave-owner.") Like statues, words are more active than they seem.

I learned at the protest that my university's founder not only owned and traded enslaved people, he also voted against abolition. And he made his fortune as a merchant importing and selling goods that were produced through slavery. Discussing the impact of the statue and name, many speakers shared how pervasive institutional racism is on campus, and how little the university has done to address it.

At the end of the protest, we were invited to write notes on Post-its and then stick them on the statue. It was a cute idea but I wanted to do something more drastic. I can't imagine myself actually destroying the statue, but I could cover it in duct tape. And not just one long strip of tape that's easy to peel off, but tons of itty little strips that take hours to remove and that leave a gross sticky layer of adhesive underneath. Realistically, that would just cause more work for the custodial staff who I imagine aren't proud to work on a campus named after a man who made his fortune as a result of slavery. I say that, but I biked by less than an hour after the protest and everything had already been cleaned off. There were no more Post-it notes – no sign of our resistance at all. Just a terrifying little statue.

SUNDAY, AUGUST 2nd
I'm supposed to meet one of my professors today to pick up some readings, but it's been raining on and off. The internet helps manoeuvre rain – both with online forecasts but also as a way to transfer files. That being said, I sometimes like

being forced to meet in person instead of just exchanging emails. It gives an opportunity to actually connect and talk about whatever it is we're sharing and – maybe more importantly – it increases our chances of talking about other things too. Digital life is too instrumental. Of course it's much faster and more efficient, but I'm already plenty productive. I don't want to rush.

*****

I got a text from Lori today explaining that a letter I mailed them became a vessel for a decomposing squirrel's skull. Their kid found a dead squirrel in Jarry Park a few weeks ago and they've been tracking its decomposition whenever they walk their dog. Last night, Lori decided it was decomposed enough and let their kid take the skull home. They had the envelope from my letter in their bag and said it was "the perfect vessel" for the job.

*****

Jonas got rid of his Instagram and is now in the process of deleting his Facebook. Before he deletes everything, he downloaded all the data Facebook has on him and was filling me in on the highlights. They know lots of intimate details – well, mostly just things related to him being gay. They have a compilation of all the messages Jonas ever sent and all sorts of lists of things he liked or attended or clicked. The strangest thing they have on him is a list of websites he visited unrelated to Facebook. I'm not sure if it's every website he's ever been to, but it's a huge list. Facebook labels this "your off Facebook activity." I didn't know Facebook keeps track of so much about what people are doing when they're not even on Facebook. It doesn't seem legal.

*****

I was on the phone with Niko today and, well, irrational paranoia is never a good sign. He has a crush on a woman he works with, though they haven't met face-to-face yet –

just online. I asked what her name is. He said he didn't want to say it.

"Why?!" I was surprised.

"Well," he replied, "when I close my laptop, it doesn't go to sleep, so it could still be listening."

I explained that he probably doesn't need to be worried about his computer listening to him when it's closed, but that even if he is worried about it, there's no reason to be worried about it hearing him say his colleague's name. He backed down and told me her name, but he defended his need to be cautious. I imagine the potential for surveillance offered by tech may be a factor in the paranoia, but because of how irrational it seems, I think there's something else going on.

I apologized for sounding like a broken record, but told Niko he should think about talking to a therapist. He apologized for sounding like a broken record, but said he probably won't.

"I've been working through things on my own and I've been making a lot of progress."

And yet you're scared to say your colleague's name out loud because your computer might be listening?

MONDAY, AUGUST 3rd

I was walking home and saw one of the homeless guys who hangs out near my apartment. He looked confused. As I crossed St. Denis at Mont-Royal, I walked right past him and gave him a smile. I don't think he noticed me, but right at that moment he sat down on the road, cross-legged, right in the middle of the busy intersection. He put his head in his hands and started to cry.

Immediately, five or six people passing by (all white men) gathered to encourage him to get out of the street. They were rubbing his back, trying to lift him up, saying kind things. I was tempted to join in, but I knew there were already too many cooks. If I tried to help now, it would be more for me than him. After a half-minute that felt much longer, he was helped to his feet and walked back towards the sidewalk.

✦✦✦✦✦

I was on a conference call for work today and I could hardly make out what one of my colleagues was saying. He's Black and his deep voice wasn't coming through my phone. Everyone else on the call (all white) sounded clear. I'm not sure if it's my phone speakers, his microphone, or what. Last year, I may not have thought anything of this, but now I'm wondering whether these technologies are designed for mid-range white voices. Wait a sec … is the idea of a *mid*-range voice designed for white people?!!

✦✦✦✦✦

Jonas just checked his ad settings on Google. They show what Google thinks they know about him when they choose his targeted ads. One of the personal details that Google somehow knows is that Jonas is in a relationship. He says he hasn't posted that to any of his social media profiles but read further and found out that, "Google estimates [that Jonas is in a relationships] because [his] signed-in activity on Google services, and on other websites and apps, is similar to people who've told Google that they're in this category." Wait, so Jonas uses the internet like someone who's in a relationship? What does that mean?!

✦✦✦✦✦

I just heard that the president of the USA is threatening to ban TikTok!? How can he do that? Can he do that? Can the American government ban an app?

TUESDAY, AUGUST 4th

I phoned my university's student service centre right when they opened and only had to wait on hold for 30 seconds. I asked the guy who answered if he could check my fall tuition bill for me. He asked me a series of verification questions and then told me I owe $2571.53 … just for the fall semester (yeesh!). I asked if the mail-in payment option is still available. He said it is but that it's not recommended because there's no guarantee the cheque will arrive on time.

"And if it doesn't make it by the payment deadline," he said, "you'll be charged interest and late fees."

The deadline isn't till the end of the month, so I'm not too worried. I'll send it express and track it, just to be sure. And if it *does* end up being late, I'll make a fuss. Though it might be hard to make a fuss without the internet.

✶✶✶✶✶

The news today is announcing that a study done in Quebec found a correlation between people who believe a lot of misinformation and people who spend a lot of time using social media. There are calls for the government to more actively regulate social media spaces to stop the spread of fake news. I don't know why, but I feel fairly cynical about the potential of this happening. Although it'd be incredibly difficult and costly to social media companies, it's probably possible. However, I just don't have faith in the government's desire to do things in our collective best interests. I know we supposedly live in a democracy, but considering the amount of money and lobbying power that big tech has, I do not foresee massive regulatory frameworks being imposed on social media anytime soon. We're at the whim of big tech and their priorities are profit, not us.

If the government does manage to introduce regulations, I can imagine some people will start complaining that they're censoring free speech. Free speech used to be about ensuring that marginalized communities weren't attacked or imprisoned for expressing themselves. Now it's become a way for communities of attackers to protect themselves from the critiques of marginalized communities. Touché!

THURSDAY, AUGUST 6th

I had a meeting today for one of my research teams and I showed up just after 4. I thought I was late but there was only one other person waiting when I arrived. At 4:10, I got a text from one of our other team members asking if I knew that the meeting was remote. Apparently the woman in charge sent out an email about it earlier today. The other person who also showed up in person pulled out her phone and saw that she *had* received an email about it, but she'd been busy all afternoon and hadn't checked.

"Why didn't she just call or text me!?" she exclaimed in frustration. "I don't get it when people just assume that everyone's checking their email all the time!"

"You're telling me!" I responded, and we laughed.

FRIDAY, AUGUST 7th
Last night Jonas and I went out for dinner. As we settled into our seats on the patio, I noticed that there were no menus. The waitress came over and explained, in French, that we just had to scan the QR code that was taped to the table and a menu would pop up on our phones.

Jonas looked at me. "Should we go somewhere else?"

*****

Fanny just texted from Toronto, "I wish I could send you a photo of the cryogenic tank buckled into the back seat (with your sperm in it!) because the clinic is closed on weekends and I'm set to ovulate sometime between Saturday and Monday! So just in case, we brought some home."

SATURDAY, AUGUST 8th
Just went to my first music store in half a year and bought a bunch of CDs and records. I love having that cozy clutter instead of streaming everything. I'm most excited about Fiona Apple's new album, *Fetch the Bolt Cutters*. Two of my friends – both talented musicians – recommended it and now I'm finally giving it a listen.

The first track is very catchy so far and I'm liking the lyrics. She brings up the classic question of whether a tree falling in the forest makes a sound if nobody hears it. She insists that it does, even if it doesn't matter in the end. I don't think she's singing about activism, but it makes me think about all the protests happening lately. Maybe none of it will have mattered, but in the meantime we have to resist – especially when nobody's listening.

SUNDAY, AUGUST 9th
Jonas and I biked down to Pointe-Saint-Charles today to hang out with my cousins. Jonas hadn't met them yet and we had a fun time chatting and playing soccer in the park. Cary seemed to be interviewing Jonas. He wanted to know what sports Jonas liked and, when we were leaving, he assured Jonas that he had been fun to play with. Although it's sort of trivial, I was glad Jonas passed Cary's test.

*****

I mailed in my tuition cheque early last week and I sent it express. I phoned the post office, keyed in my tracking number, and was told by an automated voice that the letter hasn't been delivered yet. It should have arrived by now, which makes me think something went wrong. I'll give somebody a call tomorrow.

MONDAY, AUGUST 10th
When I woke up, I phoned Canada Post again. According to their telephone tracking service, my tuition cheque still hasn't been delivered. So I phoned the Student Accounts office but got an answering machine. I tried the university's student service centre and spoke to someone who kept suggesting I email various people or look things up online. I kept explaining to him that I'm not using the internet. (Though I didn't explain why.) Eventually, he asked me to give him my phone number and he would try to find out whether Student Accounts was having issues accepting mail and then give me a call back. I thanked him profusely and gave him my phone number and my student ID. As he was noting them down in his system, he realized my tuition cheque had already arrived. It was delivered last week.

＊＊＊＊＊

I heard on the radio that Quebec's government invested in IT tools and has 100 000 devices ready to be distributed to low-income families with kids who'll be doing classes online this year. Although the government hasn't taken any steps to train teachers for remote teaching, they're confident that it'll all work out. I'm sure it will work out, but without support, it won't work out well.

＊＊＊＊＊

Jonas is thinking of getting off of Twitter. He says it's sucking up too much of his time, and he doesn't appreciate what he's reading. He even said that following all the Twitter epidemiologists is making him not want to be an epidemiologist anymore.

"It's just a bunch of angry people."

I tried to push back a bit and asked if he appreciates all the news he learns on Twitter that he might not hear otherwise.

"Yeah, maybe."

Jonas recently quit Facebook and Instagram and I worry that his recent rush away from social media might have a bit too much to do with me.

TUESDAY, AUGUST 11th

Today was the first day of some focus groups I'm helping facilitate and it reminded me how much I love being in the classroom.

There were fourteen teens and I led them through a series of activities. The project lead had printed off a facilitator guide for me but the students were all using iPads to follow along. My biggest challenge was trying to avoid looking at students' screens when I'd go around to answer their questions or help them figure things out. I didn't disclose that I'm offline, so when they called me over to ask what something meant, I'd just say, "What in particular is unclear?" and I don't think anyone was the wiser. Maybe tomorrow I'll come out.

I learned some new things today. We were talking about online behaviours and I asked whether they thought it was acceptable to "creep" someone online. They didn't know what I was talking about, but after I explained the term, they said they call that "stalking" now, not "creeping." Sounds even worse! Tech makes it so easy to "creep" or "stalk" people that it actually becomes less creepy or stalkerish. Or maybe it doesn't, but it makes it seem like it's normal to be a creepy stalker, as long as it's online. I asked the group if they thought it was okay to stalk people online.

One of the students put it best, "Just 'cause something's normal, doesn't make it okay."

WEDNESDAY, AUGUST 12th
How do people work full days? How did I used to do it?? Grad school can be tiring, but it's child's play compared to working with children. Today's focus groups went well but the participants were pretty quiet and hesitant to talk to each other. Even during breaks, they seemed more interested in their phones than each other. We did have a few good conversations though. We talked a lot about memes and I found out that the ways memes are used change so fast that particular memes don't have any consistent meaning – or at least that was the consensus amongst the focus group. They described memes as "templates."

One of the students had printed off pictures of a bunch of popular memes to help with the discussion and many of them featured Pepe the Frog. I thought Pepe was a white supremacist hate symbol from 4chan, but I asked the teens about it and most of them had never heard of Pepe being used problematically. Those who had – even the more socially conscious ones – assured me that memes don't hold onto meaning in the same way that a racist flag or symbol might. Am I just behind the times or might there be something important about recognizing the hate attached to Pepe?

Maybe I'm overthinking it. The group explained that you can't explain memes cause it ruins their meaning. One participant clarified that this is particularly true when memes are "deep fried" or "dank." Apparently, that's what you call the kind of meme that's been put through so many filters that it doesn't have a meaning anymore, and if you're looking for one, it means you don't get it.

Despite their lack of precision, or probably because of it, I have more respect for memes as a way to communicate. It seems like, unless there's a clear caption, the meaning a meme carries can be ephemeral, even sublime; you can't nail it down, and if you try, it might lose its meaning. I had no idea memes could be such a subconscious way to communicate.

When the conversation about memes was wrapping up, I finally told the group that I've been offline for the last seven months. Nobody reacted. Maybe they didn't understand what I meant?

*****

After the focus groups, I biked home quickly so that Jonas and I had could have a little bite before heading to the park to hang out with Darren. He invited us to come meet his new roommate and a couple other new friends.

When we arrived, Darren told them all about my year offline. I may not have gotten much of a reaction from the teens, but one of Darren's friends was pretty funny. He didn't realize I was already offline and asked when I was starting. I didn't realize the confusion and thought he was asking when I started.

"January," I said.

"So next year's the big year?" he asked, encouragingly.

"No, no," I clarified, "this year – I started in January."

He looked confused, "But then how are you here?"

I paused for a moment before replying: "This isn't online."

Another of Darren's friends had just started a career as a teacher, and she was excited to ask me some questions.

Unfortunately, she was a fairly archetypal west coast hippie (from Ontario, I found out) who doesn't read the news because it makes her sad. She told me she became a teacher because of her commitment to mindfulness. She had studied meditation in Asia and Hawaii and wants to bring that to her students. She talked about a project she's doing using mindfulness apps with students.

"Practising mindfulness can be so important," I said, "but I sometimes worry that it makes individuals bear the burden of bigger, systemic issues."

She didn't understand what I was trying to say and even seemed a bit offended.

"I'm not saying we shouldn't promote mindfulness," I clarified, "just that we can't lose sight of structural issues like poverty and discrimination that can't be remedied by meditation."

Darren's friend assured me that mindful meditation can work for anyone. "It doesn't discriminate," she said.

"Of course," I agreed, "but it's a 'both and' kinda thing."

Jonas was listening and jumped in, "Let's not fix racist systems," he joked, "let's just tell Black people to download a mindfulness app!"

She still wasn't getting it, so I tried something else, "Maybe my issue is just with all the focus on digital fixes. It seems a bit ironic that people need a smartphone mindfulness app to tell them to put down their smartphone." I laughed.

"I don't think that's ironic," she said, without laughing.

I tried to let it drop, but then she started talking about the democratizing potential of digital tools and I brought up the cost of smartphones and paywalls, and how that relates to discrimination.

"There's a free version of the mindfulness app," she said, "although I use the paid version."

Darren joined in, "What does that have to do with discrimination though?" he asked, "Young white men have actually become the most marginalized group in society lately, at least financially."

"That's definitely not true," I said, maybe a bit too aggressively, "especially this year, non-white people, women, elderly and disabled folks – those are the communities most impacted by everything that's going on."

"But if you think about where they started from," Darren said, "young white men have lost the most in the last six months."

"That's a bit different," I said, "but I don't think that's true either."

Anyway, I don't want to dwell. I hope I can learn from people I disagree with, and not just to sharpen the ways I already think.

✦✦✦✦✦

Fanny finally ovulated today (irregularly late) and she was able to go into the clinic to have my sperm inserted – all the way past her cervix. She said it went swimmingly! (She didn't actually use that word, but I think it's fitting.) She said the procedure didn't even hurt. The idea of sticking a tiny syringe-like straw through the cervix seems excruciating to me, but my knowledge of the female anatomy is limited. Fanny's pregnancy test is scheduled for August 28th. Eeeeeep!!!

THURSDAY, AUGUST 13th
More of the workshops today and it's been really hard to get the teens to have discussions with each other. They're talkative when we're discussing things altogether, but when we put them into groups of two or three, they get absorbed in their iPads and clam up. It's like they're working on their own, but sitting next to someone else who's working on the same thing as them, also on their own.

I suggested to the project lead that we could just use one iPad per group for some activities so that students are forced to work together and discuss things. She said that wouldn't be possible because then we wouldn't get as much data. She must think that having more data is always better, but if it's at the expense of good conversations, then it's not worth it.

The whole point is to develop an app that helps students. Gathering a lot of data on whether the app is helping students isn't as important as making sure the app is helping them.

For one of the activities, we were talking about location-tracking features on phones and about half of the teens have theirs turned on so that their parents can see where they are at all times.

A couple of the kids said they don't mind their parents knowing where they are.

"It gives them peace of mind and it's probably safer for me too."

The rest of the group disagreed. Several of them suggested that people whose parents check their location aren't doing it for safety; they're doing it for control.

One claimed that people who have trusting relationships with their parents are less likely to have their location tracking turned on. "Having a closer connection IRL," he said, "means you don't need as much of a connection digitally."

"Do you have your location-tracking turned on?" I asked him.

"Yeah," he replied, "but my parents say I have to. And they pay my phone bill."

FRIDAY, AUGUST 14th

After I finished the focus groups today, I went for a walk with a friend who's leaving town forever this week. He lived here for five years but got a job in Northern Alberta, so he's loading up his car and moving across the country. We were talking about how such a drastic change will probably be refreshing. I told him that when I move to new places, I always feel like time slows down for a little bit and I experience things more vividly or with more curiosity. David Byrne talks about the way he notices doorknobs and the colour of paper when he goes somewhere new. When things become routine, we stop noticing them. It's harder to experience life passing by.

I hadn't thought about it before this chat, but going off-line has similarly changed my pace and even space (at least digitally) in a way that's made me more aware of things this year. I didn't expect this change of pace to be so refreshing but it's almost like I moved somewhere new.

My friend told me that when he started applying for jobs, he went on a Facebook purge to delete any content he thought might make him look unprofessional. He finished going through his photos, but every day now, when Facebook shows him things he posted or comments he made "on this day" some other year, he goes through them and deletes anything inappropriate. Trimming your Facebook profile sounds like an exhausting part of growing up.

✦✦✦✦✦

Jonas' mom mailed me a list of things she'd miss if she didn't have the internet. The first thing she mentioned was talking to her kids on WhatsApp and FaceTime. Good call. Then she mentioned the same apps again, but this time for talking to her friends and extended family. The third point was about a banking app called "Revolut." (I was happy she thought about relationships first.) The fourth thing was the camera she installed to check on her mom, who lives alone and has dementia. Finally, she put NETFLIX – in all caps – and recommended a Will Ferrell movie about Eurovision.

I love that my year offline has given Jonas' mom and me an excuse to connect.

SATURDAY, AUGUST 15th
I received a near perfect letter from a woman I used to teach with in Vancouver. There were two sections in particular that I thought were very special and insightful so I've copied them down here. The first is about her experience teaching when everything went online in the spring:

"My memories of teaching online are so fuzzy *fuzzy,* and I keep trying to collect them, to make sense of that experience because I feel like I need to understand that experience in order to move forward into September with all my resources at the ready… Part of the utter joy of teaching for me is that it is a practice that engages me so fully. Because online teaching was, well, online, and under some very anxious circumstances, I feel like I made very few memories during those months."

The second part was a response to something I had sent her about how to personally get involved with making structural changes to the internet:

"What your letter brought up for me was how much I need (and my students do too, I think) to revisit our relationship with screens. I have felt my mind lose hard-earned attention span focus; I have felt anxiety so high I thought I was back in high school myself; I have been revisited by the ghosts of Comparison, Self Doubt, and Nagging Interior Monologues, fed by hours of internet use and screen time… What I think your letter offers that is especially helpful is an important sense of agency in our usage of these tools… The user experience was designed to be passive, consumptive, disembodied, apathetic, and to exploit any other vulnerabilities we bring to the experience."

But it doesn't have to be this way.

SUNDAY, AUGUST 16th

Last night Jonas and I went to Parc Jarry and ate dosas with Junior and Tyler. It was a nice evening but got a bit awkward when Junior went off about Darren. From what he explained, I think Junior has every right to feel upset, but it was still hard to hear him go on and on about one of my closest friends. Darren apparently wants to have a threesome with a couple of Junior's friends. He doesn't know them well enough to hit them up directly so he tried to get Junior to middleman it … but he didn't straight up tell Junior that. Instead he sent Junior a text saying "I want to see you today," only later asking Junior if he could invite those two friends along.

Junior was frustrated that Darren wasn't more upfront,

but he was even more annoyed when Darren ended up cancelling at the last minute. To make things worse, he checked Darren's Instagram later and saw that he'd been hanging out all afternoon with some of their other mutual friends and hadn't invited Junior along.

"I realize now that he didn't really 'want to see me.'"

Social media makes social manoeuvring tricky. You have to be careful what you post … or just honest with your friends.

✶✶✶✶✶

I went to Jeanne-Mance today with a friend to listen to Kaytranada and some other local DJs. We sat off to the side for prime people-watching. There were ravers there to see the show, as well as the regular Sunday LARPers, fighting amidst the dancers. It was a very strange mix of movements and outfits. The LARPers wore robes or armour, but the ravers looked even more bizarre. I want to believe I'm out of touch with fashion stuff because I'm offline, but I think I'm just getting old.

Things change fast these days. I just learned about calling someone a "Karen" recently and now it's everywhere. I heard it's been big in meme culture for a while but it's only now seeping into offline vernacular. Jonas explained that "a Karen is basically J. K. Rowling – an entitled, middle-aged white woman with [he paused] questionable views." He read that there's been a big drop in the number of people naming their kids Karen this year.

What else have I been missing?

TUESDAY, AUGUST 18th
Jonas is scrolling on his phone beside me on the couch, "Did you know Apple takes 30% of all sales from their app store, including purchases within apps? It's like they're the mafia."

THURSDAY, AUGUST 20th
Last night Hanni came by and we went for dinner. We wanted to try a new Thai restaurant that just opened near my

apartment. We walked over to order something for take-out, but they don't have their menu posted – just a QR code. Hanni doesn't have internet on his phone either, so we had to try somewhere else, somewhere that didn't require smart-phones. (We ended up ordering from the Peruvian place next door.)

On the way home, a guy passed us and he seemed a bit distressed. He asked us something in French that we didn't understand so I asked if he spoke English. He did and ex-plained that he was looking for an ice cream shop but every place he had checked so far was closed. I felt an affinity with the man immediately, both for his love of ice cream and be-cause he must not have internet on his phone either. Hanni and I had several recommendations for him – for hard ice cream or soft-serve – and we gave him directions to all of them.

✦✦✦✦✦

I woke up early this morning to meet with the professor who'll be teaching my graduate seminar this term. I'm very grateful she lives close and was willing to meet. Being offline for an online class is not ideal and without a supportive pro-fessor, it wouldn't be possible.

The professor seemed a bit skeptical about my ability to complete the course without the internet, but I assured her that I'll be able to phone into the lectures on Zoom and that I'll keep myself in the loop by talking to classmates. She wasn't convinced. She told me that she's anticipating bring-ing visual and text-based resources into classes at the last minute and doesn't know how I'll manage to keep up with the lecture or conversation if I can't access those resources in real time. I said I'll catch up later if I can't figure something out right away. I also brought up the neglect oral cultures get in academic spaces and said that I can use my experience phoning into online classes as a way to embrace and think with an oral approach. The professor seemed hesitantly sup-portive. I mean, she didn't roll her eyes.

As I was walking home, one of my high school friends called, but neither of us had much to say. We ended up chatting about sports. He's a classic man: he loves sports, burgers, his mother, and he's a recovering alcoholic. After we talked for a bit, we somehow started discussing slavery. I honestly can't remember how it came up, but I'm guessing it was my fault.

My friend suggested that we can't hate on all historical figures who supported slavery because then there'd be no great historical figures left to celebrate. I argued that many great historical figures didn't support slavery, especially those fighting against slavery.

If I only had friends whose values reflected my own, I'd probably feel frustrated less, but I'd also have fewer friends. And I wouldn't have as many opportunities to interact with people who disagree with me. Only befriending like-minded people is for social media. In real life, things are so much messier and more open to change.

*****

Jonas' mom phoned to tell him about the havoc being caused by algorithms at British schools recently. Because the school year was cut short in the spring, lots of graduating students didn't do the final exams that normally determine university admissions. Algorithms were therefore put to work, designed to predict what people's exam scores might have been had they completed the year. The algorithms used various inputs, but – as has become quite apparent now – the scores that students ended up with as a result were biased based on the wealth of neighbourhoods and the size of schools.

The government has had to scrap the algorithmic predictions in favour of human ones: teachers are now being asked to manually predict what students' exam scores might have been based on each student's prior performance. I'm sure there are people who still aren't happy, but it sounds like the public is a lot more comfortable with teachers predicting scores than computers.

FRIDAY, AUGUST 21st

Last night I went over to Niko's and he was stressed out about gifs. Since he started working remotely, he only communicates with his team online and uses lots of gifs to signal tone, feelings, and facial expressions that are difficult to convey with text alone. Niko was complaining about all the work he has to do to find and gather gifs to use. He said it takes him hours every week, time that could be better spent doing other things.

While he was telling me about work, Niko and I played a couple games on his new VR system. One was a music game like DDR or Guitar Hero, but with light sabres. It was surprisingly fun and relaxing, even though I failed every level I tried. The second game was ping pong. I could have played online against another human but Niko made sure all the settings were adjusted so I wouldn't accidentally slip into the interwebs. VR ping pong felt a lot like regular ping pong. The controllers even rumble a bit when the ball hits the paddle so that it feels like there's a real ball out there.

Unlike most other video games, Niko was pointing out how VR skills could be directly transferable to the real world. Someone who's really good at VR ping pong would probably be good at real ping pong too. Older systems don't have that potential. Being a great Mortal Combat player doesn't mean you can fight. Niko made sure to point out though that even old video games have a lot of positive potential – for developing persistence, problem solving skills, collaboration, etc.

There are also games that don't provide much value other than pleasure, but the same can be said about some books. Niko pointed out that people often assume a trashy book will still be valuable to a reader because *reading is good*. Whereas, for video games, he always finds himself having to argue for the value of the game.

I agree with Niko, but think that in opposition to the imbalance he sees, Niko sometimes becomes too heavy-handed in the other direction, arguing that *gaming is good* regardless of the game or context. It's hard to stay nuanced when everyone else is rushing to the poles. It's easier to just jump on the opposite side of the teeter-totter and try to keep it balanced. But balance isn't nuance.

✦✦✦✦✦

When I got out of bed this morning, I already had a bunch of stressful texts. My supervisor moved to Ontario this summer and is working at a new university, so my department's making us fill out a form about it. Both of us need to sign it, and then we need the signatures of the other two profs on my committee – one in Montreal and one in PEI. If I were online, this wouldn't be such a hassle. I asked Aviva to forge my signature, but she doesn't feel comfortable. I'll probably have to do a bunch of USB mailing. Such a headache for literally nothing. Ugh. Is it even forging a signature when the person whose signature it is has consented? Isn't that just a remote signature or something?

MONDAY, AUGUST 24th

I woke up and could smell something baking. I walked down the hall towards the kitchen and before I could see where the smell was coming from, Jonas shooed me away.

"I'm almost ready for you," he said, "Just give me a minute."

When I was finally allowed in the kitchen, the table was piled with envelopes and gifts. I can't remember the last time I had such a special birthday morning. It was probably thirteen or so birthdays ago when I lived with my parents.

31 years old! It feels … the same.

I was thinking about giving myself the day off (or on?) and using the internet. The only thing I really wanna do though is check my email. And I don't actually want to do that. I'm just already dreading having to do it in January and want to get it over with. But I'm not going to spend my birthday cleaning out my inbox.

31 is a special number. My parents are both 62, so I'm finally half their age. That means they were my age when I

was born. I can't imagine being a dad. When I chatted on the phone with them earlier, my dad made a joke about it being time for me to have kids. But then my mom got anxious and started saying that there's no rush.

"People are having kids later and later these days," she said.

"And some people aren't having kids at all," I added, "what with the end of the world and everything."

My parents didn't laugh.

"It's a quote from a movie I like."

I didn't tell them that I may very well make a baby while I'm 31. I just won't be the father.

TUESDAY, AUGUST 25th

Zoom glitched out yesterday and was down in a bunch of locations. It was the first day of school for lots of students in the US and many of them are doing classes remotely, over Zoom. Maybe Zoom crashed because of all the extra traffic? Imagine what would happen if the internet went down entirely. People might not freak out right away. Most people would probably just sit and wait until it came back on. But if it never came back on, then people would definitely freak out. People would freak the fuck out.

★★★★★

Hannibal was telling me about the comment section on the FairPhone website. FairPhone is the most ethical smartphone on the market but even they can't entirely avoid including unethical materials. When they know they can't avoid including something bad though, they identify the problematic link in their supply chain and discuss it publicly. Unfortunately, Hanni said that there are lots of comments where people get upset, "They call themselves ethical?!? Umm… They use conflict minerals!!" Does the Apple website have similar comments? FairPhones use less conflict minerals than iPhones but Apple doesn't bring attention to issues in their supply chain. It's frustrating and ironic that bringing attention to ethical dimensions of a product makes people more critical, even when the product is the most carefully-sourced product of its kind.

WEDNESDAY, AUGUST 26th
We decided not to cook tonight and got sushi for dinner. We could have just walked down St. Denis and picked one of the nearby Japanese restaurants at random, but we were feeling lazy. We wanted to order and be able to just go pick up our food when it was ready. But we had a problem. See, I like trying new sushi places, especially as I haven't been blown away by any of the ones I've already tried in our neighbourhood. However, I only had the menu for one sushi place – stacked with some other take-out menus on top of the fridge. It was a place we had gone to before that neither of us really remembered. Unless we wanted to go out and have to wait while the sushi was prepared, we were stuck ordering from the same place again.

So we did and the sushi was actually pretty good and reasonably priced. Being online may be great for variety, but without the internet it's much easier to be loyal.

THURSDAY, AUGUST 27th
A friend in California mailed me the new Bright Eyes CD. I've only listened to it a couple times so far but I think I like it. The lyrics are about the end of the world, but living on despite it. One of the songs has a line about how important it is to change our lives and act like the world isn't ending.

When there's so little we can do, we have to do all we can.

FRIDAY, AUGUST 28th
FANNY'S PREGNANT!!! AHHHHHHHHHHHHHHHH-HHHHHHHHHHHHHHHHHHHHHHH! I can't believe it!!! This is actually happening. Is this actually happening?

It was just over two years ago when Fanny and Alex first asked if I would be open to helping them make a family and it's been just under a year since we started trying. Now they're pregnant!!! It feels like we've been working towards this for a long time and like everything's happening so fast. I'm so excited for them, and also for me.

Fanny shared the news over text (millennials!) but I phoned her back and we gushed. Besides Jonas, I'm not going to tell people for the first few months, but Fanny said I am more than welcome to tell anyone who I might need to reach out to for support if she miscarries. I love Fanny and her loving directness!! What a human! This baby is going to be so so awesome!!!

I'm getting ahead of myself … and feeling narcissistic. But FANNY'S PREGNANT!!!!!

SATURDAY, AUGUST 29th

I met up with a friend for a walk this afternoon. We just wanted to catch up and chat so we strolled down St. Laurent. At one point we dipped into a shop that sells cute gift-like things made by local women so I could buy Jonas something for finishing his comprehensive exams (I got him a Celine Dion mug).

My friend has some extreme views and today he was talking about my offline year. He suggested that we may all be living in a matrix or an online simulation anyway and if we are, trying to spend time without the internet would be pretty ironic. He didn't use the word ironic but I liked where he was going.

He asked what I was planning to do next year, "Are you going to go back online?"

I told him that I was.

"If you weren't though," he asked, "do you think you could be a writer or a teacher or do the things you want to do?"

I paused, "No. I don't think I could."

SUNDAY, AUGUST 30th

When I got home, Jonas was on the phone with his mom. She was on speakerphone and I couldn't help overhearing her say she had accidentally spent a lot more than she meant to for three nights at a hotel. She was on Booking.com and saw the daily rate but thought it was the total cost for their full three night stay. She only realized her mistake after already hitting submit. (Booking.com doesn't give refunds.) She told Jonas that he should always book directly from the hotel so that he doesn't make this type of mistake. He comforted her by pointing out that websites like Booking.com are often intentionally confusing. I think travel deal websites are a gamble – once in a while, you can get a really good deal, but more often than not, they're taking advantage of you.

Jonas' mom was definitely overcharged for the hotel, but luckily she can afford it. Imagine if Booking.com has a way of adjusting prices based on how much money a user has – or rather how much money it thinks a user will be willing to pay.

*****

Yesterday, peaceful protesters in downtown Montreal successfully toppled a statue of Sir John A. Macdonald, the first official colonial leader of Canada. I only found out recently that he helped design Canada's genocidal residential school system. When I was in elementary, we learned more about his sense of humour; I remember a teacher telling our class that he was so hungover at one debate that he puked off the side of the stage, but blamed his opponent's speech for making him sick. The anecdote may have kept a bunch of 11-year-olds interested, but it romanticizes alcoholism and it's probably not even true. I wish we'd been taught about residential schools instead.

Of course the mayor of Montreal and other politicians have condemned the statue's toppling, saying that vandalism isn't an acceptable way to protest. I find it so infuriating to hear this kind of criticism. If government really represented people, then they would have already gotten rid of all the symbols that celebrate or neutralize violent racism. Don't hate on these protesters for doing your job for you!

*****

Elon Musk has installed microchips in the brains of pigs. This is to demonstrate the value of using the same technology with humans. For now it just seems to be revealing that the pigs feel happy when they're eating, but Musk promises the "Neuralink" implant will allow humans to interface with machines. We'll be able to store and access information online from the comfort of our brains. Jonas was telling me that Musk thinks becoming cyborgs in this way will ensure that humans can compete with the super-advanced AI that will surely wipe us out otherwise.

*****

It's two in the morning and I just got home from dropping off some letters in the mailbox in front of the metro station, three or so blocks away. I've determined that it's the nearest mailbox with an 8:30 a.m. pick-up time. There are a couple other ones closer, but they have afternoon pick-ups, and I have this irrational fear that if my letters sit in the mailbox for too long, someone's going to come by and light the mailbox on fire or something. (I always need something to worry about, so it's best to entertain worries I know are ridiculous.)

Jonas is fast asleep and I should probably go to bed too, but I love writing at night. After a certain hour, time takes on a different character and it seems like there's an endless amount of it ahead. When morning comes and all the day's tasks await, I have to be ready, on guard. After everything settles again though, I can write.

MONDAY, AUGUST 31st
I went for a walk with Anne and Sabrina today and heard a pretty funny internet story. Anne doesn't use the website Reddit much but logged in today to check what her ex-boyfriend has been up to. He's very secretive about his username, but Anne figured it out when they were dating. She clicked on his most recent post and was taken to a photo: a

pulsing red eye was staring into Anne's, followed by a bunch of questions. She checked and realized it was a subreddit about hemorrhoids. She was looking at an extreme close-up of her ex's bloody asshole.

September

The room, though it contained nothing, was in touch with all that she cared for in the world.
— E. M. Forster, 1909, *The Machine Stops*

WEDNESDAY, SEPTEMBER 2nd
This morning I woke up still frustrated. Sometimes I wonder how I've remained close with Darren for so long. Last night, Jonas and I wanted to see Darren before he left town to visit his family in the US. He was hanging out with a small crew of our friends and when we arrived, one of them stood up for a hug and I awkwardly told him that we're not doing hugs. He didn't seem to mind but Darren was set off.

"Then why are you even here?" Darren said.

Granted, he was drunk, but I don't want to hang out with mean drunks.

"Are you saying that besides each other, you haven't hugged a single other person?" Darren asked.

"Pretty much," I said.

"Then why did you come tonight?" he repeated.

"Well," I tried, "We wanted to see you before you left town."

Darren's next line was loaded with shade, "If you're willing to be here but not hug, then you're just posturing. If you actually cared, you wouldn't just pick and choose which rules to follow."

I told Darren that I thought he was being mean and then turned away and started talking to someone else. The tension eventually dissipated and it was an okay evening, but this morning I can't stop thinking about it. Darren can be such an asshole! (And not in a good way.)

✶✶✶✶✶

I just booked a rental car to take to Toronto next month for when my brother's baby is born. Jonas is coming with and my parents are driving in from Alberta too. I'm ready to tell them about Fanny and Alex's pregnancy now. Actually, I'm itching to tell them. But I don't want to steal the spotlight from my brother and his wife. I'll try to do it when they're in another room.

I was dreading making the rental car reservation – I thought it would be a bit of a hassle because I can't book it online. I pulled out my yellow pages and looked up the number for the car rental desk at Gare D'Autocars – the central bus station here in Montreal. I phoned and told the guy who answered when I wanted to rent the car. He asked for my name, phone number, and what kind of car I wanted, and within a minute, gave me a confirmation number, thanked me, and hung up. That was it. I didn't even need to give him my credit card or driver's license number or anything.

THURSDAY, SEPTEMBER 3rd

I don't know how – or why – I've managed to stay so social with my friends in Montreal despite having a boyfriend. Usually when people start dating someone new, they hole up with their boo and disappear. This winter I imagine we'll hibernate, but for now I still feel that social urge, and hopefully not just out of obligation.

Jonas is in the other room on Zoom for his first day of classes. I don't start until next week so I did the dishes and went grocery shopping. Despite not having class today, I still have lots of schoolwork to do, but it doesn't seem as important because it's not on a schedule – it's not urgent. I wish we valued important tasks independently of their urgency. It's hard to recognize all the household labour or emotional labour or other undervalued labour being done when we are so focused on urgent things. And if we don't recognize important labour that isn't urgent, we won't value it, which leads to unfair and unbalanced relationships – socially and globally. (I sound like a suffragette … but I'm a white dude and it's the 21st century. Yeeesh.)

Jonas' classes seem to be going smoothly, despite a few wifi glitches. While he was on break, he told me that one of his classmates had pointed out how different their breaks are now. Back when they met in person, breaks were times to chat and check in with one another – as people went to grab coffees or use the bathroom. Now there's much less potential for those kinds of informal connections.

I used to go for beers or food with classmates at least weekly after class. We weren't meeting to discuss course materials but they often became a big part of our conversations. I feel like I actually understood my courses better during these conversations than in class.

If classes continue online for a while, I wonder what'll happen to us – even just physiologically. I have a prof who wears glasses but swears that after several months in Peru without his computer last summer, his eyesight improved and he didn't need glasses anymore … until he got back and started using his computer again. When he told me this, I had a hard time believing him. But maybe I just don't want to believe that staring at screens all day might be bad for me.

SATURDAY, SEPTEMBER 5th

I had a full day yesterday and it felt like old times. I woke up and biked to Bridget's to pick up a USB stick from her, loaded with readings for the class we have together starting on Tuesday. Then I ran some errands on my way to meet Memo for lunch. Memo and I ate couscous in a park and then I biked to the canal and met Hannibal.

After looking at the water for a couple hours, we stopped to fill our tires and got chatting with an Uber Eats delivery guy who had just finished using the air.

"I've only been working for four months," he said, "and I've already done 3000 deliveries. I make $100 every three hours and I bike 50 km a day. I've never felt so good!"

If he's doing so well as a delivery guy, Uber's execs must be making a killing. (Literally?)

After I biked Hanni home, I headed to Sloane's for their roommate's birthday celebrations. I brought some gluten free dips (Sloane's roommate is celiac) and the main course was delicious garlicky donair prepared by Sloane's boyfriend.

Two of Sloane's queer friends were over and they're trying to have a baby in a similar way to Fanny and Alex. Sloane asked how the stuff with Fanny and Alex has been going. I think it's still too soon to tell everyone that Fanny's pregnant so I kept it ambiguous and said things are going well. Sloane's friends asked me some questions and I told them about the whole process – first trying at home and then through the expensive clinic. They explained that Quebec actually covers the cost of the IUI process that Fanny and Alex went through, even for queer couples who want to use a known donor.

"It's all about making more Quebeçois babies," they explained.

At first, I was impressed and pleased to find out that Quebec supports queer family building in ways that Ontario doesn't. Sloane's friends pointed out that it's actually sorta sinister; they see welcoming queers into the liberal fold as a way to keep traditionally disenfranchised people from allying with Indigenous communities. I don't hold it against Sloane's friends for taking advantage of the support, though. They're very critical of the colonial project so their kid will probably resist the Quebeçois identity anyway. Take that, Quebec!!

✶✶✶✶✶

Omar still hasn't received the jump drive I mailed him two weeks ago. I know I put enough postage on it because I took it to the post office and had the person there weigh and measure it before I sent it off. Omar thinks I should just resend it but I'm going to wait another week before assuming it's lost. If only there were some way to transport digital files quickly, conveniently, and inexpensively…

✦✦✦✦✦

My credit card is expiring and I got the replacement in the mail yesterday. The instructions that came with it explain how to activate the card using an internet browser or a smartphone app. It doesn't include an offline option. Luckily, there was a customer service phone number and the person who picked up was able to activate my card without even asking me any security questions.

Apparently they now use voice identification to ensure I am who I claim to be. WTF!!? How did they get a vocal imprint of my voice to use as a baseline? When did I consent to that? I feel like it'd be easy for someone to impersonate a voice. Or am I completely misunderstanding what they mean by voice identification?

MONDAY, SEPTEMBER 7th

In my dream last night I accidentally checked my email, although I closed the laptop as soon as I realized what I was doing. Then I shot at a police officer, but I didn't hit him – didn't intend to hit him. I was still worried, though, that I'd get caught and arrested. (I didn't get a chance to wipe my fingerprints off the gun.) As I was looking for a place to hide, I found a key on the floor and a hole for it in the wall, disguised by some cheap wallpaper. When I put the key in the hole, it unlocked a small door. I found a treasure buried behind the door in the wallpaper. I can't remember what it was, but I remember nobody else cared about it. I was the only one who even saw it as a treasure. Later in the dream, I accidentally checked my email again and had a series of messages in all caps from a vice principal I used to work for who was quite a micromanager. The subject said they were URGENT, but I read through them and they weren't urgent at all.

When I woke up, I was relieved that I hadn't actually checked my email or shot at a police officer. I was also relieved I didn't have to respond to any messages from my old boss. Email used to seem so urgent and essential to me. As soon as I went offline, I let that go. When I return to the world of the living, I'll have to remember that emails aren't as important as they seem … except when they are.

★★★★★

Our friend Junior has stopped responding to text messages from Jonas and me. He had recently done the same to Darren, but he told us about that. I can't help feeling like he decided to cut us out too now. I just don't know what we did. Maybe he's going through a tough time and it has nothing to do with us. If that were the case, though, I imagine he would let us know? He must realize that we assume these unrequited text messages are personal. Although if he is incredibly overwhelmed, then it's a bit selfish of me to assume this whole thing's about me and Jonas. I hate uncertainty!!

I've only ever been ghosted permanently by one other friend, and I still don't know why. Junior is in Jonas' grad program so he won't be able to ghost us forever. Unfortunately, he'll be able to keep it up for as long as classes remain online. I've already texted him twice and left a voicemail, but I think I'll send another text later today. I've already typed it out but I haven't hit send:

"Jonas and I are worried about you, or that we did something to upset you. Please let us know whether there's anything we can do to help!"

TUESDAY, SEPTEMBER 8th
I did too many house chores today. It was great for procrastination but feels unfair. I woke up at 10:30 and folded laundry, took out the garbage, cleaned the kitchen, and Jonas has been working on school stuff the whole time. It's 1 p.m. now and I haven't eaten anything so I have to figure that out – and we need groceries. Do I go shopping and lose even more

of my work day? If I bring it up with Jonas, or ask him to do the shop, I feel like it'll seem like I'm in too much of a rush to get our housework done and that, if I was just a bit more patient, he would've helped out. But I can't work in an apartment where there's so much that needs to get done! I wish I could go to my office or a coffee shop or the library. We may be working from home for a while, though (or forever), so I've gotta figure this out. Patience has never been my strong suit but I can work on it. It's not about lowering my standards, just delaying them.

✶✶✶✶✶

Last night I was looking through an old hard drive and found a bunch of messages I had saved in a Word document – emails I sent to straight boys I was attracted to in high school. Turns out that my younger self was a bit of a creep. The messages are all over a decade old now but still painful to read. Each one followed a similar script. They weren't so direct but basically, *I know you're straight and I know it's futile to tell you this, but I find you beautiful and I think I love you. No need to respond. Thanks, byeeeeee.*

Ugh … so cringey to read these now. I can't believe I had the courage or stupidity to send them. What was I expecting? It sounds so hopeless but I think I believed one of them was going to respond, *Now that you mention it, I think I'm gay for you too.* It just didn't make sense to me then that I could have such strong feelings for people who didn't reciprocate them. My body would never play such a cruel joke on me! I think I secretly believed that everyone was a bit gay, that this openness to same-sex attraction had just been stifled by casual, omnipotent homophobia. As if all the straight boys could be turned if the right dude came along and professed his love for them. And I thought that I, of course, would be that guy – a sexuality superhero.

Looking back on those emails, I feel pretty unabashed regret. I'm still close with a couple of the guys and I wonder if they remember. If it weren't for the convenience and immediacy of emails, I doubt I would have been able to express such bold and predatory sentiments at all. I definitely wouldn't have done it in person. Email was the perfect medium for slaking late-night lusting by sliding into somebody's private, password-protected inbox and forcing them to face my desires. Even if I knew I was unlikely to have my feelings reciprocated, there was still something that felt good to me about having them heard. Now I'm not sure that was fair.

★★★★★

I got the syllabus for tonight's course from Bridget. Before class, I went over it and noticed the professor's "Instructor Message Regarding Remote Delivery." It reads:

"I have heard that most but not all of you are feeling very well or adequately equipped for online learning. I will work to accommodate you in any way I can. For those of you who are caring for people who might be disruptive at points, know that I think appearances by children and pets (cats love Zoom) improve rather than hinder video conferences."

I feel like some of that – like the bit about "not all" of us "feeling very well or adequately equipped for online learning" – was written specifically for me. But I know there are also a couple students joining from other time zones (one Zoomed in from Nigeria). And one of my colleagues who lives on a Native reserve said that the wifi is really crappy there, so I'm not the only one experiencing friction with the internet – I'm just the only one doing it on purpose.

Class started with a "Zoom ice breaker." The professor asked everyone to point at one of my classmates on their screens.

"Don't worry," she told the student she chose, "I'm just using you as an example. I could have chosen anyone."

I couldn't participate because I was just phoning in, but that was the entire activity … just everyone pointing at one of the students. Maybe if I could have seen the visual, it would have made sense? After the "ice breaker," the professor introduced herself.

"Who am I? You might have googled me or checked out my profile on the website…"

It always come back to the internet. Because tonight's class was the first one of the term, a lot of the conversation was around new tech tools like Trello and Perusall – some of which are embedded into the course platform, some of which aren't, some which require accounts, and some which require supervisor permissions. Being offline never felt so good.

WEDNESDAY, SEPTEMBER 9th

I went down to Verdun this morning to say happy birthday to Hannibal and give him the Angela Davis graphic novel I bought him. On the metro home, I was busy reading some handwritten notes my supervisor mailed me about a paper I'm working on. The feedback was incredibly messy and I had trouble deciphering what Aviva had written.

All of a sudden, there was yelling behind me and I heard a woman saying "you people," so I spun around to glare. I noticed though that the person she was shouting at was another white woman. The yeller noticed my attention and started to explain. Allegedly, the woman she was berating had taken out her phone to sneakily photograph a woman sitting nearby who had brightly coloured hair and a matching outfit. The woman claimed that the stealthy photographer took the photo to make fun of the person.

"But I think everyone should be treated with dignity," she said.

What I originally thought was a racist Karen comment was actually kinda the opposite.

The woman went on, "I'm sure the internet can do some very good things, but I don't like how people are using it."

I was confused – had she somehow noticed that I was reading a paper about the impacts of the internet? If I couldn't make out Aviva's handwriting, there's no way she could have. There's so much I can learn for my research by just going out and looking around.

THURSDAY, SEPTEMBER 10th

I couldn't focus so I went for a walk down Mont-Royal. An Inuk guy I've chatted with before approached me and re-introduced himself. I told him I didn't have any change today and he seemed offended.

"I'm not asking for money."

"Oh, I'm sorry," I replied.

"I just want you to buy me some things at the dep."

"Oh, okay sure – what were you thinking?"

"Milk, cereal, and something to drink. What's your budget?"

This guy was good.

★★★★★

I'm always ranting to my friends these days about why they should avoid Amazon. I've had a handful of them tell me that they agree but still use Amazon.

Mark was my latest victim. He's fully aware of the disconnect:

"How am I supposed to reconcile the fact that I agree with you with the fact that I'm still using Amazon?" he asked.

I first responded with Adrienne Rich's quote about how we sometimes have to engage with hegemonic forces to disrupt them: "This is the oppressor's language yet I need it to talk to you." But then I realized that although we may need to use the internet to challenge problematic internet use, we don't need to use Amazon to challenge the fucked up things about Amazon. So instead I responded about disavowal, *I know very well, but...*

I said that "Disavowal is so fascinating and frustrating. I think it comes from feeling like we're not part of the relations ruling us. We forget how we're in control, or problems just seem so huge that we forget about them as a sort of defence mechanism. I haven't figured out yet how to remember. It starts, I think, with recognizing how our actions have impacts – some good, some bad – that we might not notice."

"I don't think that just recognizing problems makes us change though," Mark said.

"Awareness alone probably isn't enough," I agreed, "but without it, solutions aren't even thinkable."

FRIDAY, SEPTEMBER 11th

Every year on September 11th I think back to that morning. I had just turned twelve. While I was eating breakfast, we had the TV on and watched the footage play over and over. When I got to school, my first class was English and our teacher had us write down what we thought had happened. I still have the journal entry stored away at my parents' place but I haven't looked at it in years – partially because what I wrote was so wrong. 12-year-old Aron was pretty sure it was the Palestinians who flew the planes into the Twin Towers. As a pre-teen surrounded by too much Zionism, it's not surprising that my mind jumped to such an assumption, but it's still embarrassing.

I can't believe it's been almost 20 years since 9/11. So much has happened since then: I lived in Vancouver for a decade, Montreal for three years, Holland for a year, Palestine for a summer, I came out as gay, I was arrested twice, I've fallen in love, I've fallen out of love, I've fallen in love again, I became a high school teacher, I went to grad school, and I spent eight months and eleven days offline. And yet I still feel connected to that kid in 2001, condemning Palestinians like the sheltered, suburban Zionist that I was.

That was also the year my dad bought me my own domain name and I built my first website.

*****

Still no response from Junior. I hate being ghosted. It's easier to deal with explicit rejection than uncertainty. Jonas saw that Junior's been active on WhatsApp, so he's at least seen the messages Jonas sent him.

I've told a few friends about Junior and everyone has a story of being ghosted without explanation. Part of me thinks that the internet contributes to how flaky we're becoming. I may just be entertaining this idea so I don't have to take Junior's ghosting personally, but it seems that the possibilities opened by digital technologies have made it more normal and acceptable to disappear, even as they've made it more difficult. Maybe because we're so available to each other now, it can sometimes be too much and then we just have to ghost.

Socializing in the age of the internet is almost like a game with endless players, and if you have a problem with another player, you can just ignore them forever and never deal with the consequences. *Game over! Wanna play again? Swipe right for a new playmate.* However, although online worlds seem to float in cyberspace without material or human consequences, the opposite is true. The internet has quickly become one of the most impactful forces reshaping our lives.

SATURDAY, SEPTEMBER 12th
I've had to make a lot of assumptions about the weather since I stopped using the internet. The past couple days have been chilly, so I went out today expecting the same and was way overdressed. If only I could check the weather online, I'd ... probably realize that the weather forecast is just as unreliable as my assumptions.

✶✶✶✶✶

I got a text from Fanny today: "Still preggers!"

I'm so excited for her and Alex, but also for me and Jonas. Queers often have chosen families, which can be expansive.

Fanny says she's been more exhausted than ever before and is napping every couple hours. She works for the nurses' union in Ontario and is always overworked, and these past few months have been busier than ever. But growing a baby is more exhausting even than that. I replied that if it takes getting pregnant to slow her down a bit, she should start having babies more often.

✶✶✶✶✶

A friend in Vancouver phoned me yesterday. He's never slept with men before but wants to give it a shot. I suggested – contrary to my internetless ethos – that he download Grindr or Tinder and be clear about what he's looking for and what he's comfortable with.

Today I texted to see how it's going, "Got your nut yet?" I asked.

He responded right away with, "Guys are def easier to pick up than girls, haha."

I assume that's a yes.

✶✶✶✶✶

Jonas had a catch-up with his sister over WhatsApp today and, although I couldn't participate, he told me that I'd come up in the conversation. His sister works as a "stew" on a super yacht and her boss is a billionaire who often entertains fancy guests on his fancy boat. This week, they had an author on board.

"He's apparently quite famous," she told Jonas, "You should ask Aron if he's heard of him."

"What's his name?" Jonas asked.

"Stephen King."

SUNDAY, SEPTEMBER 13th

I was on the phone with a friend in New York and she asked what my upcoming semester's looking like, what with doing online classes without the internet and all. I told her it should be pretty chill. Because I'm not online, I have the ultimate excuse to be disengaged or late handing stuff in.

"You've figured it out," she joked.

Everybody's work is changing. My friend is five months pregnant and a busy lawyer, so she's very grateful to have been working from home these past few months. I heard on the radio that a majority of people in Canada prefer working from home. For students too, lots of families have decided to pull their kids out of in-person classes to do online learning instead. If we all end up living through the machines, can we then finally think about how to use the internet more responsibly? Or by then will it be too late?

MONDAY, SEPTEMBER 14th
Jonas tells me there was an accidental data breach in Wales. 18 000 people's medical and personal records were posted to a public government website and left up for over a day before somebody noticed. Whoops!! Computer glitches, amirite?

TUESDAY, SEPTEMBER 15th
My ex phoned today and we talked about boys. He's been having trouble meeting new people lately but has decided not to use Grindr anymore. He said it makes him feel "addicted" – either spending hours just scrolling through profiles without meeting anyone, or meeting up with sketchy dudes in risky situations for a quick fix. He's an actor and a server, both professions filled with gay men, but he said nobody's trying to connect in person. It's all about the apps.

He finds Grindr to be the most toxic, but even without it, my ex is still getting overwhelmed by his phone. He said that before bed is the worst and, after spending a couple hours scrolling, he falls asleep feeling anxious and insecure.

I asked whether he'd found any ways to control himself and he told me about a "time lock safe" he bought online. It physically keeps his phone away from him. He sets a timer, sticks his phone in the box, and voila, he can't access it until the timer elapses. It's like a mini version of my offline project, but just for his phone. I asked what he would do in an emergency and he said it'd be pretty easy to break the safe.

"But then I'd be out $50."

I asked where he bought it. He hesitated for a moment and then admitted Amazon. He's fixing one internet problem with another. If only I could get a time lock safe that could somehow stop my friends from using Amazon.

*****

I've been trying to navigate a couple logistical headaches today. I have to register with the Quebec government to deposit my provincial tax refund. This would be very simple to do online, but it's considerably more complicated without the internet. I had to phone someone who will mail me a form in 5–10 business days. Once I fill out the form and return it, it'll be another 30–60 business days before I'm registered. By that point, I'll probably be online again and able to register. But I already ordered the form, so I may as well go through the motions ... give myself something to journal about.

The other logistical headache – or what I thought would be one – was registering for my annual winter produce basket from a local farm that I've gotten vegetables from for the past three years. It's a biweekly drop-off with a random assortment of veggies, mostly root stuff during the winter. In the spring, I told one of the farm's volunteers about my project and asked her to let me know when it was time to register. She sent me a text today with the amount I owe and my invoice number, so I mailed in a cheque and now I'm good to go! I love helpful people.

*****

Doing a graduate degree over the phone is weird. I called into Zoom for class tonight and the professor kept talking about the internet. She was going over various things she wants us to learn this semester and kept saying, "if you google," "just google," "google google google." She never said, "if you look up..." as if we might have some choice over which search engine we use, or whether we use the internet at all. I know it's just the way people talk and she didn't actually mean we had to use Google but it sometimes feels like there really aren't any other options. Imagine if there were no other search engines, no books, only Google.

Besides the introduction, we were in breakout rooms for most of tonight's class, having small group discussions. After two minutes, or fifteen minutes, or however long the professor decided, we were "catapulted," as she called it, back into the main group. The catapult was merciless and often fired mid-sentence. In real life, we would at least have the chance to—

WEDNESDAY, SEPTEMBER 16th

"My character's name is Jojo. He's my alter ego. He's much better dressed than I am, and he has a better hairline. He's gay as fuuuck. He's even wearing overalls right now. But actually they're super cute. And actually I wanted him to look even cuter so I gave him a Band-Aid on his nose, so it looks like he was beat up, 'cause he's a little gay kid. But he's fabulous!" – Jonas as he plays *Animal Crossing*

Jonas bought a Nintendo Switch recently and decided to buy a case for it online. He's become pretty conscientious about where he buys things from and was careful to avoid Amazon. The company he decided to get the case from only sells their products through eBay, so he bought the case there. It arrived today … in an "Amazon Prime" envelope!!? The label even said it had been sent from "Amazon.com.ca" in Mississauga, Ontario.

He went back to the product's website and there was no mention of Amazon. He looked on Amazon's site and they don't sell the product. What a confusing world we live in. Thanks to the obfuscation made possible by the internet and big tech, it's becoming harder and harder to be responsible consumers. Or maybe more significantly, it's becoming easier and easier to be irresponsible.

★★★★★

"Blood Oxygen App measurements are not intended for medical use, including self-diagnosis or consultation with a doctor" – Promotional material for the new Apple watch

Apple released their latest watch and it's all about biometrics. This new watch can do all the stuff the old one could do (heart rate, step-count, monitor sleep, alert someone if you fall) but it also has some brand-new features. It can time you while you wash your hands, and it can check your blood oxygen levels (though, as the quotation above noted, its sensor technology isn't FDA approved). It all sounds marginally useful but mostly terrifying. Pretty soon insurance companies will give people deals for getting these watches. I don't want to slip into conspiracy, but I wouldn't be surprised if they start adjusting our premiums based on how much sleep we're getting, our alleged blood oxygen levels, and whether we're spending enough time washing our hands. Or we'll be able to pay extra for privacy.

THURSDAY, SEPTEMBER 17th

I was the guest speaker this morning in my friend's high school class. She teaches at an all girls school and she had her students read an E. M. Forster story I adapted. It's about the internet stopping, but Forster wrote it well before the internet existed. The main character, a mother, feels satisfied by her digital life. She does everything through the machine – ordering things to her room, reading the latest news, chatting with friends, attending lectures, etc. However, her son visits partway through the story and insists that the machines won't last forever and that they need to figure out how to live offline again. The mother scoffs and ignores her son, but – spoiler alert – he's right: the machines stop and almost everyone dies.

I wish I could have done the talk in person, but I just phoned in. It was obviously more convenient to be able to roll out of bed and do the call from home, but I was more anxious doing it remotely without the physical feedback from the group. Also, the phone wasn't loud enough and I was asked to restart my presentation partway through, speaking louder and more slowly.

Tech issues may be frustrating, but I love them. The friction they cause jolts us from our neutral slumber and reminds us that there's a machine mediating our experience. And when a machine fails, it can make people throw their devices out the window or at the wall, which may be some sort of subconscious fail-safe that our bodies have in place to make sure we don't get pulled too far from our direct, sensory experiences.

The students in my friend's class had lots of great questions but one that stood out was whether I'd recommend they try to spend a year offline too. I said no. I told them I don't think spending a year offline would necessarily be that helpful. It's an individual solution to much bigger problems; I admitted that it's ended up feeling more like a way to hide from the problems of digital life than to change them. But I added that spending one day a week disconnected from their device could be an interesting thing to try – as a way to reflect and a step towards collective action. The student who asked the question followed up by saying that she would like to try spending a day offline but she doesn't think she could because all her friends would still be on their phones, so she'd miss out.

Instead of challenging her rebuttal, I agreed: "We can't make these kinds of changes alone."

*****

I attended a surprise birthday celebration for one of my professors today over Zoom. We all Zoomed in for a "meeting" and then – all of a sudden – some music started playing and everyone shouted "Surprise!"

What a strange surprise party. It's hard to schmooze when only one person can talk at a time. Structured interactions within small groups seem much more suitable to online or remote formats than large, casual mixers.

*****

Jonas passed his exams for grad school!!! I'm so excited for him. I didn't realize I could feel this excited for another person.

FRIDAY, SEPTEMBER 18th

A friend of Sloane's was released from prison recently and part of his parole conditions is that he's not allowed to use the internet. Is that even possible? How is he supposed to find a job (let alone work that job) without going online? Socializing, shopping, bureaucratic stuff – it's all online now. It's hard enough for someone to restart their life after getting out of jail. Enforcing a no-internet parole condition is pretty much a non-starter. It shows just how far the criminal justice system has come from its alleged aim of rehabilitation. Sloane asked if I have an old internetless flip-phone this guy can use. And I do!! I often hold onto my old electronics thinking they'll come in handy one day, but they never do. Until today!

SATURDAY, SEPTEMBER 19th

Jonas is getting frustrated working from home. He misses his office and says that he's too easily distracted and isn't getting stuff done. Today we tried to do a bit of work, even though it's the weekend, and at one point I asked whether he was managing to stay focused. He said no, that he was reading an article about the founding of the USA.

"Is that something you're interested in?" I asked.

"No," he replied, "I just got caught up reading an article."

Without the internet, I wonder if Jonas would procrastinate as much. I suppose the internet isn't the main issue because, even if he was in his office, he'd still be able to go online; he'd just be better at avoiding it. It seems that Jonas' problem is actually with the physical space he's trying to do work in, not the virtual spaces distracting him from his work.

SUNDAY, SEPTEMBER 20th

Darren and I went for a walk, just the two of us. Since Jonas and I started living together, I hardly ever see Darren without Jonas, and Darren made a comment about it for a second time this morning, so I figured it was important to give him some one-on-one attention.

Darren spoke a lot about his social media issues, I guess because he knows I'm willing to listen to him drone on and on about them. He was mourning the loss of the old Instagram, when it was just people's pictures and it "wasn't political." He told me he's been going through his Instagram and muting anyone he follows who posts anything "political." I asked Darren what he meant by that word. He explained that if a post is primarily text-based and has an explicit message, it's "political" and he doesn't want to see it. I asked whether memes are a problem.

He thought for a minute. "It depends," he said.

"On what?"

"If it's funny," he replied, laughing.

★★★★★

It sometimes feels like the radio has an algorithm to tailor its content just for me. I know that's not possible, but it's surprising how relevant the radio can be even without personalizing things. I heard a documentary this morning about sperm donors and found out that there are lots of people against anonymous donations. In Canada, there's an organization actively fighting to make it illegal for people to donate sperm without agreeing to have their identity and medical history known to anyone who may be born as a result of the donation. In the UK and New Zealand, this is already the law. The people advocating to make anonymous donations illegal claim that there's something important about knowing one's "genetic history." The documentary didn't explicitly state what that value was, but it wasn't just about knowing medical histories and what health issues to expect. It was something that advocates were clearly passionate about but didn't totally understand or weren't able to express.

I don't know how I feel about this. As a non-anonymous or "known" donor, I guess I'm already on board – but I feel like the parents and family who raise a kid are way more important than biological parents, so I don't really get what the fuss is about. The documentary pointed out that the anonymity of donors has become futile in the age of genetic testing and DNA websites. So I imagine the movement to make anonymous sperm donations illegal will soon be unnecessary. Does that mean it was successful? It seems more like a happy accident! (…happy for everyone except any sperm donors who wanted to remain anonymous.)

TUESDAY, SEPTEMBER 22nd

Trapeze

This is not a trial run.
Swinging netless,
I feel hands holding mine
as if I've never held hands:

my hands and theirs, a net,
my mind and theirs, a culture,
my computer and theirs, an internet.

The crowd tries.
Theirs is not a netless run.
Swinging, holding
hands that feel held,
a net of never hands:

my hands and theirs, a culture,
my mind and theirs, an internet.
my crowd is theirs.

Trying to run
netless, not swinging,
not holding hands,
not feeling held, never holding,
as if I'm a culture of hands:

my internet hands and theirs,

my crowd mind and theirs,
swinging netless—

The crowd soars.

★★★★★

I heard on the radio about a new report from the BBC that explores the dirty gold in our phones and devices, especially those manufactured by Apple, GM, and Amazon. It turns out that much of the gold these companies use for their tech is sourced from a company called Kaloti in the United Arab Emirates. Kaloti, a gold refiner, provides a service for criminals to "clean" or "launder" their drug money by buying second-hand gold with it and then selling the gold to Kaloti for bulk cash or a wire transfer. It's a win-win-win-win for the criminals who get usable capital, for Kaloti who get a bargain on gold, for the companies who get a deal on precious metals for their devices, and for us as consumers. The only losers are the victims of the crimes by which the criminals got their illicit money and the societies who miss out on tax revenues.

According to the report, the American government knows all about Kaloti and doesn't mind. In 2014, after a three-year investigation, the US treasury was urged by law enforcement to warn the public that this was going on but they never did. The US didn't want to upset the UAE where Kaloti is based. When our governments do business with human rights abusers and ignore these abuses, we become human rights abusers. The companies that buy gold from Kaloti employ an intermediary to make the purchase so that they're not supporting crime directly, but that doesn't change anything for me. It's like how western chocolate companies sidestep their moral duties by buying blood cocoa from plantations in Ivory Coast indirectly – through intermediaries – as if they're not the ones driving the human-trafficking of children there. But, come on! Global supply chains may be composed of indirect transactions but tracing them doesn't take a degree in economics. We have to stop pretending we're not involved. Too much of our comfort and wealth is made possible by crime and suffering.

*****

Because I wake up most days around 11 a.m. and go to sleep around 3, I've started eating lunch as my breakfast, dinner as my lunch, and some snacks later, before bed. Last night, I ate a bagel and cream cheese before bed and it felt right. I've been missing breakfast.

*****

We had class tonight and, even over the phone, I got a touch of the rush I used to get in the good old days, when grad school was offline. One of the discussions ended up being explicitly about technology. In a small breakout group, we talked about whether social media helps marginalized communities. One of the guys in my group was devoted to the idea that social media is the only way for people who don't have access to mainstream news sources to have their voices heard. He was really excited about how the internet can provide people on the ground with direct access to an audience. I didn't disagree but pointed out that having a direct connection to a potential audience doesn't necessarily mean that people are getting the message. Who's listening? If it's just like-minded peers, it's not necessarily so powerful. And if the only thing people are doing is posting things to the internet, it doesn't necessarily lead to action. There's also the issue of how contagious sensational and fake news stories are. So, yea, social media can amplify people's voices, but is it amplifying the truthful ones?

Feeling the fire of discussion, I remembered how much I used to get out of sitting with a group of curious classmates, discussing big ideas, unpacking, dreaming, imagining change. If the discussion was good and the class was into it, I felt high. Although I caught glimpses of that tonight, it's just not the same remotely, as I sit with a tinny phone pressed up against my ear.

After class, Jonas and I had a long phone chat with Fanny and Alex. Fanny is eight weeks pregnant now and it seems really real, more so to them than to us of course, but still, I'm feeling it. Alex said some things on the call that made me feel really loved. They said that having gotten to know me better over the past few months, they're open to me playing as big of a role in the kid's life as I want to. I think originally they were feeling a bit guarded, but now they're ready to have me as part of their family. I'm so down.

Fanny and Alex have been talking about whether they'll let their kid use digital devices and so we were discussing some scary and exciting realities of new technologies. Alex works with youth experiencing mental health crises and says that internet- and phone-use are central to their clients' health crises 100% of the time. On the other hand, Alex and Fanny often talk about the ways digital tools help them organize against anti-Blackness. A workshop they facilitated on the basics of how non-Black people can support anti-racist organizing had 30 people attend last year and it felt like a really big group, especially in the small room they had booked. They raised over a thousand dollars at that event. This year, because the workshop was offered over Zoom, they ended up with 2200 people attending from all over the world and they raised a cool $150K. (Minus the $900 they had to pay the overlords at Zoom for a membership that would allow them to host sessions with up to 3000 people.)

I asked how they had people interact on the call considering the number of attendees and they said that everyone contributed to a collective word cloud that Alex read out, and they used a program called Mentimeter that gave people a chance to respond to multiple choice questions, displaying a breakdown of how the group responded.

2200 people instead of 30. I'd usually advocate for in-person workshops instead of the online version because it's harder to meaningfully engage people online, but if we're talking a difference of 2200 people or 30, I'd be tempted to risk a bit of meaningfulness. Besides, if one of the main goals is moving money, then this remote format is much more effective. Quality over quantity doesn't really apply to money.

THURSDAY, SEPTEMBER 24th
I'm an uncle!!!!! My brother's wife gave birth this morning to a healthy baby girl! My family sent Jonas a bunch of photos … I really wish I could use the internet today.

★★★★★

Last night I went to the park with some friends for a picnic and found out that a couple of them are moving to Toronto on Saturday for work.

"You're no longer working remotely?" I asked.

"It's still remote," my friend explained, "but now they expect me to be in Toronto for some reason."

"You'll have to go into the office once in a while?" I assumed.

"No," my friend explained, "not yet anyway. They just want us to be in Toronto."

I didn't push further but I don't get it. If people have to work remotely from home, why do they have to be in the right city? As long as the time zone's not too different, why does it matter?

Most of the people at the picnic are working remotely these days so I asked how people feel about it. The conversation was immediately focused on productivity and everyone agreed that they get more done nowadays working from home. I was surprised because I keep hearing how much Jonas wants to get back to the office. It makes sense though that people would be more productive from home: they can work longer hours, they're always available, there's less of a distinction between working and not working … people are probably more productive from home even if they're less efficient.

"And how about quality of life?" I asked, sorta trolling. I got a couple smirks, but nobody replied.

✦✦✦✦✦

I went for a walk with Sabrina and Anne today and found out more about the new system our university is using to pay their "casual" employees like us. We'll now have to log into an online portal called WorkDay and there's no longer an option for submitting paper time sheets. Sabrina said that WorkDay's been glitching hard and everybody's complaining about delays getting paid. I hope my boss can help me figure out an offline workaround. I have a feeling it may be more friction than this janky new system can handle.

In other news, Sabrina was excited to tell me about a podcast she's producing as part of her research. I probably should have asked her more about it, but instead we started talking about the word "podcast." In some of the older articles I've been reading, people talk about online audio broadcasts as "audio blogging." We tried to guess when people stopped "audio blogging" and started "podcasting." Anne brought up the fact that the "pod" comes from iPods, which don't even exist anymore, so it's probably been a while.

"It's like how we still say 'turn up' or 'turn down' the volume even if we're using buttons instead of a knob," Sabrina said.

"Or 'rewind' even if we're not playing a tape," I said.

"Or 'hanging up' a phone, even if there's no cradle," Anne added.

If I were online, I'm sure I could figure out the definitive origin of "podcasting" and whether Apple's marketing team coined the term or if they just cashed in on it later. I don't know that I'd care enough to look it up though. Or maybe it's not about how much I care, but just that I care more about discussing it with friends than looking up the cold, hard truth.

SATURDAY, SEPTEMBER 26th
My cousin told me that young people these days don't use punctuation in text messages, that they find it "aggressive"

or something. I've started paying more attention to how my younger friends use punctuation and most of them are actually quite careful and punctual – if that word meant what it sounds like it means, instead of what it actually means. However, I've noticed that almost everyone leaves out the final punctuation of the text, be it a period or question mark. (If it's an exclamation point though, it gets included!) I think I'm going to start being less careful with that final punctuation mark, or more carefully sloppy. Gotta keep up with the times

★★★★★

I've started noticing itchy bug bites on my legs again these past few days. They're not quite as angry as the flea bites I had in the spring, but they're still uncomfortable and frustrating. I can't find any new bugs but I've started using bug spray on my legs, even in the house. Every time I feel a little tingle on my ankle, I assume the worst. Despite how much I hate the itching, I'm so much more aware of my legs when I have these bumps. It's like they're shouting, "Remember us?! We're your legs." I only really notice my body when something's wrong.

SUNDAY, SEPTEMBER 27th

This morning I finished Billy-Ray Belcourt's latest book and came across a section that made me think of my journal: "The page rescues us," he writes, "The creative drive, the artistic impulse, is above all a thunderous yes to life."

I've been wondering why I've felt the need to write so much this year. At first it was just to capture my year offline but, by March, it became an obsession. I needed to get it out if I wanted to do anything else. Writing let me feel okay despite all the terrible things I was hearing on the news. I still feel this a bit, but it's less all-encompassing now. For a while, if I didn't journal every few hours, I started to feel overwhelmed. Now, I can go a day or two without writing.

I'm worried that when I start using the internet again, I'll replace my journal with something online. Getting my thoughts down here is very different than posting things on social media, but what if I can't manage both. Billy-Ray writes about wielding an app "like a weapon in the war of emotion." But I don't want to fight – I want to be rescued. If only it were that easy.

★★★★★

I'm getting weird texts from friends lately – short, few-word-long responses that don't seem to fit with the conversation. I texted a friend to tell him that I wasn't feeling up for a walk and he responded with, "Thank you." I sent a message asking another friend an open-ended question and she responded, "Sounds good." I think it's cause people have started sending more of those automated responses that their phones suggest. It's like I'm messaging with bots who represent my friends. What if I actually want to connect with someone without their personality being funnelled through an automated language model? It sounds like a ridiculous question because surely we still have control over whether we let our phones auto-complete. Don't we?

MONDAY, SEPTEMBER 28th

Jonas and I had a big talk this afternoon after getting groceries. While we were at the supermarket I could tell he was bothered by something, but when I asked he said he was fine. At home, after I asked him again if everything was okay, he admitted to feeling overwhelmed. He said that it's partially school-related and missing-his-family-related, but in his head, it's mostly connected to me.

I wasn't ready to accept that our relationship might be the problem so I got defensive and said something about feelings not being so discrete, how they spill into each other when we try to articulate them, even to ourselves.

Jonas was patient with me and even agreed but said there are certain aspects of our relationship which have started to upset him. Mostly, he feels like I make too many decisions for the both of us – what we eat, the movies we watch, the music we listen to, how we spend our evenings, etc.

He's right. I do find myself making more decisions than him but I told him (and I don't think it was as a defence tactic) that I'd prefer if he was more assertive and made more of these decisions. Jonas is a better cook than I am and I would really appreciate if he were more involved in planning and shopping for meals. In terms of the media we consume, because of my internetlessness, we pretty much only engage with movies or music that we already have on hand, so it *is* harder for Jonas to have a say without actually buying physical copies of something he wants. Next year, when I'm back online, that can change. This general dynamic though will probably linger if we don't address it head-on, so I'm glad Jonas said something.

I think Jonas internalizes discomfort and I can sometimes feel it hanging in the air, waiting in what he's not saying. I told him that I think it's better we deal with things than building up resentment or frustration. He agreed but pointed out that it's not always so easy.

TUESDAY, SEPTEMBER 29th
I'm getting excited and nervous about our Toronto trip. The prospect of telling my parents about Fanny and Alex's pregnancy is starting to become really real. They'll be excited, and I'm excited, but I'm also nervous.

✦✦✦✦✦

I was texting with Hannibal again today. He's been going through my journal to help me decide which entries might be worth sharing publicly.

He wrote, "I'm actually so curious how your day-to-day changed not because you're not on the internet, but because you're writing every day. I wonder if writing makes you feel some of the welcome changes that you're attributing to a lack of email or online distractions."

I replied, "That's a good point."

He went on, "Sometimes it felt like you were writing because you had to."

It did feel like I had to journal this year. I'm not sure if it was 'cause I felt obligated to keep tabs on my project or if I literally had to journal – unloading my fiery thoughts, giving them a healthier direction to burn. I don't know yet how I feel about this journal as an artifact, but I've come to rely on it as a ritual.

WEDNESDAY, SEPTEMBER 30th

Nine months down, three to go!! It should feel like spending three quarters of a year offline is an accomplishment, but it doesn't feel very challenging anymore. It's just become the way it is.

I went on a bike ride this afternoon to drop off a jump drive at Tyler's. It had rained earlier and smelled sweet, like autumn. For such a particular smell, it's strange that I've never stopped to think about what it comes from. My guess is wet and rotting leaves. The street I biked up and down was coated in red, yellow, orange, and a bit of green. I was nervous that my wheels might slip, but they were fine. I biked slowly and looked around me, admiring the last oozings of an overripe year.

October

I've changed my mind. I used to wait for the explosion, the big crash, the sudden chaos that would destroy the neighborhood. Instead, things are unraveling, disintegrating bit by bit.

– Octavia Butler, 1993, *Parable of the Sower*

THURSDAY, OCTOBER 1st

One of my profs had a pretty horrifying experience this week, though she seems unfazed by it. She's queer and sent out a survey to several hundred of her undergrad students asking those of them who identify as queer to respond to some questions about how to improve the university experience for queer students. People were able to submit their responses anonymously and fourteen of them shared constructive feedback. Nineteen of the responses, though, were filled with hateful slurs and death threats. These are from students whom she still has to teach for the rest of the semester or longer. If I were her, I'd feel uncomfortable interacting with any of the students now, unsure who the aggressive homophobes are. She said, though, that she's experienced this kind of thing before.

One dark reason why online classes are better: they can protect queer faculty from violently homophobic students – although the anonymity of the internet is why so many students were able to harass this prof in the first place. She has since gone back and updated the survey so that people have to log into their university account and are no longer able to submit anonymous responses. The death threats have since stopped, but so has the feedback.

★★★★★

Jonas has class this afternoon – with the prof who insists that everyone keeps their video turned on – and he came to the kitchen where I'm working for his fifteen-minute break. I made a couple cups of tea, both the same size and the same tea. When he went to pick up a cup, he reached for the one farther away from him. I asked him why he hadn't just grabbed the closer mug and he told me that the one he chose had better colours on it. Then he went back into the other room to rejoin his class. I'd heard that Zoom makes people self-conscious in peculiar ways, but this was the first time I'd seen it in action.

FRIDAY, OCTOBER 2nd

We're in Toronto and just got back from Friday night dinner at my brother's. His new baby is adorable. She's only a week old but has a full head of hair. It was really sweet to see my brother as a new father. He seems proud and fairly confident. His wife was exhausted but seemed very happy to have three generations altogether for the baby's first Shabbat dinner.

My parents are in town too and they seem more chill than anticipated. They drove Jonas and I back to the place we were staying after dinner and I told them about Fanny and Alex.

"That's such a flattering thing to be asked," my mom said. "When do they want to start trying?"

"They're actually already pregnant," I said, "I didn't want to tell you before, in case it didn't work out."

I wasn't planning to share the news right then, but I wanted to tell them while we were together in person, and didn't want to steal my brother's thunder, so I seized the opportunity. They were surprisingly unfazed by the whole thing. I assured them that I didn't enter into the decision lightly and they pretty much said that they trust me.

I also told them that Fanny and Alex are excited to meet them if they wanted to and they said they do, although probably not until next time they visit Toronto. I assured them that Fanny and Alex would love to have them as part of the baby's life. If I'm the baby's uncle, they can be a great aunt and uncle. I was very pleased with how smooth the whole conversation went. Although, when I joked that the baby will appreciate having them around for the gifts, my dad took the joke further and said that he's happy to be in the baby's life, but gifts are too much to ask. Dad-jokes never get funnier.

SUNDAY, OCTOBER 4th
This Toronto trip has been strange in a good way. We've been eating together, sitting around inside, and we've even been hugging. It almost seems like we're doing something wrong. I never imagined that getting together with my family could feel so illicit.

Yesterday, my brother's wife wanted some burgers for lunch from a place that was half an hour away. You don't argue with a new mother (especially when she's your sister-in-law), so Jonas and I went with my dad to pick them up. My dad drove and used his phone's GPS for directions. On the drive back, he missed the entrance to the expressway because his GPS gave him the directions too late. By the time it said to turn, he had already missed his chance.

We had lots of time to talk so I learned a bunch about my dad's job. He works with remote servers and cloud storage and told us that although more and more companies are moving their files to the cloud instead of having local servers on site, it's actually more expensive to store things remotely. I assumed it was cheaper and that's why companies were switching, but apparently the advantages of cloud storage are that nobody locally has to worry about patches or upgrades to the server, and cloud operators have more robust capabilities to detect suspicious or fraudulent activities than local technicians.

Because cloud storage is out of our hands, though, my dad recommends personally making a back-up of all important files. (Or even a second back-up.) Personally, I like having external hard drives and hard copies of all my important files, but I think my dad just means storing things on two different clouds, i.e. two different computers stored in mysterious fortresses far away.

By the time we got back to my brother's place, the burgers were cold and my sister-in-law had fallen asleep. But it was worth it.

★★★★★

Before driving back to Montreal, Jonas got a phone call from a number he didn't recognize. He didn't pick up, but they left a message.

It was an eerie, robotic voice repeating, "Stay safe. Stay home. Stay safe. Stay home…"

MONDAY, OCTOBER 5th

We were supposed to see Fanny and Alex while we were in Toronto but Fanny's grandmother is dying and there wasn't enough time. I've followed the legal news in Canada about medically assisted death but Fanny's grandmother is the first person I've been connected to personally who is going to take advantage of the new laws. Because we didn't get to see Fanny, I wrote her a letter:

Fanny,
I don't believe in a reincarnation where our soul or self is transposed into a new living creature after we die, but I agree with the Indigenous idea I heard from Leanne Betasamosake Simpson that our ancestors become our children and we have to trust them, respect them, and look to them for guidance – as we support them with unconditional love. I think Judaism teaches something like that too, like how we never name our kids after our parents or anyone in the family

until after they've died. And it fits with Jewish ideas about epigenetics and transgenerational trauma. If we change the way we look at reincarnation, I think most people can get behind it without even getting into anything spooky.

When I was holding my brother's baby this weekend, I could feel myself being nourished. It's pretty bizarre how much a baby – who relies on the adults around her for support – can make me feel supported and affirmed. The feeling fit with the less mystical idea of reincarnation that I'm trying to describe. Jonas commented that I looked pretty content being an uncle. And he would know, taking creeper shots of me all weekend as I held my new baby niece.

She was mostly asleep – she's not even two weeks old yet – but sometimes she opened her eyes and looked around. Once or twice, I'm pretty sure she looked directly into my eyes with her dark irises, as dark as her pupils. I could see myself reflected in miniature, a pupil in her pupils, and I started thinking about what she was thinking about. I've heard that babies don't have a distinct sense of self and see themselves as part of the world around them, of family, of nursery rhymes, of toys, of blankets, of smells, of milk.

I looked into my niece's eyes as she (maybe) looked into mine and wondered if she saw me as a part of her. I wondered what it meant to even think of a *her* that saw a *me*. I think eye contact – when we see ourselves being seen – feels intense because it's a moment that reveals the you- and me-ness of our selves. When I see your eyes, I see you but I also see you seeing me; I see myself being seen. We simultaneously affirm each other's existence.

Sometimes I get caught up thinking this way and forget how important it also is, simultaneously, to hold onto ourselves within this messy mesh of others. Jonas and I were talking about your grandmother and what it means to have agency in dying. In the face of death, there's something life-affirming about how we're all enmeshed. However, there's something about individual selves having their needs and desires honoured that is death-affirming in an equally important way.

Why affirm life? To remember that we are nothing but dust, each just a speck in the mesh of everything. Why affirm death? To remember that this whole world was created just for us, for each of us individually; the centre of the mesh shifts, is everywhere, and is certainly centred around your grandmother, and just as snugly around the soon-to-be baby that we're all becoming.

Love you lots,
<4 Aron

TUESDAY, OCTOBER 6th

Air gapped,
Gasping for breath,
Before the waves crash back over me.

★★★★★

The flowers on our front porch have started to flower again. Jonas is calling it their "last push for life." They were flowering in the spring, lost their flowers by July, and have hung around as leafy greens for the past three months. Now, as the first frosts are about to arrive, they've sprouted tiny buds and some are opening into red and yellow flowers.

There must be a metaphor in there somewhere, a flower that misses the summer and finally opens as the winter comes to strike it away. It's almost like the summer never happened, that it's still last spring and we're just crouching, waiting to spring again.

I phoned the rental car place to make sure they had gotten the vehicle I left for them in their parking garage last night. The guy on the phone asked for my last name and then after a moment said, "I've got all the information in front of me here. Didn't you receive the email we sent you with the receipt?"

I didn't want to explain too much and just replied, "I don't use email."

He paused, and then paused again, and then, "Oh. Well, yup, we've checked the car and everything's in order."

I wanted to ask him what was going through his head when he paused, and especially when he paused again. But I just thanked him and hung up the phone.

WEDNESDAY, OCTOBER 7th

Jonas received two more strange, robotic voicemails yesterday and today saying "It's time to stay safe and stay home. Stay safe. Stay home." It seems like a scam but I've never heard of a scam that tries to help its victims instead of taking advantage of them. Jonas also got a text message this afternoon from the Quebec government with some public health information. Why didn't they send me a text?

★★★★★

I called my uncle to wish him a happy birthday and after chit-chatting a bit about family, we started talking about my year offline. He was saying that, despite all the problems with the internet, it provides us with lots of opportunities that people in the "the third world" (as he put it) don't have. "And the gap between us and the third world's just growing and growing so maybe it's the internet…" He trailed off, as if to imply that having a better internet connection would give people in the Global South a chance to compete in the global economy.

I pointed out that having digital devices, while of course helping people in our communities access economic opportunities, are simultaneously limiting opportunities for workers in the Global South whose economies are captive in creating, supporting, or disposing of these technologies. I tried to bring up the IMF and World Bank to explain how rigged things are against Global South countries, but he didn't seem too interested. And it was his birthday.

I asked if he had plans for the evening and he told me about the curry chicken dish that his wife prepared and the complicated scheduling manoeuvres they both had to do in order to ensure that the crockpot was turned on early enough to let the chicken cook but late enough to ensure it didn't just turn to mush. My uncle's wife was going to rush home from work at 11 this morning but my uncle managed to get out of one of his morning clinics early and went to turn on the crockpot instead.

If only I had a crockpot, I'd have more to talk about with my uncle.

FRIDAY, OCTOBER 9th

I walked over to find a spot on the grass to sit down, past a line of cops with big, bulky pockets, cans of mace, guns, tasers, helmets, goggles, bright yellow vests, and an un-earned confidence. There were at least 25 cops and only about 100 protesters. The person leading the protest was talking about the Haudenosaunee land defenders who are standing up against land developers and now police. These Indigenous land defenders have been officially labelled as a terrorist organization by the Ontario police. As the speaker pointed out, it seems a bit strange that the "terrorists" are a bunch of peaceful people who are singing, eating, telling stories, playing lacrosse, and just existing as themselves on their land. And the police – with their terrifying outfits and unlimited power – they're the ones allegedly fighting against the terrorists.

People who stand up against state-sanctioned violence make me feel hopeful that our world might change. If that's what someone means by terrorism, then I guess I appreciate terrorism. But I recognize that not all terrorisms are equal.

SATURDAY, OCTOBER 10th

Because it's Thanksgiving weekend in Canada and people aren't supposed to be gathering, the news this morning recommended that people who are celebrating the holiday alone should refrain from using social media as it could be upsetting to see other people getting together with their families. I couldn't believe that the news actually recommended avoiding social media. I mean, I agree that if you're feeling lonely, social media may exacerbate that feeling, but isn't it meant to help people connect? Or have we all agreed now that social media's more isolating than anything else?

SUNDAY, OCTOBER 11th

I heard on the radio that some guy who used to make websites for the pope is on his way to becoming the patron saint of the internet. He's been beatified, but he has to do one more miracle before he can be the full-on internet saint. It turns out that the websites he made – those weren't the miracles. He only did his first miracle after he died.

✻✻✻✻✻

Today's protest was small, which was disappointing, but it made me more glad to be there. About 30 people showed up, mostly young people, younger than me, and there were more homeless people than I usually notice at protests.

The event started with speakers sharing their experiences as Indigenous people fighting to live their lives in ways that they find meaningful. An Inuk man around my age played his drum, and a woman who was part of the organizing team did a smudge ceremony, offering smoke for people to clean themselves with.

Only one person was arrested and he was a counter-protester who came into our circle and started telling people that "This is Canadia." Nobody responded too aggressively or even defensively, so he went over to bother the cops who were quicker to react.

★★★★★

Mark and his partner, Miriam, stopped by to drop off some articles for me to read. They were about the power of new technologies compared to the power of humans, and I mentioned something my supervisor said about computational agency being a bogus concept that just hides human agency. Miriam got a bit defensive and said that the question of whether machines have agency is like asking whether a virus has agency. I pointed out though that viruses aren't created by humans (unless the conspiracy theorists are right) and they aren't introduced to situations intentionally with particular aims or functions. Computers usually are.

Or at least that's what I thought. Hanni and I were talking about it after the protest and he pointed out that when people talk about machine learning or AI, they're talking about programs that engineers are not totally in control over. If you give a computer a whole bunch of data to work through with a machine learning algorithm, you don't necessarily tell the computer what to do with that information.

"You just keep adjusting things," he explained, "until you get the results you want."

"But then the human is still in control," I said, "even if they don't totally know what the computer's doing, they're still the ones who decide which outcomes to use or what to do with them."

Hanni didn't disagree. I think he's only slightly less confused about all this than I am. It's hard to wrap my head around what it means that the actual outcomes aren't being pre-programmed, but I still think humans are in charge, even if we're a few steps removed.

It makes me think of Marx's *Capital,* his attempt to help workers understand how they're involved in assigning value to money and commodities – even as this sense of value leads to their exploitation as workers. When they forget how they're involved in coordinating the value of commodities, the commodities "rule the producers instead of being ruled by them." Marx hoped his book might help workers re-engage their control. When I talk about AI and machine intelligence with my friends, it's the same thing. If we don't figure out how we're involved in the social processes responsible for our lives, they start to seem like we aren't involved in them. And then it's as if we're not.

People love to mystify computational agency and make it seem like it exists apart from humans, in ways that stand over us, that overpower us. And it can overpower us, but I prefer to remind people how we *are* involved and how we *can* engage control. The prospect of *Blade Runner* or *Ex Machina* coming true is terrifying, but I don't think we have to worry about that kind of thing anytime soon. Or, if it happens, we won't get dominated by machines we can't control, but by machines we've forgotten we're controlling.

MONDAY, OCTOBER 12th
Fanny texted me to let me know her grandmother died.

She wrote, "Very sweet and lots of laughs right until she closed her eyes. We got to tell my fam all about the pregnancy so it was a pretty nice day all in all."

I always find it overwhelming when people use a casual medium like text messaging to share serious news. And then I have to respond over text message too.

"Thank you for updating me," I wrote, "I'm glad to hear that even the difficult parts of life can be nice when we are surrounded by people we love."

TUESDAY, OCTOBER 13th
There's a new app in Montreal called "Bon Cop Bad Cop" and it gives users a chance to report and track police violence and racism. I was watching this news story on French TV, so I may not have understood all the details, but it sounds like it was designed to help people regain control over government services that are meant to serve and protect them.

I also heard today that Facebook has followed Twitter

and is banning content from QAnon, a right wing conspiracy group from the US. They are also prohibiting Holocaust denial on their platform. Blocking QAnon and Holocaust denial are important steps, but it isn't enough. Facebook could instead try to actually modify the algorithms that popularize sensational information. Banning particular hateful content might just be a PR stunt. Meanwhile, sexism, classism, ableism, and racism continue unchecked.

✶✶✶✶✶

Class tonight was annoying. The professor wanted us to use some of Zoom's more advanced features, including something called Whiteboard, and she didn't suggest any alternatives for me. If I were disabled or phoning into Zoom because I couldn't access the internet or a computer, I hope the professor would've been more accommodating.

This year offline has made it clearer that the university is set up for an ideal student who is non-disabled, online and often also white, male, and economically supported. Being gay used to give me some insight into how inequitable and exclusive powerful spaces can be, but since I left Alberta at 18 and moved to cities where gay white men were included under the umbrella of power, I've been re-sheltered. It wasn't until I went offline this year that I once again found myself in a place where the issues of idealized participation became loud and clear. I'm not trying to say that avoiding the internet magically makes me more aware of and able to fight against ableism, white supremacy, and the patriarchy, but it helps.

WEDNESDAY, OCTOBER 14th

A few months ago, Jonas and I were seeing Darren several times a week – making dinners, playing Scrabble, watching movies. As Darren's sex life heated up, we were still seeing him regularly, but not as often and at more of a distance. Lately though, it's becoming harder and harder to want to hang out with him. Whether he's arguing that I shouldn't protest against the legacies of enslavers because "everyone" owned enslaved people at the time, or he's calling me out in front of our friends for taking public health measures too seriously in a performative way, I feel like Darren has started to resent me, or he's just feeling bitter in a way that spills into how he treats me.

Today he may have put the last nail in the coffin. I texted him on the weekend asking if he wanted to meet up for a walk.

"I feel like I haven't seen you in forever, Darren. Wanna go for a walk this weekend or next week?"

He replied that he'd be up for a bike ride instead and suggested Wednesday or Thursday afternoon.

Well, today's Wednesday and he texted that he's going to leave work a bit early and wants to meet up around 5 to bike.

I replied, "Great! I'm there. Cool if I invite Jonas?"

He responded, "I think it'd be nice for you to come alone. It's nothing against Jonas, trust me. It's more that I'd like to spend time with you as a sole entity sometimes, ya know?"

I was a bit taken aback – I felt hurt for Jonas who considers Darren a close friend, and I also started to wonder whether Darren was trying to provoke something. He might not remember, but last time I made plans with him, he said something similar about wanting to see me without Jonas, so I went alone and we hung out just the two of us.

It gets worse. I showed up for the bike ride today, without Jonas, and Darren had invited three of his friends along!! They were all super lovely, but I don't think it's fair to ask me not to bring Jonas and then to bring three friends with.

I think I've gotta stop hanging out with Darren.

THURSDAY, OCTOBER 15th

I was reading an article (from Mark) written by a guy named Andre Staltz who differentiates the web from the internet. Staltz is trying to advocate for decentralized peer-to-peer web connections that can eventually overcome the stranglehold big tech monopolies have over the internet:

"It is not fundamentally necessary to have any intermediate company profiting whenever a person reads news from their friends, rents an apartment from a stranger, or orders a ride from a driver. This is why it is important to analyze technical systems from an economical and societal perspective: because early design decisions foreshadow certain social orders."

Staltz's article is just over three years old and it's brimming with hope, but I'm still skeptical.

✶✶✶✶✶

I heard on the radio about a survey people can take as part of a study on whether screen time helps people manage their day-to-day stresses or if it actually might make stress worse. The woman on the radio announced that they'd post a link to the survey on Twitter. I know that's normal now, but it seemed funny to me, considering the topic of the survey.

Before moving on, the radio host asked one of her co-hosts whether he finds screen time stressful or if it's something he appreciates. He said it depends on what he's doing on the screen; not all screen time is equal.

Context is almost always the secret to life. If it's not context, it's usually balance.

SATURDAY, OCTOBER 17th

My mom phoned yesterday and asked if Fanny knows that she wants to have a relationship with her kid. I was a bit taken aback by the question because I thought we had discussed that but I reassured her. The unresolved anxieties of being a non-grandmother run deep. Or maybe I'm projecting some secret anxieties of my own.

My neighbour is out on his back porch doing some tidying and singing the phrase "Baby d'amour" over and over again. He's singing to his cat, but the cat's not paying attention. This doesn't stop him though. He just keeps singing and singing and singing. "Baby d'amour, baby d'amour, baaaaaaaaaaaby d'amour, baaaaaaaaaaaay, baaaaaaaaaaaaaaaaaay, baaaaaaaaaaaaaaaaaaaaaaaaaaaaaaby d'amour, baby d'amour, baby d'amour, baaaaby d'amour…"

SUNDAY, OCTOBER 18th

People keep talking about a white-supremacist group out of the states called the Proud Boys. From what I understand, it's a group of self-proclaimed racists who show up at anti-racist protests to provoke violence. The president of the US was asked to condemn the group and didn't. In response, gay men online have pulled a prank by using the hashtag #ProudBoys to display photos of proud gay men. Besides non-white people, there's nothing that makes a white-supremacist more uncomfortable than the gays.

MONDAY, OCTOBER 19th

Everyone knows about the phantom buzz, when it feels like your phone vibrates but then you check it and there's no text or anything. I used to get the phantom buzz all the time and thought it was cause my phone was glitching. Now I'm pretty sure it's just in our heads.

I've heard the excuses. I've even made them: "But I was holding my phone when it happened!" or "I sometimes get a weird vibration feeling in my leg, but this was different!"

It's been nine months since I turned off the vibration feature on my phone. For the first few weeks, I continued experiencing phantom buzzes, but then I forgot about them. Jonas felt one today (claiming, of course, that his phone actually did buzz) and it occurred to me that I can't remember the last time I felt one. It's like having an incredibly mild case of the hiccoughs for years and finally realizing they're gone – a quiet, unexpected relief.

★★★★★

I've been pretty impressed by the mail service this year. Since January, I've mailed out over two thousand letters. Although there have been several unexplained delays and a couple dozen return-to-senders, I only know of one letter that got lost in the mail. It was a card I sent to a friend in New York to congratulate her on being pregnant.

I bumped into one of my old classmates a couple days ago and she asked me to mail her something we had worked on together a few years ago. After I dropped it in the box today, I texted her to let her know and she texted back, "Omg… Thank you for mailing it so quickly."

I think people have this impression that mailing things is a big hassle. If you have stamps and envelopes at home, mailing things is just as easy as sending an email. And you get to go for a walk!

In response to the letters I've sent out this year, I've received just over a hundred replies so far. I keep them all in an increasingly crammed shoe-box under my bed. It's like my email inbox, except I enjoy looking through it and it doesn't make me feel stressed.

✶✶✶✶✶

Jonas was emailing back-and-forth with Fanny to plan an upcoming weekend getaway we're going on with her and Alex in Prince Edward County. Jonas wanted to send a cute emoji of a menorah at the end of the message and so he typed in the word "Jew" to search through his phone's emoji database. Strangely, the only thing it suggested was a picture of a bone.

When he told me, I immediately thought about the Holocaust. Maybe that's on me, but Jonas admitted that his mind went in that direction too. Has his phone's AI just learned from a bunch of antisemites online that bones are commonly associated with Jews? When Jonas searched again with the word "Jewish," he found the menorah emoticon. Hmm…

TUESDAY, OCTOBER 20th
I phoned Enterprise to book a rental car for our upcoming trip to see Fanny and Alex. Enterprise was the same company I used a few weeks ago to get to Toronto but I spoke to a different person this time and everything was different. Last

time, the guy was happy to help me over the phone. This time though, the guy suggested I go online.

"Our rates are more expensive over the phone," he told me.

I was a bit annoyed, both that I was going to have to pay extra to avoid the internet and that I wasn't told I was paying more last time. I thanked the guy for explaining but told him that I'm not using the internet this year as part of my grad studies. He laughed and went ahead with booking a reservation for me at the reduced rate. I didn't ask how much money I saved but I thanked him for being a human.

✶✶✶✶✶

Class tonight was glitchy, as usual. I could hear everyone else fine, but the professor's voice was going in and out constantly. It made it pretty frustrating and hard to follow – especially since I'm also lacking the visual cues.

At one point during class, Bridget interrupted the discussion to ask whether it was acceptable to cook while in a Zoom class. She got mixed responses, including, "depends what you're cooking." She was making "macaroni in a box," as she called it. The professor said she wasn't sure what the etiquette was but I think that's a bit ridiculous. Of course you shouldn't be cooking during class.

At the end of class, the professor was talking about how unfair it is that so many students who work for the university are still waiting to be paid, almost two months into the semester. The school's new online employment portal has been a disaster. I know at least five students (including Jonas) who haven't been getting paid. Before I started my degree, I knew the school was a bit disorganized, but I had no idea it was this unprofessional. When people can blame the technology, they can get away with anything.

WEDNESDAY, OCTOBER 21st
"Hi Aron. I think it is clear there is a problem between us the

last month or so. It is something that has been building up for many months. I've given multiple direct hints as to what's been bothering me without any sort of acknowledgement. I believed for a while that it was your responsibility to address it, but you are either unaware or don't care enough to discuss it. I've gotten to the point where I simply feel like blocking you from my life, but I think I would regret doing so in the long run without trying to make amends first. So this is my attempt: If you want to meet to discuss it, I'm open to that. If not, then I'd prefer that you don't reach out to me in the future."

That was the text I received from Darren tonight. I was honestly shocked. What an absurd message! I knew there was tension between us but I didn't know Darren was holding like an explicit grudge about something. It's fucked how people can just "block" people from their lives now. That aspect of Darren's message aside, WHAT THE FUCK!!? What did I do? I was already feeling the need to take a step back from my friendship with Darren. I suppose he's just made that a lot easier.

"Woah!" I replied, "I'm not sure what you're hinting at and didn't know you were upset with me. I've been frustrated by a couple things you've done lately, like when you called me performative for not hugging and when you asked me not to bring Jonas along the last two times we hung out. I assumed you were just going through some stuff with your mom and boys though. Your text doesn't exactly make me want to go for a walk but I am curious what you think I've done and I'm sorry to hear you're upset."

Darren replied almost immediately, "Okay clearly you've been unaware, but like I said, we can meet up to discuss it and if not, then I prefer to not continue our friendship."

I didn't reply. Ultimatums are rarely necessary and they're about power, not communication. I resent Darren for framing things in a way that will make it seem like I'm the unreasonable one if I don't agree to his demands, but I think I can live with it.

How did I get three years deep into a friendship without recognizing how different our values are? Over the years, we sometimes had clashes but we'd always stayed close. He was the main way I met gay dudes in Montreal. Without Darren, I wouldn't have met Jonas. Although now that I've met Jonas, I don't need Darren in the same way.

After exactly an hour, he sent another text: "And the fact that I've come to you and expressed that I'm having real concerns and that I'm wanting to make things better, and your response is 'you've done things that bother me' and 'assumed you were going through some stuff with your mom and boys' and 'what you THINK I've done' and 'I'm sorry that you're upset' not that 'I'm sorry I've upset you' makes it really clear how you feel about me. Take care, Aron."

How I feel about him? I feel like he's unhinged. And I feel like he's relieved me of the obligation I'd normally feel to support him through it. And I also feel guilty, and I feel like texting him back. But I'm not going to.

THURSDAY, OCTOBER 22nd

I'm putting way too much energy into this, but Darren sent me more texts this afternoon: "Listen Aron, I realize that my message came off harsh and surprising to you, but it came from a real place of hurt and I came to you asking to talk about it. I didn't say you did anything intentionally. But there is an issue I think needs to be resolved or heard by you at least, and it's strong enough for me that if I don't get it out, then I don't think I can continue seeing you as a friend. Sometimes we affect our friends in ways we don't understand. It hurts me that instead of agreeing to meet and hear me out that you turned it around the way you did. I didn't expect that from you. It was mean. You said you were sorry I was upset and not that you were sorry you upset me. That's framing the conversation and absolving yourself. I haven't said what it is exactly because it's too complicated to be texted out. I could have ghosted you, but I respect you too much so I sent you the message to meet and I wanted you to understand that for me, it's very serious and urgent. I'll ask again, do you want to meet to talk about it? I'm free this evening."

A few minutes later he texted again: "I want you to understand that I've thought about this for months and spoken about it with friends (our friends). This is something I'm not just pulling out of my ass."

I really don't want to meet with Darren and have him berate me. I expect he'll tell me that I don't separate friendship from politics or that I talk down to him, maybe that I'm trying to hurt him. If Darren were one of my students or a classmate even, I'd treat him differently. But as a close friend, I'm going to be myself around him. The whole idea of close friends for me are the people who you don't have to walk on eggshells around. I'm not trying to say I don't like friends who call me out on things. On the contrary, I want to be able to be called out without it being a thing. I want to challenge my friends and have them challenge me, but I don't want them to berate me or attack me out of the blue.

Darren criticized me for being mean in the way I responded to his first message. But he's sending me ultimatums and threats, and telling me that he's been talking shit about me to our friends. I don't want to be friends with someone who sees the negative ways they're feeling as someone else's problem. Structural? Sure! But don't put your problems on me.

I texted back, "I'm open to meeting but this has taken me by surprise and I need some time to process it before we talk. Let me get back to you in a couple days."

✦✦✦✦✦

I talked to my friends in Berlin today – Julia and Winston – and told them about my Darren problems. They think I should meet up with him and address it. It feels like they're right even though I don't want them to be. As some of my oldest friends, it's hard not to trust them. Julia said it would of course be *easier* not to meet with Darren, but she doesn't know me to be one for easy options. I appreciate that, but I want to be a shitty friend just once! I can't always be a good friend to people who are being shitty friends to me.

FRIDAY, OCTOBER 23rd

Montreal's mayor wants people to shop locally this holiday season. "It's not the online shopping giants that need our help," she said in a news conference. She's made parking free downtown on weekends in order to promote local shopping. I hope her advice doesn't stop people from shopping locally online. And I hope the free parking doesn't promote people going downtown to shop from the large big-box retailers.

It might be better just not to shop at all this holiday season.

★★★★★

I biked down to the canal today and met up with Hanni. When I told him what's been going on with Darren, he said that he thinks I have to go hear him out.

"You owe it to your journal," Hanni joked.

If that's the motivation, then I shouldn't meet Darren. The only reason why I would is because I feel like I owe it to Darren. I feel responsible to him. Even though he's been shitty to me lately, I still feel like I'm my brother's keeper. I don't want to meet with Darren but I feel like I'm supposed to. And I don't want to be someone who knows what they should do but still acts otherwise. That's why the world's ending, or our world anyway.

This evening Jonas and I went for a walk with Yoni who is also close with Darren. I tried to bring up the situation but I could tell Yoni didn't want to talk about it. Eventually I acknowledged that I was putting him in an awkward position but asked if he could give me any clarity on what Darren is upset about.

"Is it just that I'm too political and pushy with my opinion?"

Yoni said no. He thinks it has to do with me being distant lately.

"You used to be his closest friend in Montreal."

Yoni thinks I should meet with Darren, that I owe it to him. I told him that I don't exactly feel up to it after the barrage of texts he sent. Yoni reminded me that Darren's dramatic and probably didn't mean to come across as aggressively as he had.

When we got home I texted Darren: "Do you have time for a walk tomorrow?" That was a couple hours ago. I'm still waiting for his response.

SATURDAY, OCTOBER 24th

I wore my black-and-white keffiyeh and my anti-Bill 21 pin and headed to Laurier park to meet Sloane and their friends. I got there early and was standing alone. A reporter came up to me and asked some questions about what I think "defund the police" means. I just kept repeating that community safety is important but that police are not providing that for a lot of people in our communities.

The protest was well-attended and distressing. There was a point when police in riot gear blocked our path outside their "Brotherhood" headquarters, but there was something very satisfying about hearing NWA's "Fuck the Police" blasting as we stood there, peaceful but angry.

We rerouted ourselves and marched on, chanting the names of Black and Brown people who've been killed by police, and singing along to the music.

★★★★★

After the protest, I went to meet with Darren back at Laurier park, where I'd met up with Sloane earlier. I was dreading the conversation and when I saw Darren biking towards me, my stomach sank and my heart sank into my stomach. Everything was sinking.

I asked how his day was going.

He replied, but didn't return the question. He sat down on the bench beside me, and said, "So!" and it began.

It wasn't what I expected, but it wasn't too unexpected.

He said that he hasn't enjoyed hanging out with me lately because I've been neglecting him.

"You moved in with Jonas after only two months," he said.

"It *was* really quick," I agreed, "but it was five months."

He disagreed and told a strange story about how much he hated having to wait outside a restaurant recently with Jonas while I went in to grab our food. Darren said that he has a similar issue with his dad who always brings his wife, Darren's stepmom, along to things. He said that he's told his dad not to bring her with if he wants to come visit him in Montreal.

"But Darren, I'm not your dad."

"Honestly Aron, this is what I was worried about," he said, "I didn't feel comfortable confronting you because I was afraid you'd just downplay my concerns."

"I'm not trying to downplay anything," I said, "but it's different with your dad."

I don't get it. Does Darren have a problem with Jonas?

"Remember that conversation we had at the cabin last fall?" Darren asked, "When you were giving me a hard time for being on my phone?"

"I do remember that, yeah."

Darren just looked at me smugly, as if that explained everything.

I didn't choose my words very carefully but something came out that didn't sound quite as harsh as my summary of it here:

"It sounds like we have really different understandings of what's going on in our friendship," I started, "and I'm sure Jonas has been a big factor, but I've also been uncomfortable hanging out with you lately because you've started to say and do things that upset me."

He demanded examples, so I brought up last week's bike ride and how he had asked me not to bring Jonas and then invited three of his friends along. I also mentioned the university statue protest that he criticized me for going to, and his argument about low-income men being the most disenfranchised group in society this year.

"I think we just have pretty different values about some things," I concluded.

After a pause he said, "It's really surprising to hear you say that because I don't think we have different values."

I was ready to be finished the conversation, so I changed the subject and just said, "Sorry I didn't see you more one-on-one." It felt funny coming out of my mouth, especially after we had both agreed that we didn't really want to hang out with each other anymore, at least for the time being.

But Darren smiled and said, "That's all I needed to hear."

★★★★★

I only had to bike five minutes to get to a different park where I was meeting Jonas and Junior. I hadn't seen Junior in a while. He ghosted us a couple months ago and I took it personally but he reached out recently and said he was just really depressed and overwhelmed with school and life. It was actually really nice to see him and catch up, especially cause he was eager to talk shit with me about Darren.

While we were hanging out, Jonas and I both got texts from Darren, but about different things. Months ago, Darren had asked Jonas to set up parental controls on his phone so that he wouldn't use Grindr and Instagram too much. Darren was now trying to turn that feature off but couldn't figure out how to do it without Jonas' password. Jonas doesn't remember what the password is, so just texted back apologizing for not being more helpful.

Darren's text to me was a bit more dramatic: "Hey I just want to be clear: we both think it's good to give it a break or end our friendship, but for you it's because my values don't align with yours because I questioned the validity of tearing down a statue? Is it because you believe I'm racist? Or not anti-racist? Or pro-patriarchy? Or not anti-patriarchy? Maybe just some clarity on what values you think I hold or don't hold?"

After I got home, I replied to Darren's text: "It's not just the values. It's also about how you've treated me recently. But you've done lots of really nice things too, like making me the cookie on my birthday and all the plant cuttings you've given us. So I know it's not so simple."

I don't want to hurt Darren. I care about him, or at least I used to. I had fun feeling like the bigger person and laughing at his ridiculousness with Junior and Jonas, but now that I'm home and writing about it, I feel sad and sort of small. Maybe I'm just feeling down now to absolve myself of the guilt I have over—fuck that, I have to stop constantly assuming I'm in the wrong!!

MONDAY, OCTOBER 26th

I got a call from Osama today in Berlin. I hadn't spoken to him since I visited almost eight months ago. Time goes by too fast. He phoned my cell, but through Skype. After a few minutes, the call was dropped and he phoned back from his cell, explaining that he'd run out of Skype credit.

Our call left me feeling recharged. I keep in touch with so many people too regularly out of obligation that I sometimes forget how nice it is to have a conversation with someone I really love.

★★★★★

I haven't spoken to Bradley for a while because every time he's called recently, he's tried to convince me that the anti-racist protesters in the US have taken things too far. A few weeks ago he even said he sympathizes with the militia groups "protecting their buildings," as he misleadingly framed it. I'm not sure what changed but his ideas about policing and protest have flipped. He's always identified as a "libertarian," but that used to mean something very different. I don't have enough patience for it anymore and I've been ignoring his calls.

Today he phoned though and I picked up. I felt bad that I'd been avoiding him. He didn't sound very happy and I was worried he was about to lecture me for neglecting me as a friend. But no. He told me that his grandpa died last night.

It's been exactly three years since Bradley's grandma died – three years to the day. I tried to be sympathetic and a supportive friend but Bradley said he doesn't really care about old people dying.

"We're at a point where that's okay," he said.

I tried to argue that it's ableist and ageist to argue that it's okay to let elderly and immunocompromised people get sick so that the rest of society can continue functioning as normal. Bradley didn't like being called "ableist" and started making fun of me for using the term.

"I'm just saying Bradley that it's easy for us to say that we don't want to change our lives, 'cause we're not the ones who are going to die."

Bradley reverted back to his argument about the government having too much control: "This is just like after 9/11," he said, "an imaginary fear that lets the people in charge—"

"But it's not an imaginary fear."

★★★★★

Jonas found the interview with me from the defund police protest online. I couldn't watch it, but he sent the link to his family. I wasn't sure how they'd react, but they all seemed impressed. I was surprised; I forget that the defund movement has become fairly mainstream incredibly quickly. Last year, a similar group of protesters would probably have been written off as a bunch of out-of-touch anarchists. Now though, even centrist and mainstream news stations are covering the protests in favourable ways and people are catching on. The future may not be fully fucked after all.

TUESDAY, OCTOBER 27th

Our university emailed out new guidelines for how to participate in Zoom calls and Jonas was sharing some of the highlights. They claim that webcams steal 15% of your energy so you have to put in the extra effort to make up for it. It recommends talking with your hands and being "over the top" in order to appear normal. This extra energy may feel silly but, according to the guidelines, it won't come across that way over Zoom. (Won't it though?)

✶✶✶✶✶

I can start telling people now that Fanny's pregnant! She's apparently already been in her second trimester for almost a week. I had the date off because I thought pregnancy begins at the point of conception. It turns out you start counting two weeks before that, from the preceding period. So really, a fetus begins as just an egg. The sperm is an add-on, albeit a necessary one. Makes me think the biblical idea of Eve being made from Adam's rib might've been trying to compensate for something…

Now that Fanny's in her second trimester, the chances of a miscarriage drop considerably. Fanny and Alex got to hear the fetus' heartbeat last week, and this weekend they started setting up a room in their house for the baby. I'm sure I'll still worry, but I'm feeling really good about the milestone.

I talked to my mom more about how she might be involved in the baby's life and she's feeling a bit insecure. She didn't want to say she likes control but she talked around it saying how much she likes having an "awareness of the future" and dislikes "uncertainty." I think she'll feel better once she meets Fanny and Alex. I'm going to try to set up a call between all of us soon. My parents probably won't be in Toronto again until after Fanny gives birth and it'll be nice for them all to connect before that. I think I'll wait until January though and set up a video call online. Look at me, thirsty for the marvels of the internet! But for real, it seems like meeting over a video call will be more comfortable and more meaningful than if we try to do it over the phone.

I told my mom that building a queer family (or queering a family) means that the conventions or expectations aren't so rigidly set and there'll be more flexibility to figure things out as we go. Of course there are still models, but the reality of life as a queer person can be more open to personalization, often in shared and communal ways. I think my mom would rather just follow a manual, but she's starting to appreciate that there isn't always a set way of doing things, especially when you're queer or disabled or not white, etc.

WEDNESDAY, OCTOBER 28th

It feels cranky in the apartment today. Jonas is quiet and complaining about chest pain, a headache, too much work, a funny smell, missing his family, not being able to socialize…

His loudest complaint is about the pain in his chest. He's been feeling it on-and-off for over a year now and it's starting to get really sore again lately. I suggested he see a doctor but he explained that the university clinic he goes to requires that patients first have a virtual appointment before getting a physical physical. I asked him what's wrong with that? He's not offline. He didn't explain why but said he doesn't want to do the virtual appointment.

I wanted to say that if he's not going to do anything, then I don't want to listen to him man-sulk about it. But I didn't say that. I just went to the other room.

In class last night, there was a minor mutiny and a few students recommended that the prof change the format for our final presentations. Originally, we were all just going to share our talks with the whole class but now people want to record presentations, watch them asynchronously, and then gather in small groups to discuss them. It may very well be more practical, but I want to hear about what everyone's working on. We're a twenty person cohort halfway through the second year of our program, and I still don't know what most of my classmates are researching. The people arguing for the asynchronous format were saying we need to "take advantage of the technology to save time" but what are we going to do with the extra class time? I'd rather spend it getting to know everyone than have extra lectures from the prof.

*****

My mom phoned to talk about Fanny and Alex's pregnancy again. She wanted to know whether she should be getting in touch with Fanny to see if she needs anything before we do a video call in January. I told her not to worry – try to be patient.

She said that she's been telling a couple friends and it's all very exciting – this idea of queering families, how she and my dad don't really know what their relationship with the baby will be yet, but that they'll figure things out as they go.

"Well yeah," I said, "though you and dad will be like a great aunt/great uncle kinda thing."

"Right, right," she replied, "Or however we see it."

I wanted to say more but I'll give it time – try to be patient.

THURSDAY, OCTOBER 29th

The police shot and killed a Black man this morning, not far from where I live. He had a knife. Don't the police get training in disarming people without killing them? They have tasers and mace and clubs… And if they really want to shoot someone, can't they aim for the foot or something?

*****

I talked to my uncle about Fanny and Alex getting pregnant and he seemed pleased.

"Congratulations," he said, "you're part of evolution now!"

I wasn't before? I thought he was joking and I laughed, but he didn't … and then he went on to talk about evolution. A small part of me feels excited to have my genetic material reproduced but a much larger part of me feels selfish and small for even entertaining such a narcissistic idea.

Years ago, I remember telling my uncle that evolutionary psychology – thinking about evolution as a motivating factor for why someone does something – makes me uncomfortable.

"As a gay person, it makes it seem like my sexual orientation is glitchy," I told him.

He disagreed, suggesting that gay sex can be understood to have evolutionary value, even if it's not about making babies: "It's harder to define how, but of course gay sex is part of evolution."

However, after today's comment about me only *now* becoming part of evolution, I'm starting to wonder whether my uncle's understanding of evolution is actually so generous and homo-inclusive.

FRIDAY, OCTOBER 30th

Jonas is in a better mood today. He's playing a game on his Switch where you fight insects and level-up and stuff. I feel like video games are a fairly healthy type of screen time for him. Social media is the scarier culprit. Jonas doesn't go on Instagram anymore, but he still spends a lot of time reading about it. He was telling me that Kim Kardashian posted something about flying her friends to a private island for her birthday. Jonas was laughing about the post and how self-absorbed the Kardashians are, but he still sees all these superficial people doing excessive things while he sits at home, scrolling through his phone.

At the moment though, he's fighting insects.

$$\star\star\star\star\star$$

One of Montreal's main hospitals was hit with a cyberattack earlier this week and they had to disconnect from the internet in order to protect confidential patient records. There have been lots of similar hacks in other North American cities recently except they usually involve the hospital's records getting encrypted and the hospital having to pay a ransom in order to get their files back. The attack in Montreal seems more random, or less sophisticated. There didn't seem to be a goal beyond disrupting the system. I'm all for sabotaging the state, but it's pretty low to target a hospital.

While they were under attack, the hospital had to pivot all their operations offline. I heard one doctor on the news say that he and his colleagues had to use a lot of USB sticks and were passing them around the hospital instead of sending emails. Because they were completely offline, the doctors and nurses weren't able to access or share records with other hospitals and lots of people's appointments had to be postponed. Today they announced that they have managed to vanquish the virus and their systems are back online, but there's still lots to catch up on. Imagine what would happen if the internet fully stopped? If we had to take all our systems offline? It seems unthinkable, but humans survived without the internet for ... a lot longer than we're likely to survive with it.

November

Every day we are surrounded by people who "choose" to work incessantly, not because mobile technologies mean that they can, but rather because the mere availability of these technologies suffices to make them accept that they must. The work cannot wait because mobile technology means it does not have to.

– Darin Barney, 2014, "We Shall Not Be Moved"

SUNDAY, NOVEMBER 1st

With two months to go, my friends keep asking if I'm excited to be back online. I usually answer yes, that I'm excited to stream some shows and movies that I missed while offline, but I think I say that because I have a harder time with the truth: I'm not excited.

It feels almost patronizing to tell people that because everyone else is online. But it's overwhelming to think about all the new expectations people are about to have for me, and that I'll have for myself. When you open up so much potential – for socializing, shopping, research, activism, and everything else – the world gets too big. It's daunting, especially when I'm already feeling overrun. I don't want to face the world more glaringly than I already have to. Is that selfish?

✦✦✦✦✦

It's hard to notice daylight savings time these days, now that all of our clocks change automatically. Even though my laptop is completely offline, it still knew to change itself this morning. If it weren't for the clock on the stove, I wouldn't have noticed anything was different.

MONDAY, NOVEMBER 2nd

I'm meeting up with Hanni today to get a USB from him and to give him a new one. He's read everything in my journal up until the end of March and today he's going to give me some notes in exchange for the next few months of entries. Without the internet, the jump drive exchange has proven incredibly valuable. In order to use these radical offline library tactics though, Hanni and I have to meet face-to-face … and that's becoming harder as it gets to be winter. I'm going to bike over to Hanni's in a bit, but he lives pretty far away from me in Verdun and it's going to start snowing any day now.

It's going to be a slow and quiet winter. I hope I don't end up feeling too stuck.

✶✶✶✶✶

Bradley called again today and I felt like I had to pick up. This weekend, he left a voicemail singing a song about me avoiding his calls. I care about Bradley, but I really feel like I'm just talking to him out of obligation lately. I managed to keep the call quick. We talked about the US election that's finally happening tomorrow. Like most Americans, Bradley's predicting violence. People are expecting it and preparing for it. That's often enough to spark the seeds.

Bradley and I also talked a bit about a journalist I used to like who recently left his job because his left-leaning editorial board wouldn't publish an article he'd written. Bradley was whining again about the left and how they cancel everything that doesn't fit with their vision of reality. I am curious to learn more about the controversy, but I don't think it's proof of this censorial left that Bradley's been going off about. I still think complaining about cancel culture is just an easy way for people to hide their discriminatory views in empty appeals to freedom.

A comedian on the radio today was talking about the US election and said that the biggest difference between now and four years ago is that people used to have a sense of humour.

"Now everyone has to be so careful about everything they say," she said, "or else they'll get cancelled!"

Everyone? Everything? This comedian must not be very creative. Either that or she's just really racist.

TUESDAY, NOVEMBER 3rd

There's been so much death in the news – the Halloween attack in Quebec City, terrorist attacks in Austria, Afghanistan, and Ethiopia, and all the stuff going on in France. I've pretty much stopped listening to the government press conferences lately but today I tuned in. Earlier this year, I couldn't get enough. Now I've had enough. Our leaders don't exactly inspire confidence or really much of anything except for racism and colonial bigotry.

In today's briefing, the premier was asked about Bill 21, the law that forbids religious people who wear head coverings or other religious symbols from working in public service and government jobs. This has mostly impacted Muslim, Sikh, and Jewish people. I think the recent terror attacks around the world have confused people into correlating religion and violence too directly again (or still). A group of Quebecers are challenging the law in court but the government maintains that a majority of people in the province support the restriction. Even if that's true, that doesn't make the law okay. Majority rule can be pretty tyrannical when the majority of people are racist.

There's another group who are actually defending the bill in court, arguing that they and their kids shouldn't be forced to encounter religion in public institutions like schools. I know teachers who wear hijabs and I've never felt like they were pushing their religious beliefs. Christianity, on the other hand, seems to be a huge part of Quebec's "secular" culture: Christmas concerts and vacation, the way we measure years starting with Jesus, even just the rationale behind having Sundays off. (Plus, the radio reminded me that the government's secularism bill doesn't forbid people from wearing small crosses.) If Bill 21 also included removing Christmas and Christian traditions from public institutions, that'd be a different story.

I turned off the radio when they started talking about the US election. I don't want to know.

WEDNESDAY, NOVEMBER 4th

This evening I'm doing a guest lecture over Zoom about my year offline. It's for a class studying young adult literature. The class is reading a YA book called *Feed* about a futuristic world where we all have social media news and advertising feeds installed directly into our brains. To prepare for the lecture, I borrowed a copy of the book and gave it a read. It's by M.T. Anderson and he wrote it way back in 2002, but anticipating smartphones and the constant connectivity that has since become normal. The story is very pessimistic and suggests that being constantly connected to a feed controlled by corporations will not end well. (Duh…)

Young adult literature has become so dystopic in the past couple decades. When I was a kid, dystopia was a fancy word that only the nerdy kids could define. Now it's become its own genre.

THURSDAY, NOVEMBER 5th

A 23-year-old university student from Nunuvik, an Indigenous community in Northern Quebec, wrote an open letter to the government asking them to clarify what steps they are taking to ensure everyone in the province can access the internet. Her letter points out that all the way back in 2016, the government had already declared that high speed internet was a basic service and essential to everyone's quality of life. Now the internet has become even more essential, and yet plenty of communities are still struggling to connect. The student who wrote the letter said that her community sometimes has no internet for days at a time. I have a feeling that the government isn't doing anything to address this. The tyranny of the majority often ignores rural and minority communities.

The 23-year-old goes to the same university as me, here in Montreal. Logging into her classes online from home would have been impossible, so she has now moved to the city to rent a place with internet access. So far, the government has not responded to the letter but she's received a lot of positive feedback over Facebook. These days, I think (hope?) that means the government will have to take action. Though it shouldn't have to take a public outcry on social media for the government to support Indigenous communities.

I heard about this whole thing on a local radio show, so I texted the host, telling her about my year offline and the challenges I've faced as a student. She texted right back and said someone from the show would be in touch to chat further. I always get nervous about sharing my experience publicly, especially with lots of strangers on the radio. But it's fun and I think it can even be important – especially if I make it about collective change and not just about myself.

FRIDAY, NOVEMBER 6th

Sitting quietly in the passenger seat, Jonas was on his phone reading about the election. There weren't any new results, but he was still scrolling. He called it "doom scrolling." I hadn't heard the term before but he said it's been all over the internet lately. I think people justify doom scrolling as if it's somehow a valid coping mechanism for anxiety or depression, especially in relation to something legitimately upsetting like the US election. Fine, justify it, but I don't think it's too different than just mindlessly scrolling through social media on any ordinary day to cope with anxiety or depression. Though I suppose people justify that too.

Does doom scrolling help people feel better? I feel like it would have the opposite effect. And even if it does help someone feel better, how does it affect their understanding of the world? I don't want to give the internet too much credit for all the bigotry and misinformation that's become more mainstream lately, but I think it's a factor. If you were a conspiracy theorist ten or twenty years ago, you were reading tabloids, and – even if they were convincing – you knew you were reading tabloids. On social media, the real stories and tabloids are all mixed together, often within the same platforms. It's not as easy to sift through the bullshit.

Just got to the cottage that Fanny and Alex rented for the four of us in Prince Edward County, halfway between Montreal and Toronto. We got here first and explored the area a bit and then came back in and tried the TV. We couldn't figure out if it was on the internet or not, so we turned it off and—

Fanny and Alex just arrived. I'll write more later.

SATURDAY, NOVEMBER 7th

Fanny and I were talking about how to resist capitalism. She says that racism, sexism, and all the isms are tricky, but capitalism's the worst. Her latest approach is to surrender to it in the ways that she and Alex find necessary – like by buying a car that can accommodate a car seat for a baby – while simultaneously trying not to replicate capitalist values – like by sharing the car with their housemates and friends.

I liked the idea of trying not to reproduce capitalism in our values or in the ways we relate to each other and the world. It's often hard though because we're so caught up. Without a smartphone, I don't carry as much capitalist potential in my pocket. Without the internet, I've managed to limit my exposure to the demands of the market even further, or rather I've made it harder for the coordinating potential of big companies to access me. Because I'm a student with government grants and family support, I can posture like I've sheltered myself from the organization of capital. If I'm being honest though, I'm pretty much as implicated as I was before. I've just gone into hiding.

★★★★★

Jonas just told me that the final results of the US election were at last announced. Other people's top reliable news sources are CNN or Twitter. Mine is Jonas.

SUNDAY, NOVEMBER 8th

I thought the weekend away with Fanny and Alex was way too quick but pretty perfect otherwise. Jonas said he enjoyed himself but I'm not sure he did. He told me that he felt like he couldn't get involved in our conversations – or even understand some of them. I noticed he was quiet, but Jonas is often quiet. He said that being with the three of us made him feel young and a bit stupid. I was really sad to hear him say that and told him so.

"I'm confident all of us love hearing your perspective when you share it," I said.

He added that he didn't like Codenames, the board game we played. He said it was too much pressure. Then he started talking about how the weekend wasn't as relaxing as he had hoped it would be and he felt like we didn't have enough space to ourselves. I felt frustrated that he was complaining about everything, especially cause I know how much he usually likes spending time with Fanny and Alex. I suggested he might be feeling down but that it's sometimes hard to tell what's causing difficult feelings.

He didn't disagree but kept going: "I don't want to upset you but I feel like you said some really mean things in front of Fanny and Alex. It felt like you were shaming me."

Jonas told me two stories from the weekend. I think one was just a misunderstanding but the other was about me criticizing him for his phone use. Fanny had asked Jonas whether the way he uses his phone had changed after we started dating and he replied that he doesn't use his phone very much. I jumped in and disagreed, suggesting that he uses his phone "a ton." I didn't think much of the conversation until Jonas told me how much it hurt him. Tech fragility is real.

I felt bad and tried to accept that I was in the wrong – I *did* call him out in front of our friends in a pretty callous way. I apologized and told him that I should have talked to him directly and privately. I told him I was glad to know I upset him so that I can act differently in the future. But I also think he was in a bad mood. Just last week I told a friend that one of the reasons I appreciate Jonas is because he's up-front when something's bothering him; I don't have to walk on eggshells and double-think things too much. Sure, he gets in bad moods, but I thought he was better at separating his mood from what's going on so he doesn't blame others when he's feeling down … unless they deserve it. Maybe I was wrong. Or maybe I'm letting myself off too easily. Even if Jonas' mood isn't as much about the way I treated him as he thinks it is, I did something mean and I should focus on that. It'll serve me better to think about how I can change than to try to rationalize why I might not need to.

I have to stop calling people out for being on their phones too much. Turns out it's really tough to do tactfully, even with people I'm close with, especially while spending a year offline.

MONDAY, NOVEMBER 9th

I heard on the radio that the most popular music video of all time on YouTube is no longer by Katy Perry, Justin Bieber, or a K-Pop group. It's a song that Jonas first told me about a few months ago when we started dating. Jonas sings it frequent-ly so it has gotten stuck in my head countless times even though I've never heard a recorded version. Jonas' rendition involves hand gestures, silly voices, and sometimes even a little dance:

"Baby shark, doo doo – doo doo doo doo, baby shark, doo doo – doo doo doo doo, baby shark, doo doo – doo doo doo doo, baby shark…"

If I had to make a list of the main things I missed out on this year because I wasn't online, the first three that come to mind are Baby Shark, Karen, and doom scrolling. I don't know whether any of these existed before this year, but none of them were on my radar. Now they're so common that they've escaped the internet and are part of offline conversations.

Karen seemed to get particularly popular this summer around the time that J. K. Rowling published that essay about why she's no longer a relevant cultural figure. Doom scrolling trended hard more recently in relation to the US election but Jonas said it first took off in March.

★★★★★

I'm not sure if it was in response to the open letter from that Indigenous student, but the federal government announced today that the internet is no longer a luxury (again) and they have pledged over a billion dollars of federal money for a Universal Broadband Fund to ensure that 98% of Canadians can access high speed internet by 2026. (Similar promises have been made every few years since 1996.)

While our prime minister makes speeches promising internet access for all, there are still communities in Canada – mostly Indigenous ones – that don't have drinkable tap water. My first instinct was that the government should prioritize water over the internet, but is it really too much to ask for both?

TUESDAY, NOVEMBER 10th
We had class presentations tonight but most of my classmates already shared recorded versions of their presentations online, which I wasn't able to access. I felt left out and a bit useless. Living offline in an online world can be frustrating. I did my presentation over the phone and shared nine reflections about the internet and what it's been like to live without it. Because I couldn't use a PowerPoint or anything, I came up with a mnemonic device to help people follow along: **M-A-I-L-M-A-I-L**: (1) the internet is **Mandatory** now, (2) we have **Agency** online, (3) the internet relies on **Interdependence**, (4) **Lots of data** is being

gathered on us that coordinate our online experiences, (5) there's a **Materiality** to virtual spaces, (6) we need and often lack **Alternatives** to big tech options, (7) we can learn from **Inconvenience** and friction, (8) being offline helped me rethink my **Life pace**, and (9) I like sending and receiving **MAIL**.

After I presented, one of my classmates asked a question that felt loaded. He said, "What do you think about people who have needed the internet to access work, education, and opportunities? People who do not have the privilege to buy paper books (which are very costly) or to depend on others for support in an increasingly digital age?"

I never suggested that people should follow my lead and abandon the internet. On the contrary, my presentation was about how much we rely on online infrastructures now in essential ways. We just have to be more careful. Like, for example, we can't assume that buying paper books will be more costly than digital alternatives, especially if we factor in environmental costs … and library cards. Also, his comment seemed to ignore how expensive electronics are.

I used to work at a school that was trying to be "paper-free" for environmental reasons, and I was the only teacher who pushed back. People forget that paper is a renewable resource. Computers aren't. And there's so much more exploitative labour associated with digital tech than with paper.

A lot of people get triggered when I share critiques of our digital lives and of how much we take tech for granted. The question my classmate asked made it seem like he wasn't listening to my presentation. Or maybe it was just tech fragility.

WEDNESDAY, NOVEMBER 11th
It's forgetting day today, the day we refuse to take up old quarrels with the foe, the day we sit for the national anthem, and feel terror and anger at the sounds of cannons and bagpipes. We need ways to pay respect to people who

fought in the world wars without normalizing the military. I tried to wear a white poppy at my last job but my boss told me to take it off.

"That's a slap in the face to veterans," he told me.

His father was a Holocaust survivor, so I respect his need to celebrate people who fought in WWII against the Nazis. But does that mean we have to celebrate the military more generally? Fighting against tyranny and injustice is good. Fighting to sustain global hegemony is evil. Fighting is not neutral. Remembrance Day takes fighting for granted, which is why I prefer to forget. Happy forgetting day.

✶✶✶✶✶

Issa phoned around noon today while I was working on a paper. My mind was deep in thought as I tried to hold a bunch of ideas in my head. I let Issa's call go to voicemail and just listened to the message. I'm sure she was mostly joking around, but her message seemed surprised. "Why didn't you answer my call? What could you possibly be doing right now that's more important than talking to me?"

Of course nothing's more important than being a good friend, but with everyone working from home, distractions and interruptions have become more common. It's harder to dive into deep concentration and get work done. Issa wouldn't call me at work, but while we're working from home, everything is permissible.

✶✶✶✶✶

Apparently it's already been around for ages but I just heard of a social media platform called Parler that's pretty much Twitter but without regulation; it doesn't censor comments that are racist, sexist, false, etc. Jonas told me that people who get banned from Twitter flock to Parler so it's a hot bed of conspiracy theories and hate. It just further silos things and provides a place for dangerous people to support each other. At the same time, I'm almost glad that people who want to be toxic have their own place to post terrible things far from the eyes and screens of the marginalized people they're posting about.

*****

Jonas and I met up with Mark and Miriam for a walk this afternoon and I told them I'd heard that Google has secret underground servers here in Montreal. Mark works for a Google-adjacent company and although he couldn't confirm or deny whether Google actually has servers here, he told me that the secrecy around their location is based on security concerns. Google frames it like they don't want people to target their infrastructure for attacks. I wonder though whether it also relates to keeping the servers secure from public scrutiny, keeping the myth of the cloud alive. If nobody knows about the physical infrastructures, it's almost like virtual spaces have no material or ecological consequences. Unfortunately, the virtual is physical – whether we see it or not.

*****

We went out to grab dinner tonight and were feeling poke bowls so walked over to a new spot that just opened by our apartment. There didn't appear to be any menus, but the guy behind the counter passed us a tablet with a menu opened on it.

"That's the internet," I said to Jonas, "Should we leave?"

Instead we just asked if we could order without using the tablet. He said sure but told us that they don't have any other menus.

"Can we just get two salmon poke bowls?" I asked.

They were delicious but very expensive. I don't think we'll be coming back.

*****

All day today I've had that "when I think about you I touch myself" song stuck in my head but I have no idea who sings it. I asked Jonas and Tyler and neither of them know the song. I'm pretty sure it's super famous but I might just be making it up. The lyrics seem ridiculous. Could it be a parody song? Earlier in my offline year, I think I would have felt frustrated about not being able to look it up but now I don't care, at least not as much. I really don't need to know who wrote the song. I'll just keep singing the one line I do know over and over again until somebody recognizes it.

THURSDAY, NOVEMBER 12th
Today we woke up to find our water's been shut off!!

I want to shower and pretty soon I'll really have to shit, but there's no water. I phoned the city (311) and spoke to a guy who said that the shut-off was planned and I'd been informed about it beforehand.

"But I wasn't," I said.

"You received a pamphlet about it," he corrected me.

"But I didn't."

⋆⋆⋆⋆⋆

One of my research teams has been working on a paper based on some research I helped collect. I'll be a co-author on the paper, so I offered to help revise it. The first author put the paper on a jump drive and gave it to me. I edited it but it took me longer than anticipated and when I texted her yesterday letting her know I was almost ready to return it, she told me that she was about to submit it.

The paper was strong but there were a few issues that I thought were important to address. I asked her to hold off and powered through the rest of the paper, finishing all my edits by about 2:30 a.m. last night/this morning. It was still pretty warm out – especially for a November evening – so I put on a toque and jacket and made the twenty minute trek over to her apartment to drop the jump drive in her mailbox. There's something magical about the city at 2:30 in the morning.

If I had been able to return the file over email, I wouldn't have needed to go for that walk last night. But if I'd been able to use email, I wouldn't have gotten to go for that walk last night.

✶✶✶✶✶

This year's Massey Lectures on CBC radio are about the internet and how we've lost control of new technologies. Ron Deibert, the lecturer, believes that our devices are intentionally addictive. He suggests that free choice is incompatible with compulsively using our phones, especially considering the personalized, algorithmic influence that tech platforms are trying to have over us as we use their apps or websites.

I mostly agree with Deibert but wonder why I've managed to retain choice in a tech landscape plagued with highly sophisticated "psyops," as Deibert calls them. Is it because I love to disagree? My first word was "no." And as a gay Jew growing up in a straight Christian world, I've often found myself bucking popular trends or questioning things that others take for granted. But I also know plenty of gay Jews who are glued to their devices without a whiff of criticality or disdain.

Could it be that I used tech too much when I was younger so that I got sick of it? Or maybe I have such a comfortable amount of privilege that I don't feel the need to take advantage of new technologies? I'm sure it's some combination of these things – mixed in with something personal and spontaneous that's not so structurally determined. Though that might be giving myself too much credit.

✶✶✶✶✶

Leah called from Hungary where she's doing an artist residency. We were catching up and chatting about this and that when she got serious. She told me a story about a friend of hers who has been upset by all the content Leah's posting on Instagram from Budapest. She told Leah that she couldn't help comparing herself to Leah's posts.

Leah told me that she'll be more careful now with what she's posting so as not to upset her friend. I was a bit harsh,

270

but told her I don't think she should moderate her content if she thinks this friend is being unfair. Leah agreed with me, but said she's still going to post less for a bit. I probably would too.

⋆⋆⋆⋆⋆

Bradley called again this evening and I didn't pick up. I don't feel like having someone rant at me about things I don't agree with. And I don't have the energy to defend myself against ideas that seem selfish. (Is that selfish?) Bradley left a really long voicemail and then sent a text telling me not to phone him back but to listen to his message. I was worried it would be something dramatic and it was, but as a joke (I think). His message started like this:

"Aron, do not think that your disengagement from the internet and your avoidance of my calls can stop the on-slaught of attention-seeking from me 'cause *I will* be heard *via* voicemail *every* time you don't answer. And no you will *not* need a notification when I have posted a new photo and no, you will *not* know about my upcoming events… *You cannot escape the annoyance that is being engaged with oth-er people.* That has been my purpose during this year of all these calls, annoyances. It is to remind you that *we,* the pub-lic, the acquaintances and friends you have met along the way, *we* are still here to annoy you, and we *will* do so. Let the record stand, these calls *will not cease.* Read my lips; this un-checked aggression *will not stand.* You think you can draw a line in the sand between digital realms and the analog, but it is *all for nothing.* For you will die one day and I will make a Facebook post about it and get lots of sympathy attention from people that kinda knew we were friends and stuff. *And* uhhh yea, you're gonna be a part of it. You will be complicit in your death on my social media engagement. I might even start a page for you, post mortem, so we may post pictures of you as a college student and uhh, post them again the next year and every year from then on. You *will* be immortalized in the internet realm is what I'm trying to tell you, whether you like it or not. [Long pause.] I'm running out of juice on this bit, but I need to leave you a full voicemail because that's part of the annoyance, so uhhhh I'm gonna keep going. 'Cause this is the age where we just keep going…"

It goes on from there for another five minutes but I can't be bothered to transcribe the rest. I appreciate Bradley's metaphor about the way his annoying role in my life has been like the outlandish opinions hurled at users on the internet, but I don't think the reality of our friendship is anywhere near as deep. He's come up with a fancy and poetic rationale for why I'm screening his calls because he can't accept that I don't want to talk to him if he's going to argue against anti-racism protesters or public health advice. I feel like by simply giving him an audience for his new conservative beliefs, I'm validating them. So my new strategy is just not being willing to listen.

✶✶✶✶✶

Jonas' mom told him that she's been trying not to shop on Amazon because of what she learned from me about the company's ties to ICE and the US military. She said she's committed to avoiding Amazon for all of her Christmas shopping. I know changing one person's relationship to Amazon doesn't do much, but I can't help feeling good about it.

FRIDAY, NOVEMBER 13th
Why am I spending a year offline? I get asked this question a lot and I always answer it differently. I don't know if I have a single, honest answer. Sometimes I talk about my experience as a teacher, working with teenagers whose phones seemed like extensions of their bodies. Other times I contrast my early adoption of internet technologies with my tech-skepticism these past few years. But neither of these origin stories are very honest.

One possible trigger goes back three years when Hanni told me about a blog post he read. The author suggested that every Google search uses the same amount of energy as boiling a quarter-cup of water. The claim was backed by a technical explanation but it was self-admittedly a rough estimate that Google later defended themselves against. Regardless of the amount of energy used by a Google search, there was something radical about even acknowledging that doing something simple online – something we take for granted as harmless, something we do countless times every day – has a material impact in the physical world.

I started telling everyone about the idea and most people were surprised, even defensive. I realized that many of my friends assumed that things they did online had no physical or ecological consequence. I think this is changing now, albeit slowly. Today, in the fourth instalment of this year's Massey Lectures, Deibert claimed that sending 65 emails uses the same amount of energy as driving a car one kilometre. It's not a ton of energy, but it adds up.

One of the reasons I wanted to spend this year offline was to bring attention to the energy and resources that go into the internet. Not as if going offline will solve the climate crisis – I realize that the material impact of my year offline is negligible. However, I hope my project has more symbolic potential; if more people critically reflect on the environmental cost of using the internet, we can change the system in ways that will change everyone's habits.

Beyond the environmental consequences, Deibert's lecture tonight was also about the conditions for workers involved with the mining, manufacturing, and disposal of materials used in digital technologies. There are endless examples of dangerous working conditions, armed conflict, and systematic exploitation – mostly in the Global South. How do we continue to justify our digital luxuries even as we learn about the brutal imbalance between those of us who benefit from these globalized supply chains and the people who struggle so we might have these benefits?

Deibert worries that the impacts of digital technologies threaten our "survival as a species." I agree, but would add that the negative aspects of tech do not impact all Homo sapiens equally. People like me benefit from digital tools at the expense of others in ways that reflect and exacerbate historical power imbalances. So people like me have to give up these benefits and support something different.

✶✶✶✶✶

I hate finding return-to-sender letters in my mailbox. I got another one returned today. It was from a friend in Chicago. Did he move? I know I'm not the centre of anyone else's world, but it's frustrating he didn't tell me after I put in the work of sending him a letter. Everyone's so used to everything being online, automated, outsourced, as if nothing matters when the labour is hidden. Out of sight, out of mind. And to be honest, if it was just an email that had bounced back, I probably wouldn't feel so annoyed. But that's just because I'm selfish and ignoring all the work that goes on behind the screen.

✶✶✶✶✶

I got a text from one of my ex-students today who lives down the street. She asked whether I could hear "the helicopter" from my place. I realized I *could* hear a helicopter, so I asked what was going on.

"10–12 people are being held hostage at a big gaming company, and the rest of the employees are stuck on the roof."

I texted a couple friends who work in the tech world here in Montreal and asked whether they knew anything. Tyler had already heard the story but didn't know details. Hanni hadn't heard and was a bit shook. Tech companies are known for expecting their employees to work more than is healthy, and this particular company has an especially bad reputation for that. They're also notorious for having some toxic misogynists in leadership positions.

I could still hear the helicopter when Jonas read on Twitter that it was all a hoax. Someone called in a fake threat to fuck with the company. The Twitterers called it "Swatting."

I've heard the term before but only in relation to gamers pulling misogynistic pranks where they get the SWAT team called on women who threaten their toxically masculine gamer spaces. It's definitely good to hear that it was just a troll and not a real hostage situation, but there's probably still a political message in there somehow. Or, as Hanni suggested, it might just be someone who really didn't like the new *Assassin's Creed*.

★★★★★

My supervisor spent a day offline and texted me about her experience:

"My 24 hours internet free prompted me to seek pleasure rather than distraction. What do I actually want and need right now to find happiness if I can't simply distract myself by checking my email, news, etc."

Of course pleasure and distraction aren't opposites and often overlap, but it sounds like spending a day offline made Aviva realize that the internet is often a distraction in her life, and not something she connects with pleasure.

Jonas' brother also tried spending some time offline recently and told us that he lasted a whole weekend. He constantly found himself reaching for his phone and remembering that he didn't have it on him.

"It felt like I had ADD," he said.

SUNDAY, NOVEMBER 15th

An old friend from Vancouver popped into my head today. We'd lost touch, but I still have his number in my phone. I sent him a text and he called back immediately. We started chatting and I told him I was spending the year offline.

"But then how did you text me?" he asked.

"I'm still using my phone," I explained, "Just no internet."

"Ohhh," he said, "When you said you were going offline, I thought you meant, like, all the way."

I explained that text messaging is not online, and said something about how people often forget that distinction because WhatsApp and iMessage look so similar to text messages—

"I know the difference between texting and the internet, Aron," he said, interrupting me, "I just meant that I thought you were, like, fully going offline, like 'off-grid' style."

I was surprised to find myself feeling defensive, but I let him win. "Yeah," I said, "I don't think I could manage that."

"What you're doing is still cool though," he assured me.

I'm starting to remember why we lost touch.

MONDAY, NOVEMBER 16th

I'm having a phone interview for a local radio show at 5:43 p.m. and I'm nervous!! They want me to talk about my year offline but I'm planning to mostly focus on the importance of internet access now that it's essential for so many aspects of life. And I want to try to stress that we have agency as internet users, sometimes as individuals and always as collectives. We are the internet and although it's getting harder and harder to navigate the sophisticated and hidden strategies keeping us online and on certain platforms, we can be part of the movement to make the internet more user-centred, equitable, and sustainable.

Let's see how that goes live on the radio. I just have to keep breathing and hope my subconscious takes care of the rest.

✶✶✶✶✶

I was way more nervous than I expected but the interview went well. It was a rush! I talked steadily for seventeen minutes and didn't give the interviewer much time to interject or ask questions. She didn't seem to mind.

✶✶✶✶✶

I saw a friend today who's trying to design a VR game where players battle to the death on pirate ships. He told me his theory about the future of gaming, that in the next five years all the big video game consoles will *only* be accessible online.

"You won't buy the new Xbox or PS16; you'll just connect directly to the internet."

The more the materiality of the internet gets hidden, the more likely we are to ignore its consequences, diving deeper into a virtual interface that doesn't care about the world crumbling around it. The future is looking more and more like *The Matrix*.

★★★★★

Tonight was the last instalment of the Massey Lectures, and Deibert tried to suggest how we can move forward as a society considering all the problems with the internet. He discussed "retreat" – like what I've done by spending a year offline – as "undesirable and futile." Fair. I also don't think abandoning the internet solves its problems. Instead, Deibert recommends a "reset," an internet reform based on restraint.

He shared all sorts of recommendations for building in overarching restraints or safeguards but they all rely on massive changes in political will. His lecture can be part of that, but his proposed changes didn't satisfy my desire for some practical steps to compel people in positions of power to do the reset he believes is needed. The idea of a reset makes sense to me. My offline project was meant to be a kind of personal reset. I just don't see that kind of thing happening with political leaders who are beholden to tech lobbyists and industry partners.

Astra Taylor, one of the people commenting throughout Deibert's lecture, suggested that if we reform tech companies and infrastructures, we need to choose which parts to socialize or make public (like utilities), which parts to democratize, and which parts to abolish. Again, this doesn't help me see how ordinary people might compel government or industry to reform, but I like the idea. She gave some examples of how she sees her model working: Facebook could be made public, Uber or car share companies could be democratized with unions, and she thinks that certain data gathering practices should be abolished. But how do we get there?

When people ask me that question, I tell them to avoid big tech monopolies and support companies that are trying to be more responsible, or I suggest that they try not to use the internet all the time, especially when they don't need it. More importantly though, I advocate for looking beyond personal heroics at solutions that are ordinary and collaborative. The biggest changes will be through community organizing and activism: getting involved with grassroots efforts to empower marginalized communities, to encourage critical education or art-making, to work for data justice and the regulation of big tech, or to challenge exploitative labour conditions and ecological degradation.

I think this answer is decent but it still feels forced, like I'm trying to be optimistic and hopeful despite everything. Still, giving up is even less likely to make a difference.

✶✶✶✶✶

I just got a beautiful handwritten letter in the mail from my old dance teacher. She started the letter with, "Dear Brave Aron."

I laughed and showed it to Jonas.

"Do you consider yourself brave?" he asked.

"No," I said, "I consider myself lucky."

TUESDAY, NOVEMBER 17th

Overheard on the radio: "I don't believe in cancel culture. I believe in consequence culture."

✶✶✶✶✶

My university announced that their men's sports teams will now be called the "Red Birds" instead of the racist "Red Men" name that Indigenous students and their allies had been protesting for years. It's good news, but the name of the university is still honouring an enslaver who made his fortune as a result of unpaid labour. What's worse, a racial slur ("Red Men") or honouring an enslaver? That's not a useful question to think through; they're both fucked. A better question is how can we use what we learned from the anti-"Red Men" campaign to organize against the university's name and towards a more inclusive, less racist campus.

✦✦✦✦✦

Just got a phone call from another radio show. They broadcast throughout the province and after hearing my interview yesterday, they want to have me on their show this afternoon. I don't feel as nervous this time, but I'm still excited. These interviews are like a mix of improv and a lecture. Stress, as terrible as it feels, helps me prepare.

✦✦✦✦✦

The interview went really smoothly. I talked to a couple friends afterwards who even thought it was pre-recorded. I didn't feel calm, so I'm glad to hear I came across that way. I think my autopilot is a bit more capable than my conscious self.

There were two … *incidents* though. The first was when the radio host asked me something about Christmas – how was I buying gifts without the internet? I told him I was Jewish. (Awkward silence.) I know it wasn't personal, but casual white supremacy is always a bit awkward.

The other incident was when he explained that the radio switchboards used to be analog but nowadays they're all online. He asked if he had just spoiled my internetless year by having me on his show. Luckily my brain thought to use the question as an opportunity to discuss how much the internet spills into all parts of life now and how difficult it is to distinguish online and offline spaces. We can't just run away from the problems of the internet by running away from the internet.

Jonas was listening in the other room and when I finished, he ran in to give me a hug. He said the interview went very well, and it felt really good to see him so excited for me.

It reminded me of how excited I got when he passed his grad school exams. It's like we've started to meld together. Soon we'll be telepathic.

✦✦✦✦✦

Bradley phoned again today. I hadn't called him back since that intense voicemail. He called right before the interview and I just picked up to explain why I was busy. Then, when I called him back afterwards, he told me that he had found the radio station online and listened to the whole thing.

"You killed it," he said, and he sounded genuinely happy for me.

It's hard to feel resentful against a friend who's feeling proud of you. We ended up having a casual call that felt like the old days.

✦✦✦✦✦

For class tonight, there were a few presentations that some of my classmates had prerecorded and shared with the class online. We were expected to have listened to them in advance. I didn't ask them to, but Sabrina and Anne dropped them off for me on a USB stick yesterday. It was a nice surprise, even if it meant that I actually had to do the work.

Overall the class was fine, but I got bored at some point and started sending someone a text on the same phone I was using to call into class. I didn't realize it but I wasn't muted and Sabrina texted to let me know that I was making "noisy texting noises." I was pretty embarrassed and remuted my phone immediately. I'm not sure how many of my classmates noticed, and I asked Sabrina how she knew it was me.

"Well," she said, "I don't think anybody else's phones have buttons on them."

WEDNESDAY, NOVEMBER 18th
It's below freezing out but there were still a bunch of people walking around when I went over to Memo's earlier. Memo broke up with his girlfriend again. This is the second time

now, so I imagine it'll stick. We met by his place and went to the couscous restaurant we like. I think they have other things, but Memo and I always just get stewed vegetables with couscous. It's the perfect thing for a chilly day, especially when you have to eat outside. Memo didn't seem too upset about the break up but he was glad to see me. Now that he's single again, the prospect of winter coming must be a bit terrifying, but it's probably better to be alone and lonely than snuggling with someone you don't enjoy being with. (Probably.)

✦✦✦✦✦

Bradley called again today and our conversation was not pleasant. He was going off about free speech and social media. He doesn't think it's fair that right wing conspiracy theorists are being silenced.

"Even if they're publishing things about the Sandy Hook kids being actors, they still shouldn't be kicked off of all the major platforms," he said.

I've brought it up before, but I still don't think Bradley understands who "free speech" is for.

"People are responsible for what they say," I said.

Bradley laughed as if I was being ridiculous. He's thinking of making an account on Parler. He believes the internet shouldn't be regulated.

"That was the whole dream!"

I agree that the internet shouldn't be centralized or rely on a few big tech monopolies, but I definitely think it needs to be regulated.

THURSDAY, NOVEMBER 19th
I had a disturbing dream last night that seemed to go on and on and on. I was trapped and lost in a really confusing subway system and I was being asked to sacrifice myself for a friend. However, I was hesitant to go through with the self-sacrifice because I would only have one opportunity to do it and I had some other friends with me that I knew I'd

rather kill myself for. While trying to sort out the dilemma, I was also trying to get somewhere, so I kept getting on and off subway trains, but I just got more and more lost. I'd exit the trains and study the big maps that were posted around the stations, but it didn't help. The dream didn't resolve, and I was never able to figure out how to get where I was going. And then I woke up.

I'm still feeling unsettled, like I need to figure out what the dream means and why I was so lost.

I heard on the radio that the government is moving school online again for a few weeks after Christmas and gently suggesting that employers try to allow people to work from home, if possible. One reporter asked how students without a digital device or a good wifi connection will keep up while classes are online, and the premier claimed that they've already provided tablets to every high school student who needs one (I don't think this is true) and that elementary school students aren't really able to use devices on their own, so they don't need one. It was a disappointing answer. The whole thing is grim.

FRIDAY, NOVEMBER 20th
Just got home from buying Cary a couple birthday presents. For the last three years I've given him books. This year it was a child's guide to anarchy and a Black Panther graphic novel. Every woke 7-year-old needs at least some anarchic and anti-racist literature on their shelf.

SATURDAY, NOVEMBER 21st
I'm feeling a bit off finally. Yesterday and today I've been irritable, anxious, lethargic, and my teeth have started to hurt. Everyone else has been pretty down too. I guess I didn't want to miss out.

*****

Yesterday Jonas told me that his brother's girlfriend's grandfather died. Today though, he came back to life! Not really: the hospital miscommunicated his condition and told the family he had died when he had actually just been moved into the intensive care unit. For 24 hours, everyone was devastated! Even his wife thought he was dead, and the family was in mourning. Now, they're all relieved, though I'm sure a bit frustrated by the confusion and still concerned.

MONDAY, NOVEMBER 23rd
Earlier, Jonas was cutting bagels to make us some tuna sandwiches for lunch, and he broke both the bagels.

"Jonas! You have to be more patient when slicing bagels!"

He got defensive and said, "I didn't break them on purpose!"

I'm probably not mad at Jonas, but it feels like it.

TUESDAY, NOVEMBER 24th
I was supposed to see Tyler later but when I told him I wouldn't be free until after class at 8:30, he cancelled. Tyler and I often change our plans at the last minute, but I was annoyed he didn't explain what was up. He and his girlfriend broke up recently so partially I wanna be able to be there for him, but I've also come to rely on him. I think I depend on socializing more than most people, at least more than Jonas. If I don't get enough, I feel claustrophobic and irritable. Having Jonas around fulfills part of that social need, but if I only socialize with him, I start to get negative or annoyed by little things.

At the moment, Leah and Hanni are out of town, Sloane's all the way in Verdun, Niko has a new girlfriend, Leila disappeared, and Darren's out of the picture – I don't have too many friends nearby left.

I want to see faces. I want to walk beside bodies.

This is going to be a hard winter.

I feel a bit silly about being so dramatic earlier. After going on a big walk and meeting one of my classmates for a coffee and joint, I feel much better. Socializing and exercise and drugs – the magical trifecta.

When I got home, Jonas was in a sour mood, but I just went into the other room.

✳✳✳✳✳

I ended up seeing Tyler tonight after all! I've gotta stop getting so thrown off when plans shift. He texted during class and we went for a walk afterwards. I asked why he had thought he wouldn't be able to meet and he explained that he had gone to see his ex to return some of her stuff and thought he wouldn't feel up to seeing anyone after. But he wasn't feeling too down after all, so he texted.

I remember walking across the train tracks, but I can't remember what we talked about. I remember I felt comfortable, like it didn't matter what I said or whether I said anything at all. I remember being surprised by how warm I felt despite how chilly it was outside.

Right before we parted ways, we saw a crowd of Chasidic men packing into two yellow school buses. There was a cop car behind them and when the buses pulled away, the cop car followed. Where were they going?

WEDNESDAY, NOVEMBER 25th

I've been having trouble staying in touch with Leila, even though she lives in Montreal and not even that far away. I think she's having a tough time, and her baby is just one so I'm sure that's taking a lot of her energy. But I don't really know because she never picks up my calls. A couple weeks ago, she did call me back and left a message about how much she misses me, but when I returned her call, she didn't answer. I left a message, but I didn't hear back. I don't want to be too pushy but I also don't want to abandon my friend, so I texted her a haiku:

quiet quarantine
cabin fever but cozy
'til the feathers fall

Leila responded with a poem of her own, but no further message:

a day again
some mandarins here some peeled some not but who remembers anything anymore
tea is ready

From Leila's poem I gather that she's feeling the monotony of isolation but still indulging in small pleasures, like mandarin oranges and tea. Now I want to try to phone her and find out how she's doing more explicitly, but I think I should just appreciate that I got a response at all. Sometimes it's easier to talk around things than to face them head on.

★★★★★

Bradley phoned again today, but I didn't pick up. I'm okay with talking to him once in a while, but he just doesn't seem to get the hint that I don't want to chat all the time.

★★★★★

I've been keeping a list of the movies and TV shows that people have told me to watch this year while I've been offline. January is going to be a busy month…

Movies:
- American Utopia
- Palm Beach
- Borat 2
- Bringing out the Dead
- Keeping Mum
- Downhill
- Hellboy

- The Trip
- Idle Hands
- Eurovision Song Contest
- My Architect
- Queen of Versailles
- Knives Out
- Kajillionaire
- Hausu
- nîpawistamâsowin: We Will Stand Up
- Blood Quantum
- Candyman
- Judy
- Evil Dead
- Boys in the Band
- Addam's Family Values
- Soapdish

TV Shows:
- How to with John Wilson
- Making It
- The Dana Carvey Show
- The Politician
- I Am Not Okay with This
- Ramy
- Feel Good
- The Midnight Gospel
- The Great
- Dave
- I May Destroy You
- Upload
- The Dragon Prince
- The Queen's Gambit
- Moonbase 8
- Unorthodox
- Unlisted
- Ratched
- Lovecraft Country

- Good Girls
- Pen15
- Frontier
- War of the Worlds
- Nip/Tuck
- The Crown
- Watchmen
- The Unicorn
- Baroness von Sketch Show

★★★★★

Bradley just called again and I didn't answer again. This time he left a voicemail:

"Aron, I just want you to know that your year offline is not only ableist, it's completely racist, because there are plenty of minorities that – that – that would kill a white person to have internet. The fact that you as a white person are rejecting yourrrr privilege is frankly insulting and racist and ableist, ageist, and probably sexist, uhhhh, uhhhmm, communist, there's something communist about it, fascist probably, probably a little bit—"

I didn't phone Bradley back but I texted him, letting him know that I had transcribed his voicemail in my journal. I said I'd call him another day when I'm not as busy. I know I'm not really super busy today but I know I would be annoyed if I had to spend 45 minutes listening to Bradley rant about America and the end of the world.

FRIDAY, NOVEMBER 27th

I think I know myself pretty well but then sometimes the strangest things make me cry. Like this morning, a line from Leanne Simpson's new book got me and I didn't even see it coming.

One of the characters was rejecting the idea of calling people out (or in):

"Calls should be whispers. The only one you can hold accountable is yourself. That really is your only job."

I don't know why I appreciated the line enough to cry. I could just be feeling low. I worry about the world but pretend I'm apart from it. So maybe I'm finally breaking through, joining in. It's weird that this is the line that made me tear up though. It's really plain and I'm not even sure I agree with the last part. But that's the part that catches me every time.

"That really is your only job."

SATURDAY, NOVEMBER 28th

I had another internet nightmare last night, but I didn't even use the internet this time – I just really wanted to. Somehow that was terrifying enough. When I woke up, I still felt stressed, but I had no interest in going online.

✦✦✦✦✦

One of my classmates mailed me an article about Foxconn and it made me feel angry and sad. We shouldn't be living like this, embracing digital conveniences that are only possible because of exploitative labour, mass suicides. It's sick to accept computers as mandatory and somehow just stomach the reality of how they come into our lives. But even if I only buy refurbished or second-hand electronics, what about everyone else? "The only one you can hold accountable is yourself." I've been stuck on the idea all day and keep repeating it in my head. It makes me feel hopeless … and relieved.

The only one I can hold accountable is myself.

MONDAY, NOVEMBER 30th

I was trying to make a list of all the platforms and digital portals I've been asked to use since I started grad school. So far I've come up with Minerva, MyCourses, MyProgress, YouTube, uApply, WorkDay, Outlook, Slack, Kahoot, Moodle, Doodle, Perusall, Survey Monkey, Google Docs, Google Scholar, Google Meet, One Drive, Microsoft Teams, Twitter, Nvivo, Trello, Zotero, Endnote, Padlet, Whiteboard, Jamboard, JSTOR, Prezi, Skype, and Zoom…

The list reads almost as a satire, especially since I'm making it after spending the better part of a year offline, but it's real.

★★★★★

Over a month ago, the red and yellow flowers on our front porch started to bloom again and I thought it was futile, that they'd soon be wiped out by frost. I remember Jonas and I laughing as we walked past.

"Silly little flowers. Don't they know it's too late to bloom?"

It's the end of November now and the flowers are still alive. Who's laughing now? They reached maturity and some are even over-ripe, withering from old age instead of the weather. They lived their whole lives with the precarity of winter threatening to fall on them at any moment.

I can learn something from these flowers; as long as we have the chance of blooming, there's no need to be so fatalistic.

December

Often remembered as people who were out of touch and hated technology, the Luddites were actually protesting the social costs of technological "progress" that the working class was being forced to accept.
– Ruha Benjamin, 2019, *Race After Technology*

TUESDAY, DECEMBER 1st

A letter arrived today from the teacher I trained under as a student teacher. She's in her 60s but claimed she'd only written five letters in her lifetime. I was touched I made her shortlist.

She started by writing about some of the things the internet has given her. But then she asked, "At what price? I sold my soul many times over, letting relationships, social responsibilities, and higher purpose go. I was a Borg with the drive of a Faust."

She went on, "Emotionally, I have created a lovely padded cell – perhaps a truckstop in a faded picture. I see you as the 'other' – removed, defiant, at times anxious, fearful, but always thinking, feeling, seeing, and imagining alternatives – a delightful phoenix, a tentative Adam, one small step for all kind."

I got a rush reading her letter but then started to feel that gross dread feeling when I thought about how close I am to being back online. I think I've actually been the one in the lovely padded cell this year – removed, defiant. I have more anxiety about going back on the internet than I did about getting off it.

★★★★★

I have the final online class of my offline year this evening. Next semester, classes will still be online, but I'll be online too, so things will be different, or normal? I'm tempted to still just call into classes but I don't think I'll be allowed to. I mean, I doubt there's an official rule or anything but it's almost like we have to use digital technologies if we can. There's no question of whether we *should* use them or what their consequences might be.

★★★★★

Bradley has phoned me three times now in the past three days and I haven't answered. I'm not trying to cut him out of my life, but I don't want to talk to him every day.

WEDNESDAY, DECEMBER 2nd

I think and I hope that my practice this year – developing practices that don't involve the internet – will carry over into my online life. I realize though that most people I know have been getting deeper into online practices this year and in January I might want to join in, or feel like I have to.

★★★★★

Jonas' mom sent me a Christmas gift, more than one actually, so I went out and bought her something – the new Leanne Simpson book that I raced through last week. Drawn & Quarterly has this deal where if you buy five or more copies of the same book (and say it's for a book club), they give you a 10% discount. So I bought four extra copies of the book and I'll give them to other people as gifts. I'm not going to frame them as Chanukah/Christmas presents though. I don't want to set any dangerous precedents.

I've missed out on seeing a lot of the people I love this year. Being offline probably also made me feel a bit further away. Buying and sending people books somehow seems like a decent alternative to being able to visit. And yea, I suppose I lied to the bookstore to get 10% off, but ideally I'd like to have conversations with Jonas' mom and my friends about the book. Isn't that book club enough for a discount?

Jonas and I discussed whether we would do gifts with each other for the holidays and at first decided against it. I don't usually do gifts and Jonas has been very critical of consumerism lately. A few hours later though, Jonas suggested that we each do just one nice gift for each other. Christmas is important to him and gift-giving has always been an important part of his Christmas. I agreed. I even got excited as my brain started to think about what Jonas might appreciate and how I can get things without using the internet.

A couple hours later, as I was working in the other room, he popped his head in and added that we're also doing stockings – as if that was a given. I got him to explain what that entails and it turns out I have to get him four or five gifts, beyond just the one nice one.

"They don't have to be anything expensive," he explained, "just no junk."

What have I gotten myself into?

✷✷✷✷✷

Someone from YouTube Canada was on the radio sharing highlights from this year's top videos, as viewed by Canadians. I was surprised by the top hit. With 49 million views, it was some guy's squirrel-proof bird feeder. I thought it sounded stupid, but Jonas rushed to find and watch it. He wore headphones and was totally engrossed. And it was long! When it was over, he tried to explain why he liked it, but I think it's one of those things you have to see for yourself. That being said, I'm not adding it to my list of things to watch next year.

THURSDAY, DECEMBER 3rd
There's a story on the radio about a new law that's been proposed in the US to stop the import of goods made by Uighur Muslims in forced labour camps in China. Sounds good, but

there's a but. Despite bipartisan support, companies like Apple, Nike, and Coca-Cola are trying to water down the legislation so that they can continue to use the Uighur labour … or so they won't be penalized if they "accidentally" do. I know these companies are evil, but this goes beyond even my expectations. Uighur Muslims are facing a genocide but *we need our iPhones and Air Jordans.*

This is normal.

As soon as I heard the story, I texted a bunch of friends about it – including my supervisor. I don't know what that'll do, but people need to know. I know it's not so simple, but how can such evil continue if we know we're complicit?

I got a bunch of responses. Some of my friends had already heard. Aviva was the most shocked, adding that she hadn't heard of the Uighur forced labour camps before. My friend who works in finance replied that Apple stock has gone up 100% this year. He jokingly suggested that using forced labour is "good, duh." Although I suppose he wasn't totally joking.

Omar had a similar response: "Yeeeeh, yeah, they are fucked up," he wrote, "But they are part of my portfolio so I hope they do well."

I couldn't help but bring up the Holocaust and wrote back, "It's like if we were buying things made in Auschwitz, but we're all like, 'but come on, have you seen these savings?'"

Omar replied, "The issue is that they are ALL like that."

I knew what he was trying to say, but I got defensive and ranted back, "They're all bad, but not like this. This is forced labour and genocide!"

Omar didn't respond, so a few minutes later I softened my tone. "Anyway, I'm not trying to hate on you. I just sometimes get these waves of overwhelmedness about how casually evil we are."

Eventually Omar wrote back, "I don't have a stock portfolio, Aron! Who do you think I am?!!"

Turns out he was joking.

★★★★★

Bradley phoned again this evening. He's relentless! And the call wasn't very pleasant. He was eager to tell me about coming across a dead guy with his girlfriend on the side of the road in Mexico last weekend.

"We got there even before the police," he bragged.

Other than that, I just felt goaded into conversations I didn't want to have. After he told me the Mexico story, I asked whether there were still lots of people from California crossing the border. He said that the state's health authorities don't recommend it but did his little rant again about how our individual actions don't make a difference and the government has too much control. Then I did my little rant to counter his, and it all felt aggravating and futile and I didn't want to keep talking.

Our actions *do* have consequences. Small changes *do* make differences. Different people are situated differently to make changes, but our actions matter. We just have to figure out how to change our actions, and how to change them collectively.

FRIDAY, DECEMBER 4th
A silverfish just crawled out of my laptop!! EW!

SUNDAY, DECEMBER 6th
Cary's birthday was exhausting. It was lovely – with a treasure hunt, a piñata, and home-smoked pulled pork – but Cary has an endless amount of energy and we had to play with him for six hours straight. He particularly likes Jonas and chose him to be on his team for everything. I was a tiny bit jealous, but mostly just glad that Cary approves of my choice in men.

AJ updated us on Cary's school situation. He's enrolled in the public school's remote learning program now, which involves online classes for three hours a day, four times a week. Cary didn't seem too excited about it when I asked him, but he does seem to be getting a lot better at reading. When I was Cary's age, I was already reading but it might be harder when you're bilingual. Or when your school's been disrupted and you're learning to read on an iPad.

It was late when we finally got home and Jonas was quiet.

"Everything okay?"

"Yeah, just tired."

"You sure?

He looked lost for a moment and then admitted he was feeling a bit overwhelmed. He stressed that he really appreciated getting to spend time with my family but that it was a lot.

As we discussed the afternoon, our conversation tumbled into something about Jonas hardly knowing anyone here except through me, that our schedules are too different lately, that we haven't been connecting enough. I was a bit taken aback but brought up how much mood can affect perspective and how hard it must be to spend time with my family when his is so far away.

"But I feel like we *have* been connecting," I insisted, "though I know that isn't something I can decide on my own."

While we were talking and listening to each other, I turned on the bath. It fills slowly and by the time it was ready, we didn't have much left to say. We got in the tub together and smoked a joint, mostly in silence. I was feeling a bit down, but small pleasures still feel oh so sweet.

TUESDAY, DECEMBER 8th

So many people just text emojis now, without messages – especially as replies to questions or to finish conversations on a cute note. My phone doesn't have data, so it registers emojis as empty rectangular boxes. I end up having to respond, "Sorry, that didn't show up on my phone. What were you trying to say?" Or I just imagine what the emoji might have been.

I do have some friends who've been more conscious of

the fact that my phone doesn't get emojis. They still insist on using them, but they write them out in words: "shy face emoji," "hug emoji," "eye-rolling emoji," "laughing cat emoji," or as Jonas texted me today when I told him I was on my way home, "gif of me dancing on ceiling." I also have a couple friends who write out their own cute little emojis that just involve punctuation. ^_^ It's a dying art. 8==>-----

WEDNESDAY, DECEMBER 9th

I bought Jonas his Christmas gift today, an electric keyboard so that we can finally play music together. It's a selfish gift, because I've been wanting someone to jam with, but I know Jonas misses playing piano, so hopefully he'll appreciate it too.

Normally, I'd look on Craigslist or Kijiji but instead I went to a couple of pawn shops in the neighbourhood. Keyboards are more expensive than I expected. Most of them were between $500–$1000. I only wanted to spend $100–$200.

The one I ending up buying seems decent. It was snowing out so I had to cover it in garbage bags to get it home. Now I've hidden it in the closet. However, once I wrap it and put it under the tree, it'll be pretty obvious what it is. There aren't many other things shaped like a keyboard.

✶✶✶✶✶

WARNING! We had the TV on while we were eating lunch and a warning flashed across the screen. Jonas' phone buzzed at the same time. WARNING! WARNING! WARNING! I looked at my phone, but there was nothing. No warning, no concern for me, no fear. Why didn't I get a message? I have a Montreal area code. Is it because my phone's not connected to the internet? I assumed I was still being tracked regardless, but maybe my phone doesn't have the location services feature that the government's using to determine who gets the warning message? I'm not complaining, but part of me would like to be included in the government's emergency alert system.

*****

I spoke with Fanny and her belly bump is finally showing. Her anxiety's been really overwhelming so she's started meeting with a pre-natal psychiatrist and is already feeling a bit better.

I had to cut the conversation short to join the quarterly meeting for one of the research teams I'm on. Painful call. It took a while to get started because half the team thought the meeting was on Google Meet and the other half thought Zoom. (I was just phoning in.)

Before I knew what was happening, everyone was crying and thanking the team leader for "hand picking" each of the "fabulous" team members who will "change the world." It was pretty cringey. We're just developing an app! At least no one could see me rolling my eyes.

*****

I went for a walk with Tyler and saw a guy using a payphone. It didn't strike me as odd until I was walking home later and noticed the same guy, still talking on the same payphone. I don't know if it's just a Montreal thing, but there are still a lot of payphones and plenty of people using them. Who are these people? How many Montrealers don't have cellphones?

THURSDAY, DECEMBER 10th

Just walked up to the Mile End to get bagels with my cousins. The first thing Cary said when I met up with them was, "Where's Jonas?"

"He's working," I said.

Cary proceeded to mope down the sidewalk for the next ten minutes. Eventually he got bored of sulking and joined our conversation. We were talking about the internet, of course. AJ likes to tease people to show his love and he was joking that the person interviewing me on the radio must have thought my project was a "stupid waste of time."

I gave him a look but didn't respond.

"Do you think the expectations people have for you are going to change in January?" AJ asked.

"Absolutely, yeah," I said, "Yesterday I had a call with one of my research teams and three people separately made comments about how much more I'll be able to be involved next year. One woman – probably the oldest member of the group – told everyone how excited she is to be able to email me again so we can get going on a paper we've been discussing. I didn't say anything, but couldn't we have already been working on the paper? How did she collaborate with people before the internet?"

"It sounds like some people have been giving you a break this year?"

"Some people," I agreed. "But I—"

AJ cut in, "It's like you're disabled."

I didn't know how to respond.

"Maybe," I said, "being offline *does* make it harder to do what society expects. But, I chose to be offline, so it's different."

★★★★★

I really hope there are still movie theatres after all this. Streaming has come a long way since Kim Dotcom and Megavideo. Warner Brothers just announced that all the films that they're releasing next year will be available for streaming over HBO Max as soon as they're released in theatres. Disney has a similar plan for Disney Plus. I know these changes have been coming soon for a long time, but it's jarring to see it happening now so suddenly.

FRIDAY, DECEMBER 11th

In a strange turn of events, there's some good news coming out of the US today. The government is challenging Facebook's monopoly-like control of the internet; 46 states and the federal government are suing the company. They're looking back to when Facebook acquired Instagram and WhatsApp and they're claiming that Zuckerberg and his team engaged in predatory behaviours that forced smaller companies to sell to Facebook. Lawyers and politicians are talking about the "Wrath of Mark" that was unleashed on Facebook's competitors if they refused to bow down to emperor Zuckerborg.

If the internet's going to live up to its potential, it needs to change dramatically. Breaking up Facebook would be an epic step towards more free and fair futures online, but will Marky Mark let that happen? His money and Facebook's lawyers are going to fight hard for the status quo. In our society where lobbyists can legally bribe politicians to favour corporate interests, I'm not optimistic that justice will prevail. But I'm more hopeful than I was yesterday.

Alex and Fanny both texted me today.

Alex's message: Aron! Guess what?! We were originally going to wait to find out the sex of the baby … but then we caved and found out today at the 20 week anatomy scan. We're having a girl!!! (Or someone with a vulva, which sounds less exciting)

Fanny's message: Omg baby girl!! :S crying face, quivering lips, so happy face

Fanny also texted Jonas a photo of the ultrasound and he said the fetus looks just like you'd think a fetus would look like. "She could be a fetus model."

I asked Alex and Fanny what made them change their mind and find out the baby's sex. Fanny said it was actually Alex who really wanted to know. Alex is non-binary but that doesn't mean gender and sex aren't important to them.

I was surprised though by Alex's reason for wanting to find out. "I realized I was getting really anxious about having a boy," they said, "We would've made it work of course, but I needed some time to prepare myself. I mean, how do you raise a boy who won't rape?"

*****

I walked all the way down to Verdun today to see Sloane. Our friend John met us too. It was a long walk just for a little hang but definitely worth it. We talked a lot about school stuff and we actually understood all the shop talk and insider references. I felt like I could really vent, like vent meaningfully to people who understood what I was talking about. It was just so nice to be socializing. I love Jonas but I also love variety.

★★★★★

I've been getting way more "Happy Hanukkah" texts than I thought I would. I feel like non-Jews love being in the know enough to send their Jewish friends holiday greetings. I don't mind. I even appreciate it, although Chanukah's never been a particularly important holiday to me.

I noticed that all the texts had "Hanukkah" spelled the same way. I bet it's autocorrect. Being a Hebrew word, "Hanukkah" has lots of different spellings when transliterated into English. There's even a fun song about all the different spellings. I know it's not a big deal, but I'm sad that smartphones are standardizing how people spell Chanukah. Who made them in charge? Oh right, we did.

SATURDAY, DECEMBER 12th

I had a long call with Omar today and we got to talking about Apple and the forced Uighur labour again.

"It's all so corrupt," he said, "but I need my iPhone."

"Need?"

"I'm an addict, Aron!! It's like you're telling a meth addict to stop using because you have ethical concerns about how people manufacture meth."

While scrolling through news earlier (on his iPhone), Omar saw that Indian police have arrested a hundred workers from a Taiwanese manufacturing plant that produces iPhones. The workers were protesting because they haven't been paid in the past four months. Apple's not directly responsible, but considering how much money they make on each device sold, they are absolutely responsible. I feel self-righteous writing this on my Lenovo ThinkPad, but I'm sure they're just as evil – just less powerfully so.

SUNDAY, DECEMBER 13th

Last night's internet dream was different. It was after midnight on December 31st, so technically I was allowed to be back online, but when I logged on, one of my friends got mad at me. I can't remember who, but it was someone I trusted and knew well. I felt dishonest, but tried to rationalize it. When I'm back online, I expect to experience a lot of that. I don't know how much I'll have to explain myself to people, but I know I'll have to justify my internet use to myself.

It's a Sunday and I've been sitting here plugging away at work all afternoon. I had a coffee, which always makes me work like a firecracker. In a few Sundays, I'll have a near infinite selection of things to do and read and watch, all constantly available from the comfort of my couch. Without that compulsive need to use the internet, there seems to be so much more space in my Sunday afternoon. I almost can't remember the temptation – that *need* to go online – or the awareness that it's always on and always available. Today I'm thinking my own thoughts, uninterrupted. It sounds almost greedy or solipsistic, but it actually works the other way round; I've found space to consider how I'm connected and how I might act with more respect for others.

In a couple of weeks, the floodgates open and I'll have to exercise a new type of self-control, a more reactive one, one that I've been neglecting lately. I'm not feeling super confident.

Or it could be the coffee.

★★★★★

Jonas is grumpy. He was going to spend the afternoon out buying Christmas presents, but has decided to do his shopping online.

"I hate shopping," he said, "it's too stressful. I always get overwhelmed and then end up spending a bunch of money on gifts that aren't even very nice."

He's in the other room now. I'm in the kitchen writing and listening to the radio. There's an expert on, talking about the environmental impacts of shopping. She claims that online shopping can cause less pollution than in-person shopping under certain circumstances – like big or bulk purchases that are delivered in one go from a local store. However, if you can avoid driving, in-person shopping is more environmentally friendly even than that. Even if you have to drive, shopping in person is still better than buying things from a big company like Amazon that promises expedited shipping and that's liable to send out different parts of your order separately.

I know lots of people don't feel comfortable with the in-person option these days, and that's fair. The internet has probably saved a lot of lives this year. However, we can lean into the internet without carelessly embracing its worst parts.

MONDAY, DECEMBER 14th

Google was down this morning. For over an hour! I slept through it … and it wouldn't have impacted me anyway, but hearing about it on the news got me giddy with excitement. How are people supposed to figure things out without YouTube?

I texted my friends in Berlin who were awake for the outage, but they all missed it. Winston hadn't even heard about it until I told him.

"Sounds like it affected you more than me," he replied.

Right now Jonas and I are at our friend Chris' place. He asked us to come water his plants while he's out of town. It's a very cute apartment – on-brand for Chris. Unfortunately, he has a bunch of Google Homes. I've noticed at least three. I'm being careful not to trigger them and whispered to Jonas that we should avoid saying the words: "Google," "okay," or "hey."

✦✦✦✦✦

I got a phone call out of the blue from a guy I've never met. It was a strange call, especially at first. He told me he'd been cleaning up the contacts on his phone and came across my name. He couldn't figure out who I was, so he looked me up online and read about my year offline. He was interested, so decided to give me a call.

I asked, trying not to sound too suspicious, why he had my number in his phone. He said he got it from our mutual friend John, but couldn't remember when or why. We ended up talking for half an hour and it was actually a cool chat. He's a housing activist and works as a real estate developer. For some of his new projects, he's had to start spending a lot more time on social media, and I think he was hoping I would tell him something that would encourage him to take a step back from the internet. I brought up the environmental and labour impacts of digital tools (he hadn't heard about the forced labour camps for Uighur Muslims in China, let alone the fact that they're manufacturing Apple products), but I said that I think we've gotten to a point where we need to use these tools in order to change them. I don't know if I totally believe that but it felt like the right thing to say.

I asked if he'd done any activism related to the internet and he brought up a project he started years ago. I'm not sure if I'd call it activism, but he created a Facebook group called "Facebook Explorers" that was meant to give people a chance to see the world from somebody else's perspective by sharing Facebook login credentials. Nobody but him joined the group.

He laughed that we had only really spoken about tech, "For someone who's offline, you sure think a lot about the internet."

TUESDAY, DECEMBER 15th
We were both still asleep when my phone rang. It was in the other room, but it woke me. I thought about getting out of

bed, but decided to let it ring. After it stopped, Jonas' phone started buzzing and he woke up, confused. I jumped out of bed and grabbed Jonas' phone. The call display said it was our landlord. I threw it to Jonas and told him to pick up.

Apparently, there was water pouring into the apartment below us from the ceiling. I went downstairs and it was bad. The ceiling paint was ballooning into big round balls of water, and one of them had burst, ripping through the paint. I went back upstairs and turned the knobs that I think turn off the water in the whole building, and now we're just waiting for the plumbers to arrive. I feel guilty, stressed, and frustrated. Though if I'm being honest with myself, mostly just frustrated.

✶✶✶✶✶

The plumbers are downstairs. They found the problem and it's unrelated to us, but they've had to turn our water off and expect the repairs to take several days. Fuck!!! Considering the Christmas construction holiday, they might not even start until January. Our landlord has said we can stay at his house, but it's quite far away. The other option is that Chris is out of town and we have his keys. We could ask him if we can stay there until this gets sorted, but I don't want to do that either. I just want to stay at home. I feel silly getting so upset about such a "first world problem," although I suppose not having running water isn't really a "first world problem."

✶✶✶✶✶

Our landlord has a friend who lives in New York but owns an empty apartment in Montreal, about five minutes away from us. He says it's a small studio, but we can use it. Hopefully we don't have to stay there for long. He warned us that he may not be able to get anyone in to do the repairs until January. He's making it sound unavoidable but then he brought up a company that can do the repairs this week but they're more expensive than he expected. When he drops off the keys later, I'm going to tell him that we would really like to be able to spend the holiday break at home, especially cooking our Christmas turkey and everything. I know I can be pushy when I need to be, but it makes me feel guilty, stressed, and frustrated. Though mostly just frustrated.

WEDNESDAY, DECEMBER 16th

Last night we stayed at our landlord's friend's apartment. It was tiny! Jonas and I were laughing about how much more difficult the past few months would have been if we lived in such a small place and both had to work from home. He called the apartment "a relationship killer," but it was fine for a night.

We tried not to snoop, but the guy had a VCR so I peeked in his closet to see if he had any movies worth watching. I didn't dig too deep, but found *The Usual Suspects*, *Big Daddy*, *The Diary of Anne Frank*, a few unlabelled tapes, and a final one that Jonas and I had never heard of. We chose the last one and watched it all the way through. It was very bad – so bad that it was fun. The dialogue was melodramatic, the acting was hilarious, and whoever was in charge of continuity didn't pay attention to the actors' haircuts. The plot was about two Black boys in New York City, one rich and one poor, who become friends despite their differences. In the end, the poor boy dies saving the rich boy from his gangster brother, but it was so poorly done that Jonas and I couldn't help laughing. We didn't understand why this guy had a copy of such a terrible movie. We knew his name though and when the credits started to roll, we realized he was the director!

It was still early, so we tried the unlabelled tapes and found a homemade wedding video and some gay porn. It felt a bit invasive to be watching this guy's porn and personal wedding videos, but it didn't feel as disrespectful as watching his feature – and he commercially released that.

It's just after noon now and we still haven't heard from our landlord about when the water will be fixed. We're back at our apartment though, just waiting. I've done hardly any schoolwork since yesterday morning when this started, and I know I'm being a bit of a baby, but I can't focus. The situation makes me appreciate the value of stable housing and running water, even just for getting work done, let alone living.

It would be a lot more difficult to deal with this if we didn't have such lovely neighbours. We hardly ever speak to them, but the woman above us and the woman below have both welcomed us into their homes to use their sinks and toilets. The neighbour upstairs is even letting us use her apartment while she's not home. I've always been told that it's important to connect with neighbours, but I can't think of the last time I actually experienced the value of those connections. It feels good to be dependent.

✦✦✦✦✦

It's just after 4 p.m. now and our water's back!! It's just a temporary fix (they'll come back to do it properly in January) but I'm hoping it holds. When we turned the water back on, it gurgled out all haltingly – like there was a lot of air in the pipes. We've run it for a while now, but it's still gurgling. I like having something to worry about so I'll hold onto this for a while, but I feel so much different now, so much better. I also feel a bit silly realizing how distressed I was. It's like my whole world changed.

THURSDAY, DECEMBER 17th

Jonas told me that he read about a Huawei employee who resigned in protest of a facial recognition tool called the "Uighur Alarm." The tool was designed to use AI and CCTV to find Uighur Muslims based on a racist and essentializing understanding of what they look like. The technology is expected to be used as a way for the Chinese government to round up Uighurs and put them into camps. The article Jonas read didn't say whether the Uighur Alarm is actively being used yet, but the government's campaign against the

Uighurs is well documented. The only reason I can think of why they might *not* be using their Uighur Alarm is because it probably doesn't work very well.

$$\star\star\star\star\star$$

My phone rang and that familiar wave of anxiety rose in my stomach. I took it out of my pocket and saw it was Bradley. I didn't want to answer but he's so persistent. I think this is the third or fourth time he's called since the last time I answered. I feel like a dick writing it down. Anyway, I answered the phone and at first felt closed off, but I warmed up. At one point though, Bradley started talking again about the dead body he and his girlfriend found in Mexico. He said something about people in Mexico not caring about murders as much as people in the US, as if some people don't care about death as much as "we" do. I was annoyed, so I challenged him on it. He backed down immediately and we went back to some small talk. It was a short call.

$$\star\star\star\star\star$$

I've started making a list of things I'm going to do online, not right away on the 1st, but in the first few days after I get back online. Here's what I have so far:

- Check out the course outlines for the two courses I'm planning to take next semester
- Register on my university's registration portal so I can submit my candidacy papers this semester
- Check I have enough money in my account to pay my credit card bill and my next tuition instalment
- Pay tuition
- Watch funny things
- Email some people from my grad school cohort to start a reading group
- Book a rental car for my January trip to Toronto
- Get a new email account that's not owned by a big tech company

- Buy some records on Discogs
- Learn about my treaty obligations as a settler
- Buy an N64 on Kijiji or Craigslist
- Write a piece about what it's like to be back online, and post it online
- Go through all my emails

FRIDAY, DECEMBER 18th

Jonas and I had our dictionaries out this afternoon as we chatted about Fanny and Alex and how babies are made. We were going through parts of the female anatomy that we thought we should know. We started with the vulva, the outer part of the female genitals, including the openings; then the vagina, the inner canal; followed by the cervix, which is like the neck of the uterus; with Fallopian tubes on either side connecting the uterus to the ovaries – where the egg comes from.

I probably learned all this in school but little gay Aron didn't think he'd ever have to know about getting sperm past the vulva, vagina, and cervix to meet an egg in the uterus.

"You tried to get Fanny pregnant a lot of times before going to the clinic," Jonas said, "and it all ended up being unnecessary."

"I don't think Fanny and Alex would have gone with the clinical option though if we hadn't first tried it at home a bunch of times," I said, "so it *was* necessary." (I can justify anything.)

It's intense to think about all the trouble we went to, time-after-time, and then how quickly – and abruptly – the clinic was able to help.

*****

This afternoon I phoned into what I imagine will be the final Zoom call I do during my offline year. It was a holiday party for one of my research teams. Hearing everyone's voices reminded me what a warm group it is, but when it was my turn to talk, I shared that I was *not* looking forward to being back on video calls. Nobody said anything and I couldn't see what people's faces were like, so I started to feel awkward and back-tracked; I added that I was also looking forward to being able to see all their faces when I can.

After we all had a turn speaking, there was a holiday card-making activity. Because I couldn't see the facilitator's screen, it was hard for me to follow. I might have enjoyed participating, but I worked on some of my own art instead – a collage I'm making from the envelopes I received in the mail this year. I wonder if I would have gotten more out of the call had I been able to see and be seen by everyone. It's such a lovely group and I think that makes the difference. For other calls I've been on, I've been glad that I didn't have to show my face. For this one though, I think I would have liked it.

✹✦✦✦✹

Darren's been popping into my head a lot lately. It's annoying because all the memories that come up are silly and positive. It's harder to remember the issues we had. I miss him but I'm still glad we "broke up."

When Jonas and I are joking around, I often use a high-pitched voice that sounds like a Jewish mother from New York, like George's mom on *Seinfeld.* And I always do it without thinking – it just comes out. But Darren used to do that voice too and now every time I catch myself doing it, I think of him. It makes me feel sad and a bit nauseated. I'd rather not think about him so much.

SATURDAY, DECEMBER 19th
Christmas shopping has become very stressful – even though I already bought all the presents I needed to get. This afternoon I went to water Chris' plants without Jonas so that he could go find some last-minute gifts for me and his parents. When I got back, I was surprised to find Jonas already home, frustrated and empty-handed.

He was in the kind of bad mood where when I said, "I'm

sorry you're in a bad mood," he replied, "I'm not in a bad mood." (He admitted that he had hardly eaten anything all day … I had a poutine while I was out.)

JONAS: I hate Christmas shopping. I'm so bad at it. I have no idea what you want or where to look.

ARON: I didn't even want to do Christmas presents, and now I feel bad cause you're struggling to find me something.

JONAS: I'm not trying to make you feel bad, and I wanted to knit you something, but I just didn't have time.

ARON: I'm sorry. I didn't mean that you're making me feel bad. It's just stressful to see you stressed, especially when I know it's because of something you're trying to do for me.

I gave Jonas a bunch of suggestions of things that I would like – an N64, a yoga mat, records, a gift certificate for a massage, a new belt – but having to help Jonas figure things out spoils the gift-giving for me, at least a bit. Also, discussing all this less than a week before Christmas feels sort of futile. I know I didn't want to do gifts, but now that I got Jonas some cool things, I feel like I deserve something special. When I think about feeling deserving and special though, I mostly just feel self-righteous and small.

*****

Hanni's eyes have been hurting, so he asked if I could print out my journal for him so he doesn't have to read it off a screen. I don't have enough ink left, so I'm going to wait until January when I can order it online. Having to buy printer ink in person this year has been over twice as expensive as the knock-off brands that are available over the internet (even without using Amazon). I feel like I'm cheating by waiting until I'm back online to print this off – especially since I'm printing my journal *about being offline* – but it's hard to justify the extra cost.

As much as I try to exist otherwise, my mind always comes back to money.

MONDAY, DECEMBER 21st
Jonas is glued to his phone, reading and re-reading the news. I can tell he's anxious because he keeps picking at the hairs on his neck and chin. I can't imagine that constantly checking to see if there's any new news is helping him feel less anxious. He keeps checking though because he can, because he's anxious, because the online news cycle is constant regardless of whether things are changing, because compulsive smartphone use is normal.

Technologies drive our actions, and they are under our control.

Whenever I start to think about what it'll be like to reconnect to the internet, I get a bit overwhelmed and anxious. I'm sure it'll be fine, and I can't put it off forever, but I already have too much to do without adding the infinite potential of the internet. I feel like it's a bit irrational to be stressing, so I tried to boil it down to what I'm really dreading and I came up with three things:

1. being able to read news and watch stuff endlessly
2. being too available to colleagues and people who want me to do things for or with them
3. feeling unable to avoid contributing to all the fucked up ecological and labour conditions that make it possible for us to go online.

I thought this list would help, but it actually makes me feel worse – like my anxiety may not be so irrational after all. I think I would be okay with staying offline forever if I didn't have to be online for work and school.

✶✶✶✶✶

I had a long phone call with a friend tonight whose parents used a known donor to get pregnant, and the donor was one of their close friends. I thought my friend might have some advice for me going into this relationship with Fanny and Alex's kid, but he didn't have much to suggest. He was just really excited for me. He said that thinking about me as a "bio-dad," as he called it, made his heart "wet." He talked about some of his early memories with his bio-dad and how special and normal the relationship seemed to him. He also told me that he didn't refer to his bio-dad as "uncle" and thought that was a weird idea. I don't want to worry about what the kid will call me though, not yet.

I asked him how his relationship is with his bio-dad now, and he told me that they don't really talk.

"Not for any particular reason," he said, "We just haven't kept in touch."

TUESDAY, DECEMBER 22nd

Jonas and I are running out of stuff to watch. I collected a lot of movies and TV shows before I went offline, but now that I've looked through my collections so many times, nothing seems exciting anymore. I miss Blockbuster.

✳✳✳✳✳

Jonas' mom sent a message around to his family chat this morning about an online clothing company that their family likes. She saw a headline about how little their textile workers earn and was suggesting that their family boycott the store. Jonas replied with a list of several other clothing companies that they should also boycott for similar reasons. Jonas' little sister says she already buys all her clothes secondhand from "charity shops," as they call them in the UK, and it sounds like the rest of Jonas' family is on board too.

"Only buy from small brands then with good credentials," his mom told everyone at the end of the conversation.

I don't want to give myself too much credit, but I wonder if they would be thinking about these things if Jonas and I weren't dating. I know modesty's important, but in terms of our impact on the world, I think we need to start taking more credit too. Systems – like those driving fast fashion and sweatshops – are made up of so many people that our parts within them seem negligible. Somehow though, because they're fairly negligible, humans have started treating it like our actions actually don't have impacts. It's one of the simplest and most complicated things I've tried to wrap my head around this year: how we have control despite all the ways in which we don't.

I'm with Marx though – enough with blaming the system. It's obviously oversimplifying things to say that we, alone, are in control, but ignoring our control as individuals will lead to our collective self-destruction.

WEDNESDAY, DECEMBER 23rd

Jonas and I heard someone talking about "foxy boxing" on the radio but didn't know what it was. We looked it up in all our dictionaries, but couldn't find it. I was glad Jonas didn't check his phone. Instead we imagined what we think the phrase might mean. I'm picturing a degrading boxing match between two scantily-clad women – à la mud wrestling. Jonas thinks it just refers to foxes boxing. If I remember, I might look it up when I get back online, but I almost prefer just wondering – and I can't imagine a scenario where it'll be important for me to know what foxy boxing actually is.

I got a text message from the professor of the online course I took this term but it was an MMS, so it just showed up as a blank message. I texted her back and explained that my phone can't get data messages. I assumed she had tried to text me an attachment or something but she replied that it was just a really long text with feedback on my final assignment. (When a text is too long, it gets converted into a data message.) I suggested she could split it into a couple messages or print it off and I could come by to pick it up. She suggested we wait until January and she'll just email it to me then. I didn't resist, but it made me feel sad, like my offline year is already over.

I was hoping my internet habits wouldn't just revert back to "normal" as soon I got back online, but it feels like they're already turning on me and I don't have a say in it.

✶✶✶✶✶

I got a call from a popular national radio show that wants to have me on next week!! They asked if I would prefer to do the interview live or record it before. I said I'd much prefer to pre-record it so I don't have to deal with the stress.

After I got off the call, Bradley phoned again. I couldn't remember how many times he'd called since I'd last answered but I picked up, more out of guilt than anything, and we had a nice chat. It was chill, nothing heated, but warm. We didn't talk about the weather, but we didn't get too deep. I'd be okay talking to Bradley more if he didn't call so much. Is that a paradox?

I wasn't sure if I'd told Bradley that Fanny was pregnant, so I brought it up and he'd already heard, but not from me – he found out from Fanny's Instagram. I didn't know she had a public Instagram profile, but I'm not too surprised. I'm more surprised that Bradley's been creeping her profile. He and Fanny aren't even friends.

THURSDAY, DECEMBER 24th

Jonas and I have a turkey in the oven. According to its weight, it could feed thirteen adult humans. I have a feeling social media's about to be flooded with ideas for what people can do with their holiday leftovers.

We knew dinner would be a lot of work, so we walked over to a Viet sub place for lunch but when we got there, the internet was down and the guy's cash register wasn't working. I offered to just pay cash, but he said he wouldn't know how much to charge us without the machine. I was about to explain how to add two numbers together and calculate 15% tax, but Jonas sensed it and pulled me out the door. I just can't get over the fact that the guy couldn't make us sandwiches … because the internet was down!??

★★★★★

I got a text from my older brother today asking if I would be the backup guardian for his daughter if he and his wife die. It's a big question, and it felt wrong to answer it over text, but I wrote back that I would, of course.

I don't think of myself as a superstitious person but I sent him a second text that said "knock on wood/poo poo poo and all that."

"haha thanks," he replied.

FRIDAY, DECEMBER 25th

Jonas and I exchanged presents and had such a lazy morning. I gave him a pipe, which we christened, and I also gave him the keyboard, so we spent a bit of time jamming. In his stocking, I got him a daytimer, a candle shaped like a baby's head, a wooden and gold-looking mouse pad, some jam, a mint chocolate bar, and a graphic novel about science.

Jonas got me a graphic novel too and I devoured it immediately. It was about a futuristic world where everything is automated according to secret algorithms. He also got me a poetry book, a new (bigger) lava lamp, some records, a framed photo of the two of us, a pen, and some erasers shaped like fruit.

After we showered and ate some leftovers, we went for a walk on the mountain. We passed Darren, who was out for a run. I wasn't wearing my contacts, so I didn't notice him until the last minute. He waved but it was too late – we'd snubbed him. I felt bad and tried to talk about it with Jonas but he didn't engage. He changed the subject and when I brought it up again, he said he wasn't too bothered. I guess I'd been friends with Darren a lot longer than Jonas, but I also think Jonas and I hold onto things – or people – differently. I'm a sentimental man.

I thought about texting Darren to apologize for not waving back, but I don't want to open any doors, at least not yet. Also, this way, he can smugly think of me as a dick, like he was the bigger person for trying to say hello. If I text him now, I'll be taking that away from him. (I love making self-righteous excuses for my fear and laziness.)

✳✳✳✳✳

My uncle is a die-hard Apple user and he was a bit defensive when he found out that I no longer use an Apple laptop. My aunt had phoned to wish Jonas and me a Merry Christmas and my uncle joined partway through the call. I started defending my ThinkPad by saying it was easier to service than an Apple device, but eventually admitted I was mostly concerned about Apple's ethical standards – like how some of their products were apparently made in forced labour camps by Uighur Muslim workers. My uncle had heard about the Uighur forced labour, but he claimed it was just one rogue subcontractor and they'd lost their Apple contract. I was ready to finish the conversation so tried to say something agreeable.

"Well, at least things are a bit better now that the subcontractor was fired."

My uncle disagreed though. I was surprised. His logic was that if Apple stops working with subcontractors who get in trouble for exploitative labour practices, the workers end up getting nothing at all. He compared it to child labourers.

"It's not like these kids have another choice," he said, "If they can't work, they starve."

But kids *should* have other choices. They shouldn't have to work. Is that too idealistic?

I tried a different approach:

ARON: We're not talking about underpaid child labourers though; these are *un*paid Uighur labourers – these people are being held against their will and forced to work for free. If they lose their jobs, they don't get paid any less.
UNCLE: They're still being fed and given a place to sleep. If they can't work—
ARON: But they're in a forced-labour camp.

When you're clever, you can justify anything. And I know it's easy for me to say this from my couch, sipping a glass of Woodford Reserve and listening to the Erykah Badu album Jonas bought me for Christmas. But it's strange to have to argue against normalizing things we would never accept as normal if they were happening to us. My uncle is one of the nicest, most generous people I know, so I imagine I just backed him into a corner.

"I definitely agree that your heart's in the right place," he said, "Where we disagree is on the mechanisms for regulation and the intentions of the company."

The other difference is that I don't own Apple stocks.

My uncle insisted that Apple is run by "a bunch of hippies." I don't think one of the biggest corporations in the world is being run by "a bunch of hippies," at least not anymore. That they've managed to hold onto that image despite how powerful they've become is a pretty nifty little trick.

SATURDAY, DECEMBER 26th

The last two times Jonas and I had sex, I got a really intense headache immediately as I came. The pain swelled in a horizontal line at the base of my cranium, on the back of my head. I remember hearing from a friend years ago about something similar but I can't remember who it was. The internet would be perfect for looking into this kind of thing. (If I'm able to sift through the sites that tell me I'm dying.) It seems awkward to text a bunch of friends and ask whether they know anything about orgasm headaches. If I weren't about to be back online next week though, I might do it. Really, I don't think any of my friends would mind, so I don't know why I feel like this is the type of issue that's best kept private. Hopefully the headaches stop and I don't have to worry about it. I'm tempted to jerk off before bed to see if it happens again. It's like when I have a sore in my mouth and can't stop touching it with my tongue. I don't want to feel the pain, but sometimes I can't help myself.

SUNDAY, DECEMBER 27th

I had another one of these headaches this morning and it left me super nauseated. I think it might have to do with my neck muscles tensing up and blocking the surge of blood-flow that comes with an orgasm. This morning's was painful enough that I decided to ask a few friends about it after all, but none of them had heard of orgasm headaches before.

✶✶✶✶✶

There was a car bombing in Nashville this week. An RV filled with explosives caused a lot of property damage, and one person was killed. On the radio, they were saying that an image of the RV was found on Google Street View, leading police to the residence of the people responsible for the attack. I wonder if Google is actually partnered with the police or if the police are just taking advantage of the technology.

MONDAY, DECEMBER 28th

I woke up from a wet dream last night and was pretty surprised. I hardly ever have wet dreams, and usually they only happen if I haven't masturbated in several days. I wonder if it had anything to do with the orgasm headaches; I told myself I wasn't going to ejaculate again until I'd figured out what was going on, so maybe my body revolted. Luckily, I didn't get a headache when I came in my dream. I'm still planning to avoid coming again until I've figured out what's going on, but I wouldn't mind another wet dream in the meantime.

✶✶✶✶✶

The guy from the radio show called to reschedule my interview. The host is no longer available to do a pre-tape so they've asked me to do the interview live on Wednesday morning at 8:30 a.m. I know the adrenaline will help, but oy, that's early for me. I hope my brain will be awake enough to perform.

TUESDAY, DECEMBER 29th

I was reading Aaron Swartz' afterword to Cory Doctorow's novel *Homeland* and don't know how to take it. Swartz writes with hope about the power we each have as internet users to make the online world a better place – a place that isn't about the big guy exploiting the rest of us.

"It's up to you to change the system," he wrote.

But then he killed himself. I try not to let that discredit his optimism, but words aren't as memorable as actions. I'm trying to keep both parts of Swartz in mind though and have realistic hope. *Realistic hope* – that isn't an oxymoron, I hope.

There are less than three days left before I have to go back online. Everyone I talk to asks whether I'm looking forward to it. Instead of shouting "no" and telling them to leave me alone, I've been trying to reply in an honest, but gentler way:

"Not exactly," I say, "I'm actually pretty anxious for all the new potential it'll open up."

Of course, being online will be helpful for my research and for connecting with friends and family, but it's over-whelming. I don't want to be so easy to reach and I don't want people to assume that I'll use the internet for every-thing just because I can. Pushing back was easy when I could tell people that I wasn't using the internet at all. The month of January will involve a lot of negotiations and com-promise, but hopefully I'll still feel hopeful by the end of it. *Realistic hope...*

✶✶✶✶✶

I think something happened to our neighbour – the one who feeds squirrels from inside his kitchen and sings to his cat, "baby d'amour." A couple nights ago I noticed cops out-side his place and then yesterday I saw his sister and anoth-er woman cleaning out the apartment, leaving several big garbage bags on the street along with a bunch of furniture. I nodded as I walked past, and she nodded back, but we didn't smile. After they left, nobody's been home and there's no sign of the cat.

The blue and white lights on their Christmas tree were still on when I started writing this entry, but now the whole apartment is dark. Is someone there? I can't see anyone, but I don't want to be a creep and stare at the window for too long.

There's a clock ticking behind my head and I usually don't notice its sound, but today I'm tempted to take the batteries out.

WEDNESDAY, DECEMBER 30th
What a thrill!! I was on the radio for fifteen minutes at 8:45 this morning and then spent the rest of the day texting and talking to friends and family about it. I had told a bunch of people I'd be on, but I couldn't believe how many random people from my past heard it and got in touch to let me know. I even got messages from people whose numbers I don't have in my phone.

When the interview ended, I thought it had gone poorly. When it aired in Montreal an hour later though, I was actually pretty happy with it.

A close friend texted afterwards saying, "You managed to publicly announce you're gay and Jewish all in 15 minutes, then provided an online link. Have fun with the trolls!"

Most of the people who sent me messages made me feel warm and even a bit high. I usually have a hard time with compliments, but today I soaked them in. I also had some critiques, like that the interview was too much of a "feel good" piece, or too "fluffy." My Russian friend called it a "joking dessert." I don't disagree, but I tried to balance the interviewer's interest in Zoom, Netflix, and TikTok by talking about equity in internet access and colonial labour in the supply chain for digital devices. It was tough with only fifteen minutes, but I hope I at least made some people curious enough to learn more.

My ex in Vancouver sent me a text that I really appreciated. He wrote, "Although a lot of people are aware of what's wrong with social media, very few think of the conflict minerals and terrible labour. I think you may have planted an idea."

One of my favourite texts came from a professor of mine who's been living in the Maritimes this year. She wrote, "A great interview Aron!!! My partner and I both enjoyed hearing you and a letter from you arrived yesterday in our lovely rural route mailbox." Even without the internet, I was still able to reach her in a couple different ways.

My supervisor heard the interview and texted, "In case you didn't know, you need to list each of these on your CV as media engagements and/or invited research communication opportunities." Aviva is very critical of the neoliberal university and its obsession with cataloguing all our experiences and valuing them towards tenure track positions. I suppose you have to really know something to critique it. But can you really critique something while engaging in it?

Jonas told me that his whole family gathered around a speaker to listen to my radio interview, streaming it over the internet. Their connection cut out partway through, but he said they loved what they heard.

At some point after the interview I got a call from another journalist who was doing an online piece about my year offline. (Ironic, I know.) He hadn't understood the part of the conversation where I talked about trying to text a friend in Berlin and accidentally using WhatsApp.

"But what's the difference?" he asked.

I explained that text messages are sent through the same network that is used for phone calls, whereas WhatsApp uses the internet. He still didn't seem to understand the difference. The article he wrote though is really good … says my mom. I won't know if it's actually any good until I can read it on Friday.

Jonas told me that the article's headline refers to me as *this guy*, "This guy swore off the internet…" I'm clickbait!! What a way to end my year offline.

THURSDAY, DECEMBER 31st

Bridget texted, "Wow dude, the article about you has skeptical internet comments already!!"

I wrote back, "Woo! You know you're doing something right when you have haters!"

She told me that people are questioning whether I actually spent a year offline. One person commented, "It's amazing the lengths uninteresting people will go to hoping to give the impression they are interesting."

"Another person," Bridget explained, "has an issue with you sending letters because it anticipates returns and people would have to change their behaviour to do that."

And there were more. Apparently, several readers were annoyed that I was making a big deal about something as trivial as spending a year offline, and a handful were upset about the photo they included with the article because I was wearing a hat indoors.

I'm glad I'm not online to comment back because that wouldn't help anything. I don't care if strangers believe me. And Jonas knitted me that hat! When I get back online, it might be amusing to look through the comments – I might even learn some things about people's attitudes towards the internet – but I'll try to avoid it. Fighting with trolls or fixating on how I'm being represented online will just distract me from doing things I find more meaningful.

When I sent out letters to friends and colleagues about my year offline, the responses I got were sometimes critical, but always in ways that felt thoughtful and constructive. As soon I shared my experience online though, the trolls dominated the conversation. It's like the internet nurtures a certain way of treating people that's all about one-ups and put-downs. Being connected like that makes it hard to connect.

As I was chatting with Bridget, I realized that I lied about something in yesterday's interview. While I was talking about my experience driving to Toronto with paper maps, I said that I hadn't used paper maps before, at least not as an adult. Bridget asked if that was actually true, and after saying yes, I realized it wasn't; I've used paper maps plenty of times before this year.

"We forget so quickly," Bridget said, "The internet seems so normal now, it's like we've always been using it."

✶✶✶✶✶

I had a long talk with Fanny today about life and yesterday's interview and the pregnancy. She's been having some rough days but sounded pretty positive. I told her I'd spoken with a friend who has two moms and a known donor. My friend brought up how much he appreciated being around other queer families when he was little, how it made him feel like there was nothing wrong with him or his parents. A queer family may be queer, but it's also normal.

✶✶✶✶✶

It's my last afternoon offline and I have a stomach ache. I often get diarrhea when I'm anxious, but I'm not quite there. I feel tired and lazy, like it's a Sunday in the middle of a several-months-long snowstorm. It's still "the holidays," so it's normal to be as unproductive as I've been, but I'm dreading tomorrow.

January

But unless I learn to use
the difference between poetry and rhetoric
my power too will run corrupt as poisonous mold
or lie limp and useless as an unconnected wire
  – Audre Lorde, 1978, *The Black Unicorn*

FRIDAY, JANUARY 1st

Jonas and I spent New Year's Eve separately. We aren't in a fight or anything, but had different people we wanted to see. I went to Sloane's for some drinks and then met up with Hanni and Kat for dinner. After midnight, I took the metro halfway home and then decided to walk the rest of the way.

As I was getting off the train, I got a text from Jonas, "Congratulations on completing your internetless year, it was so much fun to experience it with you and I'm so proud you stuck to it despite the many challenges and reasons not to."

I replied immediately, "Love love love you too!"

As I walked past the mountain, there were pockets of people gathered – drinking, laughing, and shouting. Once a few people started, the wave of noise didn't stop. One group would take over as another group gave up, and the sound roared on. I felt warmer than I should have and walked slower so I could take everything in – the laughter, the shouting, the traffic. But there was no wind. It was perfectly calm.

✶✶✶✶✶

The first thing I did when I got online was check my email. I wanted to make a performance out of it, so I tried to live-stream myself over Twitter. I couldn't figure it out though, so instead just tweeted out a few videos of me checking my email. I had 1503 new emails in my university inbox, 748 in my personal Gmail, and 585 in my professional Gmail. That's not including several hundred more that were automatically filtered out as spam.

After I posted the videos to Twitter, I closed my laptop. I didn't read through any of the emails – I just went for a walk. When I got back to my apartment, I didn't want to go inside and deal with online things, so I kept walking in the other direction.

While I was out, my mom phoned to ask how I was feeling. I told her I was overwhelmed, and she said that I should take it slow. I appreciated the advice, but then she suggested we do a video call when I get home. My anxiety levels spiked and I got that feeling you get when your mom asks you to do something you don't want to do. I said sure but that I didn't know when I would be back from my walk. She didn't catch on and suggested we use Zoom. My dad, in the background, suggested we use Google Meet. I suggested we wait until tomorrow.

They agreed but continued to discuss what platform we would use. My mom likes Zoom because "it's so easy" and my dad thought Google Meet or Microsoft Teams would be better because they produce less "digital exhaust." I'd heard the term "digital exhaust," but couldn't remember what it means.

"Is it something to do with the environment?" I asked.

"It's not," he explained, "Digital exhaust is data that's being gathered on you and sold, often behind your back."

We agreed on Google Meet or Microsoft Teams (I can't remember which), and then discussed what time to schedule the talk. Normally my parents just call me and I pick up the phone, or vice versa. This feels so much more complicated.

*****

When I finally got home, I dove into my laptop immediately. I didn't want to, but couldn't resist. I think that's what the word "abject" means. I started going through the 2836 emails I had waiting and they've pretty much all been junk. There were a couple from people welcoming me back online, and one from a friend offering me $5000 "if you respond to this message before the end of December." But the only email that was even a bit serious was from my university saying I needed to add an address to my student account. Before I went offline, the university definitely had my address and I haven't moved, so I don't know what that's about.

It's a bit infuriating to think of all the energy used just for me to receive all these emails. As Ron Deibert would say, it's like driving almost 45 kilometres for no reason. If we actually had to face the amount of resources we're using so carelessly, I hope we'd act differently. Imagine if every student received 1500 paper memos a year – that's at least four every day, even on weekends. With the virtual though, everything's hidden.

When I got sick of skimming through emails, I did a bunch of small bureaucratic tasks: I added my missing address for the university's records, I paid tuition, and I emailed two of my friends in Berlin asking when we can have a chat. I joked that we could use Skype. When I went offline, that was the default. Now it's a joke.

Afterwards, I made myself a snack and sat down to watch something. I wanted to find a show called *How To with John Wilson* that one of my favourite comedians produced. I've had half a dozen friends recommend it this year, more than with any other show. I searched on Crave, the streaming service Jonas subscribes to, and it was there! Jonas was out, but he had left me his account information. I logged in, found the *How To* show, clicked on the first episode, and … it didn't work. Jonas only has the basic Crave package. Apparently, this show is premium content.

I scrolled through the rest of the comedies and found a stand-up show that looked funny. I clicked on it, waited, waited, waited, but nothing happened. I think I need to update my laptop.

I closed the browser and watched an old episode of *The Simpsons* that I have on DVD. It was pretty good.

SATURDAY, JANUARY 2nd
Before bed last night, I read the comments people left on the article about my year offline. There were some kind ones, but the majority were not nice, and the mean ones had way more "likes" than the supportive ones. The most popular comments were the ones speculating that I was a phony and hadn't actually spent a year offline. It *is* hard to believe, but it's also hard to believe that people took the time to refute it.

After going through all the comments and feeling a bit deflated and amused, I started to watch porn on Twitter. A few months ago, I heard that Twitter had become the best place for porn, so I decided to do a bit of "research." I just wanted to take a quick look – it was already 1 a.m. and I was tired – but I got stuck and didn't go to bed until after 2.

This morning, as soon as I woke up, I grabbed my laptop and checked my email. Winston in Berlin emailed me back. I don't know why I felt the need to get back online again so quickly this morning. After a year of hardly any cravings, I didn't think the compulsion would return with such force. Now that I've checked my email though, I'm going to head out for a walk and try to ignore the internet for the rest of the day … except for the video call I have with my parents at 1. Ugh. Why can't we just talk on the phone?

*****

I got home just in time for the chat. My parents both seemed very glad to see me.

"I know we talked yesterday," my mom said, "but it feels like you've been away."

"It's nice to finally be talking 'in person,'" my dad said.

I didn't feel like the call was very different than a regular call with my parents, except that I had to make eye contact and couldn't do other things while we chatted. And it felt like the call had to be a lot longer than usual.

We talked about digital exhaust again and the way that companies like Zoom, Facebook, or Google gather and sell user data in order to make their "free" services as lucrative as possible. I'm so much more skeptical of free services online now, but also more appreciative of services like Wikipedia that are legitimately free. I've been looking into getting a paid email account with Protonmail because if I'm not paying for my email service, it's making money off me.

My dad was explaining that, although lots of people are focusing on anti-trust laws that could break up the Facebook monopoly, Google is just as concerning. He said they recently made a deal to purchase user data from credit card companies and are adding it to the profiles they have on us. It sounds like a conspiracy, but I believe it. These big tech companies think if they get enough data, they can make us do anything.

After the call, I went for another walk and phoned Yuki in Toronto. She has a premium subscription to Crave and gave me her password so I can watch that *How To* show. (She was one of the people who recommended it.) Friends used to lend each other VHS tapes or DVDs. Now we share passwords for streaming services.

*****

I keep getting distracted by the internet. I pulled out my laptop to write in my journal but the internet dragged my attention away for nearly an hour before I was able to start journaling. I don't know what I did for that hour. Even when I was video calling with my parents earlier, I was tempted to open other tabs and felt distracted just thinking about what I could be doing online.

Last year, if I was doing other things while I was on a call, I always felt like I could listen and focus. The unknown newness that's constantly available on the internet feels more distracting than more familiar distractions – distractions from our physical surroundings, ones that we can see coming.

★★★★★

Just watched the first three episodes of *How To with John Wilson* on Yuki's Crave. I loved it. Such a strange and careful show. The music is also really beautiful and Yuki told me that her partner has a song in the final episode. I'm tempted to skip ahead to hear it, but I'm sure I'll get through the season quickly enough.

Crave does that autoplay thing where the next episode automatically starts partway through the credits of the previous episode unless you get up and manually turn it off. I really like the show so far, but I don't think I would have watched three episodes if I was in control. And of course I was in control, but it takes more effort to get up and stop the next episode than to let it keep playing.

SUNDAY, JANUARY 3rd

My sister-in-law texted me today asking if Jonas and I want to do a video call this week. "The baby has gotten so big!" she wrote, "You'll be surprised when you see her."

I've never video called my brother and sister-in-law before. What changed? Oh right, they had a baby.

★★★★★

I finished going through all my unread emails and didn't find anything important.

One strange email I noticed was from a classmate of mine who's in her fifties. The email was from partway through last year, and it included a job posting that she was asking me to help pass around to potential applicants. In her message, she wrote: "Not sure if you are up to helping with this in your year without internet, but maybe you can print them off (or ask me to) and hand them out..." I spoke with her a couple times since this email, but she never mentioned it. It's too late now anyway, but I wonder how she thought I could've checked my email without internet.

✳✳✳✳✳

Jonas was out tonight and I ended up watching Twitter porn again. I even used some hashtags. I felt like a pervert, even though I wasn't doing anything too out of the ordinary. It's almost like the internet's the pervert and I'm the victim … but that's letting myself off too easily. I have control.

✳✳✳✳✳

Sloane texted me this afternoon, "How's the internet life? How're you?"

"Internet life's okay!" I replied, "Got trapped a couple times, but trying to stay away. The schoolwork I have to do already feels more oppressive, even though nothing's changed yet."

SLOANE: Just remember, it doesn't have to be an all or nothing thing – like me with drinking.

ARON: lol

ARON: I was reading the course outline for one of the courses I'm in this semester and the professor is insisting that we blur/replace our background while on video calls for class. Do you know what that's about?

SLOANE: It's supposed to be an equity thing. People (myself included) have been cautioning teachers and people who force students to have their cameras on because people might not have a place they'd want to share.

SLOANE: But … forcing someone to use a background also doesn't get at it since a lot of lower end computers can't run backgrounds on Zoom.

SLOANE: Mine can't.

ARON: Thanks for explaining! That makes sense, but yeah, frustrating how the rule backfires and outs the people who have shittier tech.

Sloane: Exactly.

Sloane: I think there's been a lot of scrambling from an equity perspective in the rapid shift to online teaching.

*****

I think having access to internet porn has made me more horny than usual. "Horny" might not be the right word, but I've jerked off five times in the past three days.

I completely forgot about the orgasm headaches, but I guess they went away on their own.

MONDAY, JANUARY 4th

I've been checking my email way too much. Every time I open my laptop now, I feel like I should check. And my Twitter. There's usually nothing new, but I keep doing it. It's making it hard to journal or do anything else on my laptop. Inevitably, after checking my email, my internet browser is open so I do something else online. Today I read about a grant that I think I might apply for. I looked up the James Bay hydroelectric project that Quebec uses and learned about the Indigenous led activism that's been opposing it since construction began in 1971. It's important stuff, but it really eats away at the day.

*****

I was looking through the syllabus for one of the courses I'm starting next week and saw that the section on electronic devices had mostly been crossed out, but it wasn't deleted. The professor wrote:

"Use of Electronic Devices Laptop computers may only be used for taking notes and working on assignments. Any internet-related activities such as Email, Facebook, Twitter, Instagram/etc, and text messaging, are strictly prohibited in class. The instructor maintains the prerogative to inquire about your laptop or MC2 use if such use appears to be distracting or disrespectful to the classroom commu-

~~nity."~~

I appreciated him leaving the note on the syllabus, even though the course is now entirely online.

We ordered pizza for dinner tonight and used the internet both to find a spot and to order. When the delivery person arrived, I realized that this was the first time Jonas and I have ever ordered food to the apartment. I know you don't need the internet to get food delivered, but we never even considered it before.

TUESDAY, JANUARY 5th

Jonas and I FaceTimed with my brother and his wife. Their baby was there too, but she didn't say much. She made a cute sucking noise with her mouth, like she was nursing or blowing kisses.

Yesterday I was arguing with my mom that videos don't add much to conversations, but getting to see my adorable niece made me rethink that. Like anything, it's about context. Talking to my brother and sister-in-law is one situation that's definitely more enjoyable with video now that they have a baby. (Nothing against them when they didn't have a baby...)

*****

Jonas was talking to his family and one of his sisters' boyfriends said he thought it was cool that Jonas and I had developed our whole relationship without the internet.

"You never looked me up?" I asked Jonas.

"Well I did," he admitted, "but not until we had already been dating for several months."

Jonas pulled out his phone and tried to look me up again to see if the results had changed, but our internet wasn't working and he couldn't get the results to load.

*****

I got an email from Hanni and I responded immediately. He wrote back right away, saying he was surprised to get an instant reply.

"I can't help myself," I joked.

✶✶✶✶✶

I got another orgasm headache tonight while Jonas and I were fooling around. This time, the headache wasn't so bad, but I looked it up online. It sounds like they're pretty common and rarely serious. I just have to figure out some new moves and angles. There were some people online who suggested going to a doctor, but I think I'll wait. Orgasm headaches seem important, but not urgent.

✶✶✶✶✶

There's something else I had to look up online but I can't remember what it is…

WEDNESDAY, JANUARY 6th

I spent way too much time on Twitter today. I've never gotten into slot machines, but I imagine it would feel like this: I open Twitter and there's nothing. So, I close the window, but then open it up again just quickly, in case there's something now. And then I close it and open it on repeat until I snap out of it or just succumb to scrolling my feed.

I still haven't followed anyone, but I found some academics I like who have very active profiles. I'm tempted to follow them, but I also worry that'll just lead to me spending more and more time online. For now, I just liked and retweeted a bunch of their posts.

While I was exploring Twitter, I had the radio on and heard that there was something going on in Washington, D.C. For the first time in over a year, I was able to watch the chaos unfold online. I started looking through Twitter at photos and videos of rioters inside the Capitol Building. The first thing I noticed was that everyone looked white. At least one person has been killed – a woman who was shot in the neck by guards. However, the majority of the rioters seem like they're enjoying themselves. If the protesters were Black or Brown, would the police be as gentle and forgiving?

I went to LiveLeak and watched footage of the woman who was killed. I feel sick now and wish I hadn't looked it up. It's not the internet's fault, but if I weren't online, I wouldn't have so casually been able to find footage of someone dying. Direct access to all the knowledge in the universe seems so promising, but I didn't learn anything that I hadn't heard on the radio; I just wasted a bunch of time. And yet, I'll probably go back online later and read/watch more from the riots. What's wrong with me? It would be so much easier to just blame the internet, but I think that's letting us off the hook a bit too easily. We have some degree of control, even if it's hard to activate. I thought spending a year offline would help me have more willpower to avoid wasting the day away online, but I think the opposite happened; I've forgotten how to use the internet in moderation. Luckily, I still don't have a smartphone, so I'm somewhat insulated.

I told Jonas that I watched the video of the woman being killed and he gave me a weird look.

"Why did you do that?" he asked.

"I don't know," I replied, "I was curious." He didn't respond, so I added, "I wish I hadn't."

I need to develop more self-control.

✦✦✦✦✦

Because of the role that the president's tweets may have played in today's riot, Twitter has suspended his account for twelve hours and he's been warned that further violations of Twitter's rules will result in a permanent ban.

✦✦✦✦✦

I tried to update my website today with some of the things I wrote during my time offline. My password wasn't working, so I reset it … but it still isn't working. I tried to find a number to call my web hosting company, but their website says that problems can only be reported over email. I had all sorts of plans for this morning, but instead I just spent an hour struggling. Since I've been back online, I feel like I haven't been able to get much done.

THURSDAY, JANUARY 7th

When I woke up, the first thing on my mind was email. I knew I wanted to check to see if there was anything new, and I knew I had a couple emails I wanted to send, but mostly I was just—I don't know, craving it. Now, an hour or so later, I'm sitting at my computer and actively avoiding opening a web browser or checking my email. I've told myself I can only check email and Twitter after 4 p.m. today. In the meantime, I cleaned the kitchen, and once I finish writing this, I'm going to do some readings that I've failed to focus on this week because I keep getting distracted.

Yesterday Jonas said, "I didn't realize how addicted you are."

I got defensive and tried the excuse that I'm just making up for everything I missed last year. As I said it though, I knew it wasn't true.

✦✦✦✦✦

I made it all the way to 4 p.m., and at that point I actually had to check to find out whether or not I have class this evening. Turns out I do.

It was my first time trying Zoom for real. The class is about arts-based research methodologies and it seems like it'll be really cool, but I wish I didn't have to sit still in front of my computer for three hours. The professor asked that we all leave our videos on throughout the class, so there's no escape. Besides feeling stuck behind my screen, I also felt self-conscious in a way I never had before. My hair was a mess, so I put on a toque. I didn't want to be one of those obnoxious people with a carefully curated background, so I sat in front of a blank white wall. Throughout class, the biggest distraction was my own video.

One of the exercises we had to do for class was to imagine our research roots. I enjoyed the activity, even if the details I included seemed a bit arbitrarily chosen. I wrote about being really young and lying in my parents' bed in the morning, playing on my dad's Newton – an early Palm Pilot kind of device made by Apple. I'm not sure if my parents were trying to sleep and I was just given the Newton to keep me busy, but I remember feeling important when I held the device. I don't really recall what I did with it. I have a clear image of myself drawing lines and shapes, numbers and letters, but was there more to it? I don't remember there being any games. At that age, and considering the technology of the time, just drawing squiggles may have been enough.

Because class is online, people can join now from anywhere, but I didn't expect that so many students would be Zooming in from out of town. There were a few people in Ontario and California, and even somebody joining from Beijing. This makes class so much more accessible but I worry that it's also making the experience more transactional – like online shopping – instead of feeling like a journey that you share with classmates. That being said, class was still really warm tonight. It made me feel like I was part of a community, which is something I've been missing lately.

Partway through class, the professor singled me out and asked if everything was okay. I unmuted to say it was, but didn't know why she had thought something was the matter. I must have done something strange with my face. In person, our faces reveal things we don't intend to as well, but it's more obvious on a close-up screen. Ideally, I don't want to have to worry about controlling my facial expressions, but now that I was called out I'll be more careful.

FRIDAY, JANUARY 8th
As long as I don't let myself check my email when I wake up, I feel much less addicted. I waited until after 6 p.m. today and then when I finally got online, it wasn't so bad. It's

like potato chips or tobacco; as long as you don't get started, you're fine. Once you pop, though…

I spent a bit more time than I would have liked trying to find a website that would sell me a Samuel Delany book I'm looking for called *Heavenly Breakfast*. It's available for cheap on Amazon, but that isn't an option, so I went through several other websites that either didn't have the book or that don't ship to Canada. I ended up finding a copy from a seller in the US through a website called Abe Books.[1] Shipping only costs $2 somehow. I also bought a book called *Cruising Utopia* by Jose Munoz. I had read about it in a Billy-Ray Belcourt book and figured I was already ordering another book, so why not. Online shopping makes it easy to spend money without realizing it. Or is that just credit cards in general? Either way, I have 60 dollars less than I did a moment ago, and I haven't left the couch.

✦✦✦✦✦

I talked to a friend today who's also a student and he told me he doesn't have a webcam. My first instinct was that he must be lying. Why would he lie about his webcam though? I wasn't asking him to do a video chat. It didn't make sense, but I couldn't wrap my head around it.

"But you're doing online classes, aren't you? How can you do that without a webcam?"

"How did you do it without internet?"

Touché. He admitted that it would be easy enough for him to buy a webcam, but he doesn't want to. I respect that. It's good to be able to set boundaries. As a university student, it's not like having a webcam is required … is it?

SUNDAY, JANUARY 10th

Jonas told me that the first anniversary is the paper anniversary, so I got him a card with a crude drawing of two men kissing and the words, "Love you." Has it only been a year? That night at Darren's apartment seems like a lifetime ago.

---

1. I found out later that Abe Books is a subsidiary of Amazon. Noooooo!

Since I met Jonas, I helped Fanny get pregnant, I became an uncle, I had a falling out with Darren, and there may have been a couple other things that happened. (The personal overshadows the global every time.)

I can't get over how casually things between Jonas and I got so serious. He moved in after six months and now we spend all day together every day without getting on each other's nerves … too often. I was looking back at my journal entry about the day we first met and I think I knew that this was it, even then. I wouldn't call it love at first sight, because love is something active that takes work, but I knew I was ready. And he was worth the work.

Jonas and I have cooked lunch and dinner every day this week, so we decided to order out tonight. We found a Thai restaurant on one of those union-busting, third-party delivery apps with all the hidden fees. I had to make an account and felt annoyed, but it wasn't too much of a hassle. After we placed our order, they showed us in real time what was happening. First the order gets confirmed by the restaurant, then they prepare the food, then the delivery person drives to the restaurant, then they collect the food, and finally the food is delivered.

MONDAY, JANUARY 11th

When I woke up today I got on Twitter and started reading. An hour later, I told myself I couldn't use Twitter again until tomorrow. I appreciated what I was learning, but if I'm not proactive about it, I could spend all day scrolling.

✶✶✶✶✶

A friend called me around 1 p.m. today. I had just eaten and asked if he was on his lunch break.

"No," he said, "but I'm working from home so as long as it looks like I'm staying busy, it's all good."

"What does 'staying busy' look like when you're working from home?" I asked.

"Funny you should ask," he said, already laughing, "We

use Teams and my boss can see if I'm active, like, typing on a Word document or something. So I just put something heavy on my keyboard that makes it keep typing. That way, if my boss looks at my name on his screen, there'll be a little green circle around it, which he 'knows' means I'm staying busy."

I laughed, "And what heavy object do you use?"

"An upside-down stapler. It works perfectly."

We chatted for almost an hour before I told him I had to get back to work. After I hung up, he texted to let me know that his stapler had typed 25 pages of the letter M.

★★★★★

I had some technical difficulties joining tonight's call for class, but after creating a new Zoom account, I made it in. Everyone had their cameras on, so I turned mine on and noticed myself getting a bit shaky. When it was my turn to introduce myself, my voice faltered. I got through it, but I felt way more nervous than usual.

TUESDAY, JANUARY 12th

I walked to campus today for the first time in months. For one of my courses, the professor asked us to come pick up a bag of supplies she'd prepared for each of us. Her email said that she had made special arrangements so that we would be allowed to come to campus, and the supplies would only be available this week. She offered to mail the package to students living outside of Montreal, but I didn't mind coming in. It had just snowed and the sidewalk was covered in a comfortable crunch.

It took about an hour, round trip, and I waited until I was home to check what I got in the professor's package. There were two lined index cards, a mini pad of Post-it notes, four sheets of white printer paper (two of which were slightly thicker), one sheet of decorative card stock, a glue stick, a pencil, and a Ziploc bag filled with an assortment of buttons and a long black hair. I've worked with this professor before and we get along very well, so I was a bit perplexed to see that she had insisted we trek to campus to pick up things we probably have around the house. Anyway, I don't know why I'm complaining. I appreciated having an excuse for a walk.

When I sat down at my computer just now, I wanted to open an internet browser but didn't. First, I journaled for a bit. After I wrote about the walk and supplies though, I checked my email. I responded to a couple, then I watched the headlines on Democracy Now while drinking a glass of kombucha. Now I'm scrolling through Twitter. If I find that Twitter starts taking up energy that I want to put into community organizing or other work, I'll stop checking my account. For now though, it's helping me learn about important activist projects and I'm feel motivated. I'm also feeling anxious.

At first I thought I didn't want to follow anyone on Twitter, but I've decided instead to follow everyone who follows me. It feels more consensual. When I started going through and following my list of followers though, Twitter stopped me. I looked through the website's policies and found that they don't let users follow more than 400 accounts a day. But I got stopped after just 26! I kept reading and found that Twitter's "limits are based on the rate at which you are following new accounts, as well as how many followers you have." So the automated, personalized Twitter AI doesn't trust me!? It probably thinks I'm an AI too.

WEDNESDAY, JANUARY 13th

Okay – Twitter may be more distracting than I can handle. I keep setting arbitrary rules and then breaking them almost immediately. I've told myself twice in the past twelve hours that I'm done with Twitter for the day, and both times I found myself back on and scrolling. I'm not even getting notifications or interacting with anyone – I'm just reading tweets and looking through profiles. I know I don't want to keep going back, but something inside me is stronger than that. Though I'm not sure if it's actually something inside me or just forces playing with my subconscious – like Twitter's engineers and their algorithms.

Now that I've spent a couple hours scrolling, I really need to commit to staying off Twitter until I get through the three readings I have to do before class tomorrow. I'm just glad I don't have Twitter on my phone.

✶✶✶✶✶

I did a guest lecture for one of my colleagues' Globalization in Education classes today and it went great ... once I was able to connect. Right before I was supposed to Zoom in, the wifi in our apartment stopped working and we couldn't figure out how to get it back on. We tried turning the modem off and on again, unplugging the phone line and plugging it back in, unplugging the modem from the wall and plugging it back in. Nothing!

Jonas luckily has lots of data on his phone so he just turned on a hotspot and I used that to connect, but how fitting that I struggled to get online for a lecture about the problems with going online.

After I finished the call, my colleague sent me a text saying thank you, and followed it with a data message that my phone couldn't read.

"What was that?" I replied, "My phone still can't do data messages."

She replied a few hours later: "It was a photograph of the late afternoon sun coming in through our window."

THURSDAY, JANUARY 14th

I had two meetings today – one for a class project and one for a paper I'm collaborating on. The first was on Teams and the second on Zoom. Then I got an email from Aviva with feedback on a paper I've been working on, as well as a note about how glad she is that I'm back online. With such an internetted day, I find it hard to remember how I managed to get things done last year. I remember being on my phone a lot and sending lots of letters, but it all seems so implausible now. It's only been two weeks and my memories are already fading.

✶✶✶✶✶

Darren dropped off my Scrabble set today. I found it leaning against the door when I went out to check the mail. He had borrowed it a few months ago, but after everything that happened, I didn't think I'd get it back. I brought it inside and opened the box, expecting a note or a turd or something, but it was just Scrabble.

It feels weird not to have Darren in my life anymore. I'm not about to reach out to him or anything, but it seems like there needs to be an ending to his story line. I guess this is it.

FRIDAY, JANUARY 15th

I "attended" a Zoom webinar this afternoon that I read about on Twitter. I had just "pinned" a Tweet about the ways the internet contributes to the ongoing colonization of Indigenous land and resources, and all of a sudden I was seeing Tweets about a Montreal digital media artist/scholar whose research imagines Indigenous tech futures.

At the event, the speaker shared his experiences moving from critiquing computer-related design to organizing Indigenous-led design teams. Because he's based here in Montreal, I didn't realize there would be people joining the call from all over the world. There were folks from Australia, Brazil, Afghanistan, Turkey, Mexico, France, Estonia, Ghana, and the US. I don't even think there were any other Canadians. The idea of having a casual event like this with attendees from all over the world would be unthinkable without the internet.

The speaker shared his early experiences working with digital technologies and meeting too many white people who didn't think Indigenous people would be interested in tech, as if Native people are trapped firmly in the past.

"There've been Indigenous technological innovation since time immemorial," he said.

His current work is focused on imagining the ways that

digital technologies can be used by Indigenous people to support their lives and cultural identity. He pointed out that Western technologies have often been used against Indigenous people, so it's not so simple to just embrace these tools. First the technologies need to change so that they are designed by and for diverse people in equitable ways.

✶✶✶✶✶

Our new N64 console arrived in the mail today. My childhood console broke last year and I tried to find one locally, but N64s are rarer than I expected. When I got back online, I looked at Kijiji and Craigslist but the cheapest ones were over 125 bucks and far away in the suburbs. Jonas checked on eBay and found a seller in Ontario who had several old N64s for $80 each. We bought one and it was shipped in under a week.

I have a lot of work to do today, but as soon as the N64 arrived, I plugged it all in to make sure it works. When the screen lit up, I got a rush of tingly nostalgia. I saw flashes of Rainbow Road and Slippy the Frog and the Golden Gun. But I've gotta get some work done before I play.

✶✶✶✶✶

Leah shared a link with me for a disability arts festival called Unlimited. It's normally in the UK but went digital for the first time this year. I "attended" two events: a dance duet called 111 that was audio described, and a virtual tour of an exhibition presenting artifacts from the history of disability activism – mostly related to a collective I'd never heard of called Reasonable Adjustment. The exhibit presented posters, TV clips, and even weapons from the group's demonstrations, like the bombing of an inaccessible train station and the shooting of a geneticist who was advocating for euthanizing—

Scratch that!! I was pranked. The artifacts were all made up. The curator is an artist, not a historian, and I'm not the only person he fooled. I was trying to read more about Reasonable Adjustment online and found several articles and a

Reddit thread about it as if it were real. Then I checked on Wikipedia and read:

"Reasonable Adjustment is a fictional disabled armed resistance movement…"

Wikipedia is awesome. Imagine if everything online was publicly and transparently moderated. Social media would be unrecognizable.

✶✶✶✶✶

About two hours into class tonight the professor's video stopped working, and then ten minutes later her sound starting glitching too. It sounded trippy but we couldn't make out what she was saying. Eventually, her connection dropped entirely and she was booted from the call. The rest of us stuck around for ten or fifteen minutes and had a candid conversation about the course. It's funny how much easier the conversation flowed once the professor left the room. If she had planned it, abandoning the class could've been an interesting experiment. Even unplanned, I appreciated the experience. Glitches are so much more memorable than business as usual.

Later in the evening, the professor emailed us explaining that her wifi had completely cut out.

"Sorry all. I lost my internet – never has happened before."

Jonas and I have also been having lots of wifi problems recently. It'd almost be easier to just go back offline.

SATURDAY, JANUARY 16th

I attended my first Zoom games night yesterday. Sloane organized it and there were eight of us in total. I laughed so hard at one point that I had to hide from the camera. Jonas pointed out that we didn't get to chat very much while the games were happening but I didn't mind. (It didn't hurt that I kept winning!)

One of the games was about being funny, one was a drawing game, and the last was trivia. I'd forgotten how competitive I can get. Jonas didn't like the funny game, but he enjoyed the other two. He and his friends stopped doing Zoom games months ago, but Sloane and their crew have kept up with it.

*****

Our internet connection's been really shit the past couple days. I asked Jonas whether we should get in touch with our internet provider and upgrade our service, but he thinks we would still have the same problems if we paid more. I don't know how he knows this, but I don't mind trying to adapt to our slow and glitchy internet connection.

This morning, I was on a Zoom call and got booted off a couple times. It was a webinar about Palestinian political prisoners and I was just listening, so getting kicked off wasn't a big deal, but it was annoying. Despite my unstable internet connection, I still managed to ask a question in the Zoom chat:

"How do you see 'digital activism' contributing to these causes? How can we ensure there is a meaningful place for online activism (such as this event) without having online things stand in for material/offline actions?"

It was cool to hear the event's organizer share my question with the panelists. One of them (who was Zooming in from the West Bank) insisted that the internet is a very important tool – especially now – but it doesn't replace offline efforts.

"It's just a tool," she said.

I appreciated the event. I learned a lot and connected with some front-line activists who I'm now following on Twitter. I can imagine how this could be a problem though, how it might fool me into thinking that I'm actively supporting Palestinian human rights when really I'm just sitting on the couch, watching a video on a screen.

*****

Hanni and I played Mario Kart against each other over the

internet this afternoon. We talked on the phone while we raced and I think I appreciated the chat more than the Kart, but gaming is a good pretext for conversation. There's no way we would've had such a long phone chat if we hadn't also been playing.

SUNDAY, JANUARY 17th

When I woke up, I joined a lecture with Justin Edgar, the artist who set up that fake disability activism exhibit I saw a couple days ago. He seemed genuinely shocked that so many people thought the history he'd presented was real. There were lots of comments in the chat from people who were offended by the work, but I appreciated it – how he managed to provoke important conversations in a transgressive and respectful way. I mean, the artist is disabled, his event provided audio descriptions, two sign language interpreters, and live captioning; these formal features seem more important than whether or not everyone agreed with the work.

Immediately after the talk, I joined Jonas for a Zoom trivia call with his mom's extended family. They do these trivia things every few weeks but Jonas has only joined once or twice. I really liked it, even though lots of the questions were a bit too UK-centric. I'll prepare a category about Canada for next time.

This evening Jonas and I have been binging a terrible Netflix show called *The Circle* where a group of people spend a few weeks isolated in their apartments, only communicating with one another over social media. Each episode shows them stressing about messages and speculating who's being authentic and who's insincere. Some of the contestants are catfish, pretending to be people they're not, while others try to cut through the bullshit – or so they claim – and present themselves as they "really" are. The show is incredibly brainless, but it shows how people who try to be themselves online can be just as phony as the catfish.

✶✶✶✶✶

I haven't done any reading for fun since I started using the internet again. Okay, a lot of the reading I do online is for fun, but I mean that I haven't read any novels or nonfiction, except for articles I've had to read for class. I know that there are plenty of critical and creative things to read online, but I've mostly been reading Twitter.

MONDAY, JANUARY 18th

I went on an eBay shopping spree last night before bed. I was looking for a copy of Paper Mario to buy Jonas for his birthday, but after I found that, I also bought albums by Young Thug, Final Fantasy, Dead Prez, Tierra Whack, Sloan, and Guster. Over 200 dollars later, I was still sitting in the same position, and nearly asleep.

This morning, I looked back through my eBay purchase history. If I could live last night over again, I'd try to stop myself about 100 dollars earlier.

✶✶✶✶✶

My friend in New York is expecting any day now so I went to the post office to mail a little wooden boat toy for her baby. The clerk at the counter was someone I'd seen there before. He's a serious-looking white guy, younger than me, and he always seems a bit on edge. I've seen him over-police the line-up and get frustrated with customers who don't speak French. When I got to the front of the line, I handed him the box (prepacked and addressed) and he asked for my customs form.

"I was hoping to get that from you," I said (in broken French).

"Mais non," he started, "you have to do that online beforehand." And with that, he looked past me and called to the next person in line.

"Excuse me," I said, no longer trying to speak French, "But I've mailed things to the US plenty of times and never had to fill out customs forms in advance. Is this something new?"

"It's not new," he said, and started to help the person who was behind me in line. When he noticed I wasn't moving, he added, "If you go to the Canada Post website on your phone, you'll be able to fill out the form and then you can get back in line."

"I don't have a smartphone," I said.

There was an awkward pause. The customer behind me (who was now being served) didn't say anything. The clerk didn't say anything either but just took out a paper copy of the customs form – the one I've filled out dozens of times before – and passed it to me. I wanted to say something self-righteously, but I just thanked him and filled out the form.

As I walked home, I passed two little parks that were filled with snowpeople. There were dozens and dozens of them in all shapes, sizes, and genders. It was around noon and a Monday, so the people who had made the sculptures were no longer around, but the parks didn't feel empty.

When I got back to my place, I looked on Canada Post's website and couldn't find anything to suggest that you have to fill out a customs form before going to the post office.

*****

I tried to teach an online drama class to Cary over Google Hangouts today and it was difficult. The idea of teaching something that's usually collaborative, like drama, to just one student was itself a challenge, but trying to also teach something physical and movement-based through the narrow field-of-view of a webcam felt nearly impossible.

We started with stretching, did some vocal warm-ups, and then played around with miming and tableaus. Cary enjoyed himself and after we sped through the activities I had planned, he seemed excited to just chat about tone and how the way we say something changes its meaning. It definitely wasn't a waste of time, but it didn't feel like a drama lesson, or at least not any drama lesson I've taught before.

Cary is doing classes online this year, but it's only for a few hours a day. He said he likes his online classes, but he gets nervous when he has to talk over webcam to people he's never met before in person. He said he was excited that I was his teacher today because he already knows me. We decided we'll have an online class like this for an hour or so every two weeks.

*****

I participated in my first "Twitter Storm" in honour of Martin Luther King Jr.'s birthday this afternoon. According to my Twitter analytics, 42 people saw my tweet in the first hour after I posted it. In real life, that's a lot of people, but online, the difference between 42 people and 0 is negligible.

*****

In class tonight, most people had their cameras on, but I turned mine off during the lecture because I kept getting distracted by my face. While we were discussing things though, I turned it back on to avoid seeming rude. Towards the end of class, my internet cut out and I got kicked off the call. I wasn't able to get the wifi to reconnect, so I borrowed Jonas' phone and used his hotspot. By the time I got back though, class was over.

Not having a reliable internet connection is frustrating. I wish I could just phone it in.

TUESDAY, JANUARY 19th
The internet is particularly distracting when you have a lot to do. It makes procrastination easy and almost productive. (But only almost.) I keep trying to read things for class online but I should really just download all the readings so I can print them off and avoid getting distracted. Whatever happened to those course packs professors used to prepare? In my undergrad, we'd go to the bookstore and buy a plastic-wrapped package of articles for the term. People complained because we had to pay for copyright permission stuff, but I spent half an hour today trying to figure out how to access just one article that I'm supposed to read. I'd pay a

bit extra to avoid the hassle and to have a hard copy of the readings.

Now I've spent another five minutes procrastinating by writing about all the time I've spent procrastinating. Time for another break to go online and procrastinate!

✶✶✶✶✶

One of my favourite things to do on Twitter is look at the stats on how many people have seen my posts or interacted with them. Twitter calls these "impressions" and "engagements," respectively. Even though I'm not doing too well, I still like checking. And then five minutes later I like checking again. And again. And again. Again. Again. Again. Again. Again. Again. Again.

WEDNESDAY, JANUARY 20th

Last night after Jonas went to bed, I spent two hours doing actually nothing online. Those late-night hours used to be my most productive time for writing. Now it's like I've lost all my time. And I know that's not true, but I'm having a lot of trouble controlling myself. I won't blame the internet; it's not the internet's fault that I'm wasting my time. But it's not helping! It's hard to be self-motivated when the whole wide web is just sitting there, waiting for me. Every five or ten minutes, I get the urge to check my email or Twitter. I sometimes resist the urge, but because most of the work I have to do isn't time sensitive, it's easy to convince myself to take just a little break. And then that break turns into an hour of mindless scrolling.

One of my ex-students saw my retweet about an anti-racism event I signed up for this evening and texted to let me know she's planning to come.

"You've been quite active on Twitter," she added.

"I know," I replied, "Ugh. I'm actually just journaling about it now, haha. It's addictive and a tiny bit useful, but mostly not."

"I was extremely addicted to Twitter last year, having never used it before," she texted, "and then I reached a breaking point and just stopped using it completely. Now I've been checking it once in a while."

"I'm trying to figure out whether I should get off of it completely," I wrote, "or if I'll be able to self-regulate and use it in moderation."

I don't know if I can control myself... No, I know I can. I've just been failing lately.

✶✶✶✶✶

This evening's webinar featured a professor in Toronto who spent most of her early academic career in Montreal. It was about what higher education is like in Canada for Black and Indigenous people and how we can change institutions to make them less racist.

I missed the first twenty minutes because I couldn't get into the Zoom. Turns out I had my display name as just my first name and – as I found out when I reread an email from the organizers – they were using display names to verify who had registered before letting people into the event. I added my last name and got in right away, but then my sound didn't work. I restarted my computer but still couldn't get the sound to work, so I called Jonas to help. He did the same things that I had just done but it worked for him. I hate when that happens but I was too relieved to care.

When I started listening, the main speaker was sharing a history of my university as a colonial institution. Then the event moved into a Q&A that focused on how students have more power than many of us realize. Especially in Quebec, she reminded us that students have managed to collectively organize in order to pressure powerful institutions to change.

"Organize, organize, organize," she said, "There are ways to put pressure on institutions."

They'll push back, she admitted, but we have power.

As the event was ending and everyone was signing off, I heard one of the event's organizers tell the speaker that this was the first time she's left a Zoom call feeling energized.

✶✶✶✶✶

I just spent another two hours on Twitter "unheedfully," as they say in the Bible. Earlier today I told myself I wouldn't waste the night again but again the night was wasted. Enough is enough. If I keep insisting I have control, then I have to use that control. Tomorrow it's over.

THURSDAY, JANUARY 21st

I've been feeling more anxious recently. Every morning, I'm already thinking about the internet as soon as I wake up, and although there's nothing in particular stressing me out, I feel an old familiar pressure coming down on me constantly. If I can control the amount I go online, maybe I can also control my anxiety.

✶✶✶✶✶

And it's down!! Usually, when the internet stops working, I'm doing something online that I don't need to be doing and I sort of appreciate getting kicked back to whatever I got distracted from. All of a sudden, I have so much more self-control. When the wifi stops working during class though, that's when it's the most annoying. But those moments are also when I think about the internet with the most clarity, feeling both its importance and frivolousness. Instead of getting frustrated, I'm trying to take every glitch as a reminder to use digital technologies carefully and intentionally.

FRIDAY, JANUARY 22nd

The internet has been crashing more and more and we finally caved and phoned our service provider, a small company based here in Quebec. Despite being a regional provider, the technical support person I spoke with was in Egypt. At first I thought she meant that she was from Egypt but then realized that no, she was actually on the phone, talking to me from Egypt. She was incredibly personable and asked whether I'd been to her country. I told her I hadn't, but that I'd spent some time in Jordan, camping in the desert. She told me that the desert camping in Egypt is even better.

"You will love it!" she said.

Although I really enjoyed the chat, she wasn't able to fix our internet. She could see, all the way from Egypt, that our connection had already cut out five times today (and it wasn't even 2 p.m.). However, when she tried to reset things, she got an error message from Bell, who – she told me – own the phone line that our internet is connecting through. She said that Bell have a monopoly on this kind of internet service in Canada. I commented that she knows more about Canada's internet infrastructure than most Canadians and we laughed. There's nothing funny about the ever increasing unaffordability of something that should really be a public utility, but it felt good to laugh together.

At the end of our call, she escalated my service request and told me to expect a call from the overlords at Bell. A woman from Bell phoned (fairly quickly afterwards) and tried to troubleshoot with me, asking mostly the same questions. After she ran all her diagnostic tests, she sent a link to Jonas' smartphone that allowed us to live-stream a video of our modem directly to her computer. She watched the stream but said she couldn't see any physical issues that may have been causing our problems.

After 45 minutes, she conceded that she couldn't fix the problem remotely and we needed an actual human service technician. Less than an hour later, he showed up. He's still here, fiddling around with wires, pliers, and strange-looking gauges. He doesn't look very hopeful but it's hard to tell what's going on under his mask.

*****

The internet technician is gone, but I'm not sure if the wifi's fixed. He didn't speak any English so I tried to talk to him in French. I sort of understood him, but I missed a few crucial words. In a couple hours I'm doing a Zoom presentation for my teacher friend's Grade 6 class in Vancouver. If I get booted from that call, I'll know that the fix failed. I'm presenting about my offline year, so if my internet glitches during the presentation and I get dropped from the call, it'll be annoying but sorta perfect.

✶✶✶✶✶

The call with my friend's class went well although it was a bit more intimidating than I expected. He forgot to mention that he'd invited three other teachers to join with their classes, so my presentation was to four classes of students – each in their own classroom. I wasn't shook by the audience size, but it was confusing to make sure I was interacting with people in all four of the rooms at the same time. I had to orchestrate who would speak when and ask the teachers to call on students, and then remind the students to unmute themselves, and then to mute themselves again when I called on someone else.

Once we got underway, things started to flow a bit and I tried not to focus too much on what was happening on the other side of the screen. I managed to ask the students what they would miss about the internet if they were offline and they all said things related to entertainment: YouTube, Netflix, and ebooks. We then discussed the environmental impacts of the internet for most of the class, but I also brought up some of the colonial problems that even "sustainable" energy projects have caused for Indigenous communities. In Montreal and Vancouver, we use hydroelectricity that's considered by many to be environmentally responsible. However, people rarely discuss the ongoing opposition that both hydro projects have faced and continue to face from Indigenous groups whose lands and rights were/are violated by the construction and operation of these dams. Beyond flooding important lands and resources, both hydro projects are known to be poisoning the surrounding fisheries and agricultural areas. I don't see how that can be considered "sustainable."

After I finished my talk, the students had time for questions and I was asked a lot about what it meant to be offline and what challenges I encountered:

"Could you still use your phone to call and text people?" "How did you do school?" "What was the biggest road-bump?" "Was being offline painful?"

My favourite question was about how resisting the internet might impact people's exposure to knowledge and information:

"Aren't you worried that if people use the internet less, people will become less intelligent?"

I answered this by discussing the personalization of our Google search results and social media feeds:

"It's so important that people can access information, but we have to ask *who* is able to access *what* information and at what cost to who."

My internet did glitch a few times during the call, and there were a couple of frozen, laggy moments where I got warning messages saying my connection was unstable, but I never got completely booted. As far as I can tell, our internet is fixed.

At the end of the call, when I was saying bye and the kids were thanking me for joining, they all started doing a strange dance move that I hadn't seen before. It looked a bit like dabbing, but upside-down. It made me think of a two-handed Nazi salute.

✦✦✦✦✦

Jonas and I went for a big walk on the mountain with some friends, and when we got home we sat down at our internet portals – me on my laptop and Jonas on his phone. After I checked my email and Twitter, I realized I was still online but in the most useless way possible: I was just clicking through different tabs as if something was going to happen. And of course nothing was happening. So I forced myself to close the browser and put my computer away. But it was hard.

SATURDAY, JANUARY 23rd

We took the metro today to pick up meat from a farm just

off the island. While we were waiting for the train, I noticed that every single person on the platform had their head in their phones, including Jonas. I even had my phone out to write myself a note about everyone being on their phones.

✶✶✶✶✶

This social media reality show *The Circle* is too good. I mean, it's terrible, but I could do my whole thesis about it. All the "real" people are sucking up to each other and basing their strategies on loyalty, while all the "fake" people are self-admittedly phony and seem much more socially aware.

One of the runners-up sounded particularly hypocritical. In the final episode she explained that she "tried as hard as possible to be genuine." What does it mean to be genuine if it takes a lot of work? The funny thing is that what she's saying probably makes sense to most viewers. People know that it takes a lot of work to appear genuine online. (*Being* genuine is another matter entirely.)

The host asked her what she learned about social media while on the show and she answered, "Don't trust nobody, not even myself at some points."

She's genuine AND she can't be trusted??

SUNDAY, JANUARY 24th

I was just reading about the recent spike in attacks on Palestinians in the West Bank. Notably, a Palestinian family in the South Hebron Hills had their house raided by a group of ultra-nationalist Israeli settlers and when the family turned to the Israeli military for support, they were threatened and told they would be evicted if they tried to involve journalists or activists.

I immediately wanted to go to Twitter and post the video of the soldiers threatening the Palestinian man whose home was raided but I stopped myself. I'm applying for some funding and I had to give the adjudication committee my Twitter handle, so now I feel like I have to be more careful about what I tweet. I know there's nothing wrong with posting in support of Palestinian human rights, but I also know many people from across the political spectrum (perhaps including the people who sit on grant adjudication committees) who mistake criticism of Israel for antisemitism and practically treason, as if uncritically supporting Israel is part of what it means to be Canadian. And, in a sense, I suppose it is – both in terms of where our taxes are going and in terms of the similar logic we use to justify our own colonial project here in "Canada."

As my mind churned out reasons why I shouldn't post something about this to Twitter, and why I needed to, I reminded myself that tweeting isn't meaningful enough to warrant such a debate. I'm sort of embarrassed to even be journaling about it.

MONDAY, JANUARY 25th

I got stuck on Twitter this morning. After 45 minutes, I urged myself to close the browser, but before I did, I tweeted a quote that I wrote in my journal back in June: "I'm just as cynical about the possibility of a revolution happening as I am about the possibility of the status quo working." Now that I've shared that ambiguous message with the world, I can get back to work.

★★★★★

I logged into my online banking and got really anxious-feeling about nothing in particular. Getting the monthly paper bills this past year didn't make me feel much, except organized. I don't know what's so different about looking through my purchases online but I've decided I'm going to stick with the paper bills, even though they cost a couple bucks each time. This way, I only have to deal with my bills once a month, not every time I feel the urge to check.

★★★★★

A year and a half ago, one of my friends completely ghosted me. He didn't text me back, so I gave him a call and left a voicemail. He didn't call back, so I emailed him. He didn't email back, so I gave up. It was confusing though and it hurt. I chatted with some other friends who knew him and they said he was still in touch with them, so I couldn't help but take it personally. Anyway, while I was offline last year, I pretty much forgot about it, especially after I deleted his number from my phone. Now that I'm back online though, he keeps popping into my head. I sent him an email a week ago to check in and see if he's willing to respond now but I didn't hear back. Today, my Gmail "nudged" me, reminding me that I had messaged him and he hadn't responded. It asked if I'd like to follow up and send him another message. So I did. Now that I've sent it though, I wish I hadn't. Stop pushing me around, Google!!

✶✶✶✶✶

An ethical tech organization started following me on Twitter, so I checked out their profile and learned about a working group they're organizing that's trying to improve social media. I sent the leader a message about the project and now I've been invited to their Google Doc, Slack team, and a weekly video chat. I would love to sit in a room with a bunch of people and work towards a better internet together, but doing it online makes me feel a bit less motivated. It's not that we're using the tools we're critiquing – I came to terms with that contradiction long ago – but I just don't feel as excited to work with people I've never met. I know, I know – getting together online allows a bunch of people from all over the world to meet and organize collectively in ways that would be practically impossible without the internet. But I can't shake this uneasy feeling I get when I think about it.

✶✶✶✶✶

The bell just rang notifying me that I have a new email, and when I heard the noise, I felt a pleasure/anxiety pang shoot through me. Was that rush always so intense or did I reset my dopamine receptors last year?

★★★★

I've been working on an assignment with a classmate over Google Slides this afternoon and it's making it super easy to work together despite not being able to get together. I know I love to hate, but this is super handy.

★★★★★

I bought an old copy of Samuel Delany's 1979 text *Heavenly Breakfast* online and it arrived today. It looks like it's never been read, but the pages are yellow and they smell delicious, like musty adhesive. The moment I took it out of its envelope, it took hold of me and I started reading. I have more schoolwork to do before class, so I put it down after a few chapters. The internet may be more relentless, but a good book is pretty powerful too.

★★★★★

Imagine a huge underground labyrinth of stuffy computers, whirring fans, and a gazillion eyes of red and green – blinking or steady stares.

★★★★★

I started following a woman on Twitter this afternoon who's the leader (or "Nap Bishop") of a group called "The Nap Ministry." She sees naps as resistance against capitalism and white supremacy and an approach to reparation – individually and collectively. I'm already loving her tweets. Two that she posted today really resonated with me.

The first was about the power of phone calls (without video) in a "disconnected, tech-run world." I appreciate the framing of the tech world as disconnected. But I more so just really love old-fashioned phone calls. There's something about doing video chats that's stressful in a way audio-only calls aren't. That "FaceTime fatigue." Not to mention all the equity issues with video chatting. But even for someone like me with all the privilege in the world, I still feel anxious and frustrated by the expectation to do video calls or have my video on during class. Like with my parents who keep suggesting we do video calls instead of just chatting on the phone – I'm okay with it once in a while, but I'm not going to let our weekly chats casually make their way online.

The Nap Ministry's second tweet was making fun of people who send cold emails to her and then follow up 24 hours later. It's that terrible consequence of more potential … more expectations. Because the internet makes us able to do more, we feel like we have to do more to keep up. Rest is such an appealing form of resistance to me. Part of me thinks its just because it's easy and pleasurable, but in my life I don't find rest as easy as it should be. Sure, it's a passive resistance, but it takes a lot of work to get to a place where I can be passive and really res(is)t.

I originally heard about the Nap Ministry from Hanni when we held a "nap-in" demonstration in February. We set up an air mattress in our faculty's lobby to provoke students/staff to think about the ableist and disabling pace of life expected on campus. Hanni had made a sign quoting a tweet from the Nap Bishop and we used it as a conversation starter with people passing by. At the time, I wasn't able to go on Twitter and check her out, but I phoned Hanni today to tell him I didn't forget.

"Have you still been following the Nap Ministry?" I asked.

"I'm not using Twitter anymore," he said.

"Oh." I paused, "Is it an anxiety thing? Like when you post things?"

"I never really posted things," Hanni laughed, "I just read things."

We both paused. Hanni often pauses so I've learned not to rush in to fill the space.

He continued, "But yeah, anxiety – I was just always doom scrolling. It was too much."

I know the goal should be moderation not abstinence, but it seems like the people who are best at moderating their social media use don't use social media at all.

✶✶✶✶✶

In class tonight I felt like I couldn't turn my camera off. I wanted to. I feel like it would've helped me focus, but most people had their cameras on and I felt like if I turned it off, the professor would assume I'd left the room or wasn't paying attention. And that wouldn't be the case, but I can't escape appearances and assumptions. It's a pass/fail course, so my grade wouldn't even be affected, but I don't care about the mark. Wait – so what do I care about? Appearances? Or maybe it feels like I'm supporting the class more by having my face visible?

I told a classmate about my year offline and how I've been having trouble controlling how much I go online now that I'm back. She seemed surprised.

"You must have quite a lot of self-control though to have been able to last a whole year."

"It's sometimes easier to do something drastic," I responded, "than to make more moderate changes."

I think I'm getting back to a better place though. The last few days have felt more measured and my pace of life is beginning to feel under control. I miss being offline, but I'm enjoying a lot of the internet activities I'm doing, despite the guilt. One issue, however, is the new back and neck pain that may or may not have to do with how much time I'm spending online. I probably should get a new office chair or at least figure out a better way to hold my laptop.

✶✶✶✶✶

Looking back at all the entries in my journal today, I'm feeling a bit discombobulated. I don't think of myself as someone who has problems focusing, but the internet pulls in so many directions that it's hard to stick with any one thing for long; there's always something else.

I'm impressed with myself and how much I got done today. I'm also feeling worn down and ready for bed. I'll just check the internet one last time first.

TUESDAY, JANUARY 26th

Will this be the year that big tech companies get reined in? The US is making a bunch of flashy moves to regulate the big five. These monopolies have helped normalize and incentivize extremism all over the world, but now that they're impacting the US – where the companies are based – American legislators are finally like, "hmm, maybe we shouldn't let big tech execs control everything? I mean, they are paying us a lot, but we're supposed to be a democracy." (And politicians wonder why so many people have no interest in electoral politics.)

✶✶✶✶✶

I thought I was doing better at controlling my time on Twitter, but I spent over an hour on there earlier, so now I've been forcing myself not to check it again until tonight. *Not* checking something would seem passive, but it's taking a lot of effort. Every time I lose focus, my first instinct is to take a peek, and every time, I have to actively tell myself not to. And it's working! I'm slowly developing more restraint. Earlier this month, I couldn't manage myself, but now that I've had some time to practice, I'm regaining control.

✶✶✶✶✶

I was just out on a long walk with Tyler. I'm a big talker and Tyler's often not that talkative so I sometimes worry that I'm talking too much and being overbearing. When we said bye and headed our separate ways, I started feeling super anxious. It probably had to do with my insecurity about whether Tyler enjoyed the walk, but as I made my way home, I found myself dwelling on something completely unrelated…

I follow Yuki's boyfriend on Twitter and he posted something earlier about the band Young Marble Giants. I'd never heard of them, so I listened to one of their live shows on YouTube, recorded at a venue in Vancouver where I used to take free jazz classes. The show was really weird and charming. (Jonas said it reminded him of video game music.) I tweeted back with a lyric from the show about how some people relate to the world like cogs in a machine, even though we're so much more complicated than that. I imagine Yuki's boyfriend didn't think much of it, but while I was walking home I started to get anxious that I had fucked up. I haven't figured out all the conventions of Twitter. What if he was making an inside joke that I hadn't understood?

When I got home, I checked to see if he'd interacted with my tweet but there was nothing. The social media anxiety that people talk about is real! It's like, you put something out there without context and then you have no control over how people read it. You can delete it, but you can never take it back.

THURSDAY, JANUARY 28th

It was a hectic day with meetings, a webinar, and class. After I finished everything, I was about to get down to work, but noticed an email from my old supervisor. Because our university has a new payment system, she needed me to do some online paperwork in order to get re-hired for a research position that I've already been doing. After a year of glitches, the new system is supposedly working now ... but not for me. I spent two hours trying to figure it out, but couldn't find the right buttons to press.

With so much happening this term, I feel like I'm just treading water. It's going okay, but if another wave comes along, it might be too much. Without email, I felt protected, like I wouldn't get caught by anything – at least not by surprise. Now though, I'm feeling very exposed. Even just the expectation of a wave is making it harder to breathe.

FRIDAY, JANUARY 29th

Am I actually getting better at self-control or have I just been deluding myself, trying to stay positive? I don't think I'm spending nearly as much time online as I was a couple weeks ago, and I haven't even felt tempted to watch porn or TikTok videos. I did, however, spend over two hours on

Twitter this afternoon and haven't gotten any work done. I announced aloud that I'm not going to use Twitter again today. Jonas is in the other room so I don't think he heard me, but now that I've said it out loud (*and* written it in my journal), it has to be true.

✦✦✦✦✦

My friend in Vancouver called this evening and partway through our conversation, her boyfriend – another close friend – got home, so we had a three-way. While we were talking, a fourth friend phoned and I was able to make my little Nokia add him to our call too so that all of us could chat.

I think I like the classic conference call more than a group Zoom. I know I could just turn off my video and then it'd be the same, but sometimes that's not an option.

SATURDAY, JANUARY 30th
Jonas was talking about Putin's palace this morning, so I looked it up and then spent the next hour reading about Putin and his ex-wife and his daughter and his daughter's ex-husband and then I realized what I was doing and closed the browser immediately. Why do I care? I don't care.

✦✦✦✦✦

I tweeted at Ruha Benjamin today. She posted something about her idea of the New Jim Code, that digital tools often speed up or heighten racism while hiding it in the technology's objective- or neutral-seeming programming. She has 50,000 followers, so I didn't expect her to notice, but she did! She liked my reply … and then she actually started following me!!! It's so not a big deal, but I feel giddy.

February

We live, learn, and organize in a web of contradictions.
– Aziz Choudry, 2015, *Learning Activism*

MONDAY, FEBRUARY 1st
I joined a video call today for the working group I'm part of
that's trying to make social media more "human" – whatever
that means. Everyone involved is committed to concepts like
"equity" and "wellness," but we're also all industry people or
academics – so we're pretty served by the system as it is. It's
hopeful to be part of a group like this, but I have a hard time
imagining that social media will change.

Within the first minute of the meeting, I was booted off
the call. I thought it was my internet glitching again, but
realized the power had gone out in the whole apartment.
I phoned Quebec Hydro and found out that my street was
experiencing an outage and that it wouldn't be fixed for several hours.

Power outages weren't such a big deal last year, but now
they feel like a disaster. I'm going to miss the call, I'll have
to reschedule the drama lesson I have with my cousin Cary,
and I'm thinking I should reschedule another Zoom meeting I have later too, just in case. Plus I have class tonight, also
online. Without the internet, I'm pretty much useless. How
did I make it through a year like this?

So much can change in a month. So much can change in
a moment. So why is it so hard to imagine that things will
ever change?

Acknowledgements

Being able to spend a year offline was only possible because of support I had from the people around me and my privilege doing funded graduate work at a Canadian university. This sets me apart from many of the communities that rely most on the internet – both directly in their everyday lives and on the exploitative labour involved in its operation.

Ruha Benjamin notes that "the capacity to refuse rests upon a prior condition of possibility – that one has been offered something in the first place. Such offering, in turn, implicitly sets one apart from those who have been altogether neglected and excluded, so as not even to have the chance to refuse." There are over three billion people today who do not have regular access to the internet, many of them living in the countries most impacted by the problematic labour practices and resource exploitation associated with the industries of the internet. I would like to acknowledge them and the imbalanced relationships on which our digital lifestyles depend.

I wrote most of this book on unceded Indigenous land in Tio'tia:ke/Montreal, an area that continues to be a home and meeting point for many Indigenous peoples including the Kanien'kehá:ka of the Haudenosaunee Confederacy, the Huron/Wendat, the Abenaki, and the Anishinaabeg. The internet – as a dispersed network of computers – is contributing to the displacement of various Indigenous communities depending on where users live and where data centres and other internet infrastructures are located. Beyond that, the resources and energy that make the internet possible are still often acquired through colonial projects. I hope this book can help challenge the normalization of our ongoing roles in colonialism.

I am so thankful for the support I've received from my family and friends throughout my year offline and while preparing this book. Thank you to my colleagues and professors for helping me through the challenges I faced while offline, especially when it meant doing extra work to accommodate me. Thank you, Mom and Dad for supporting me to pursue decisions that don't always make so much sense. Thank you to my partner for playing along with my internetlessness and standing behind me, beside me, in front of me, etc. This book (/my life) wouldn't be as meaningful without you. Thank you to the friends and family who helped me go through my journal, fixing typos and deciding which excerpts to share. And thank you to David Stover and Rock's Mills Press for making that sharing a reality.

Finally, I would like to thank all the writers, activists, artists, family, and friends whose ideas grounded my thinking in this journal. And in turn, thank you – dear reader – for picking up my journal and making its ideas your own.

References

Abraham, A. (2021, June 15). Douglas Coupland: Slogan Project. *AnOther*. https://www.anothermag.com/art-photography/gallery/11771/douglas-coupland-slogan-project/0

Ahmed, S. (2006). *Queer Phenomenology: Orientations, Objects, Others.* Durham, NC: Duke University Press.

Anderson, M. T. (2010). *Feed.* Somerville, MA: Candlewick Press.

Apple, F. (2020). I Want You to Love Me [Recorded by Fiona Apple]. On *Fetch the Bolt Cutters* [Album]. Los Angeles; Tornillo, TX: Epic.

Barney, D. (2014). "We Shall Not Be Moved": On the Politics of Immobility. In A. Herman, et al. (Eds.), *Theories of the Mobile Internet: Materialities and Imaginaries* (pp. 15–24). New York: Routledge.

Belcourt, B. (2020). *A History of My Brief Body.* London: Hamish Hamilton.

Benjamin, R. (2016). Informed Refusal: Toward a Justice-Based Bioethics. *Science, Technology, & Human Values, 41*(6), 967–990.

Benjamin, R. (2019). *Race After Technology: Abolitionist Tools for the New Jim Code.* Hoboken, NJ: John Wiley & Sons.

Blake, W. (1793). *The Marriage of Heaven and Hell.* London: Self-published.

Boyle, D. (Director). (2000). *The Beach* [Film]. 20th Century Fox.

Butler, O. (1993). *Parable of the Sower.* New York: Four Walls Eight Windows.

Byrne, D. (Director). (1986). *True Stories* [Film]. True Stories Venture; Warner Bros.

Byrne, S., Harcourt, T., Lambert, S., Lilley, D., Price, S., Fenster, C., Foster, R., & Ireland, T. (Executive Producers). (2020–). *The Circle US* [TV series]. Studio Lambert.

Cazabon, L. (2006). Interview with Hasan Elahi. *Public,* 34, 26–37.

Choudry, A. (2015). *Learning Activism: The Intellectual Life of Contemporary Social Movements.* Toronto: University of Toronto Press.

Coates, T. (2016). *Black Panther: A Nation Under Our Feet.* Modena, Italy: Panini Comics.

Current, M. (2006). Email Message. *Public,* 34, 84–7.

DeForge, M. (2020) *Familiar Face.* Montreal: Drawn & Quarterly.

Deibert, R. (2020, November 10–16). *2020 Massey Lectures – Reset: Re-*

claiming the Internet for Civil Society. [Radio Broadcast]. Canadian Broadcasting Corporation.

Delany, S. (1979). *Heavenly Breakfast: An Essay on the Winter of Love.* New York: Bantam Books.

Doctorow, C. (2019) *Radicalized.* New York: Tor Books.

Dostoevsky, F. (1866). *Crime and Punishment.* Moscow: The Russian Messenger.

Douek, E. (2021, January 11). Trump Is Banned. Who Is Next? *The Atlantic.* https://www.theatlantic.com/ideas/archive/2021/01/trump-is-banned-who-is-next/617622/

Dunn, S. & Al-Kadhi, A. (Writers) & Dunn, S. (Director). (2020, January 17). The Son (Season 1, Episode 8) [TV series episode]. In J. Bearman, J. Davis, L. Eisenberg, E. V. Gordon, S. Heder, K. Nanjiani, A. Spector, & A. Yang (Executive Producers), *Little America.* EPIC Magazine; Universal Television; Apple TV+.

Dyer-Witheford, N. (2015). *Cyber-Proletariat: Global Labour in the Digital Vortex.* Lutsen, MN: Between the Lines.

Fielder, N., Reinking, C., Wilson, J., & Koman, M. (Executive Producers). (2020–). *How to with John Wilson* [TV series]. Blowout Productions; John's Movies.

Forster, E. M. (1909). *The Machine Stops.* London: The Oxford and Cambridge Review.

Gardner, A., Schneider, D. (2005) How Do You Spell Channukkahh? [Recorded by The LeeVees]. On *Hanukkah Rocks* [Album]. New York: Reprise Records/Warner Music Group.

Garland, A. (Director). (2014). *Ex Machina* [Film]. Film 4; DNA Films; A24; Universal Pictures.

Gibson, W. (1984). *Neuromancer.* New York: ACE.

Gilbert, J. (2012). *Collected Poems.* New York: Alfred A. Knopf.

hampton, r. (2020). *Black Racialization and Resistance at an Elite University.* Toronto: University of Toronto Press.

Hess, J. (Director). (2004). *Napoleon Dynamite* [Film]. Fox Searchlight Pictures; Paramount Pictures; MTV Films.

Hua, J. (2018). *The Foxconn Suicides: Human Vitality and Capitalist Consumption. Women's Studies in Communication,* 41(4), 320–323.

Huawei: Uighur Surveillance Fears Lead PR Exec to Quit. (2020, December 16). BBC News. https://www.bbc.com/news/technology-55332671

Invisible Committee. (2009). *The Coming Insurrection.* Los Angeles: Semiotext(e).

Judge, M. (Director). (1999). *Office Space* [Film]. Judgemental Films; 20th Century Fox.

Klein, E. (2018, February 19). How Technology Is Designed to Bring Out the Worst in Us. *Vox.* https://www.vox.com/technology/2018/2/19/17020310/tristan-harris-facebook-twitter-humane-tech-time.

Laaksonen, T. V. (2014). *Tom of Finland: The Complete Kake Comics.* Cologne, Germany: Taschen.

Lerman K., Yan X., Wu X-Z. (2016). The "Majority Illusion" in Social Networks. PLoS One.

Lohmann, L. (2019). Labour, Justice, and the Mechanization of Interpretation. *Development, 62*(1–4), 43–52.

Lorde, A. (1978). *The Black Unicorn.* New York: W. W. Norton Co.

Marquez G. G. (1967). *One Hundred Years of Solitude.* (G. Rabassa, Trans.). New York: Harper & Row.

Marx, K. (1976 [1887]). *Capital* (B. Fowkes, Trans.) New York: Random House.

Meyer, D. S., & Rohlinger, D. A. (2012). Big Books and Social Movements: A Myth of Ideas and Social Change. *Social Problems, 59*(1), 136–153.

Moxham, S. (1980) Colossal Youth [Recorded by Young Marble Giants]. On *Colossal Youth* [Album]. Welshpool, North Wales: Rough Trade; London, UK: Universal Music Publishing.

Muñoz, J. E. (2019). *Cruising Utopia.* New York: New York University Press.

Nap Bishop. (2019, December 1). Observations From My Month-Long Sabbath. *The Nap Ministry.* https://thenapministry.wordpress.com/2019/12/01/observations-from-my-month-long-sabbath/

Nap Bishop. (2021). Twitter user profile. https://www.twitter.com/TheNapMinistry/

Navarro-Remesal, V., & Zapata, B. P. (2018). Who Made Your Phone? Compassion and the Voice of the Oppressed in Phone Story and Burn the Boards. *Open Library of Humanities, 4*(1): 11, 1–30

Noy, O. (2021, January 24). When Police Kill a Settler, Settlers Rain Terror on Palestinians. *+972 Magazine.* https://www.972mag.com/settler-violence-tawamin-west-bank/

Oberst, C. (2020). Dance and Sing [Recorded by Bright Eyes]. On *Down in the Weeds, Where the World Once Was* [Album]. Bloomington, IN: Dead Oceans; New York: Kobalt Music.

Odell, J. (2019). *How to Do Nothing: Resisting the Attention Economy.* Brooklyn, NY: Melville House Publishing.

Ore, J. (2020, December 30). This Guy Swore off the Internet for All of 2020. Then the Pandemic Hit. CBC Radio. https://www.cbc.ca/radio/thecurrent/the-current-for-dec-30-2020-1.5857232/this-guy-swore-off-the-internet-for-all-of-2020-then-the-pandemic-hit-1.5857330

Postman, N. (1997). *The End of Education: Redefining the Value of School.* New York: Vintage Books.

Pun, N., Shen, Y., Guo, Y., Lu, H., Chan, J., & Selden, M. (2016). Apple, Foxconn, and Chinese Workers' Struggles From a Global Labor Perspective. *Inter-Asia Cultural Studies, 17*(2), 166–185.

Pynchon, T. (1965). *The Crying of Lot 49.* Philadelphia, PA: J. B. Lippincott & Co.

Rich, A. (1971). The Burning of Paper Instead of Children. *The Will to Change: Poems 1968–1970.* New York: Norton.

Riley, B. (Director). (2018). *Sorry to Bother You* [Film]. Significant Productions; MNM Creative; MACRO; Cinereach; The Space Program; Annapurna Pictures.

Roberts, S. T. (2016). Digital Refuse: Canadian Garbage, Commercial Content Moderation and the Global Circulation of Social Media's Waste. *Media Studies Publications*.

Safdie, J., & Safdie, B. (Directors). (2019). *Uncut Gems* [Film]. A24; Elara Pictures; IAC Films; Sikelia Productions; Scott Rudin Productions.

Scott, R. (Director). (1982). *Blade Runner* [Film]. The Ladd Company; Shaw Brothers; Blade Runner Partnership; Warner Bros.

Seven, J., & Christy, J. (2013). *A Rule Is to Break: A Child's Guide to Anarchy*. San Francisco: Manic D Press.

Simpson, A. (2014). *Mohawk Interruptus: Political Life Across the Borders of Settler States*. Durham, NC: Duke University Press.

Simpson, L. B. (2011). *Dancing on Our Turtle's Back: Stories of Nishnaabeg Re-creation, Resurgence and a New Emergence*. Winnipeg, MB: Arbeiter Ring Pub.

Simpson, L. B. (2020). *Noopiming: The Cure for White Ladies*. Toronto: House of Anansi.

Smith, B. (2021, January 12). We Worked Together on the Internet. Last week, He Stormed the Capitol. *The New York Times*. https://www.nytimes.com/2021/01/10/business/media/capitol-anthime-gio-net-buzzfeed-vine.html

Spicer, M. (Director). (2017). *Ingrid Goes West* [Film]. Star Thrower Entertainment; 141 Entertainment; Mighty Engine.

Staltz, A. (2017, December 18). A Plan to Rescue the Web From the Internet. *Staltz*. https://staltz.com/a-plan-to-rescue-the-web-from-the-internet.html

Swartz, A. (2020). Afterword. In C. Doctorow (Author), *Little Brother & Homeland* (pp. 641-643). New York: Tom Doherty Associates.

Taffel, S. (2016). *Invisible Bodies and Forgotten Spaces: Materiality, Toxicity, and Labour in Digital Ecologies. In Security, Race, Biopower* (pp. 121–141). London: Palgrave Macmillan.

Titeux de la Croix, S., & Ameziane, A. (2020). *Miss Davis: La Vie et les combats de Angela Davis*. Monaco: Éditions du Rocher.

Tuck, E., & Yang, K. W. (2012). Decolonization Is Not a Metaphor. *Decolonization: Indigeneity, Education & Society, 1*(1), 1–40.

Turner, F. (2006). *From Counterculture to Cyberculture: Stewart Brand, the Whole Earth Network, and the Rise of Digital Utopianism*. Chicago, IL: University of Chicago Press.

Unlimited. (2021, January 22). Justin Edgar: Reasonable Adjustment – The Disabled Armed Resistance Movement. *Unlimited*. https://weareunlimited.org.uk/commission/justin-edgar-reasonable-adjustment-the-disabled-armed-resistance-movement/

Verity, A. (2020, September 22). FinCEN: Why Gold in Your Phone Could Be Funding Drug Gangs. BBC News. https://www.bbc.com/news/business-54238918

Wakefield, J. (2020, June 11). Edmonton Police Chief Says Defunding Would Hinder Diversity Initiatives. *Edmonton Journal*. https://edmontonjournal.com/news/local-news/edmonton-police-chief-says-angry-voices-shouldnt-dominate-reform-discussion

Weise, J. (2018, September 24). Common Cyborg. *Granta*. https://granta.com/common-cyborg/

Wikipedia contributors. (2021, January 4). James Bay Project. *Wikipedia*. https://en.wikipedia.org/wiki/James_Bay_Project

Wikipedia contributors. (2021, September 2). *The Last of Us: Part II*. *Wikipedia*. https://en.wikipedia.org/wiki/The_Last_of_Us_Part_II

Winner, L. (2020). *The Whale and the Reactor: A Search for Limits in an Age of High Technology*, 2nd Edition. Chicago: University of Chicago Press.

Printed in Great Britain
by Amazon